C000227234

A LIGHT IN THE WILDERNESS

DAVID M. HIRD

Balnakeil Press

First published in 2008 by
Balnakeil Press
2 Balnakeil
Durness
Sutherland IV27 4PT

Copyright © David M. Hird 2008

www.balnakeilpress.com

The moral right of David M. Hird to be identified as the
author of this work has been asserted by him in accordance
with the Copyright, Design and Patents Act 1988

All rights reserved.
No part of this publication may be reproduced, stored
or transmitted in any form without the express
written permission of the publisher.

ISBN 978 1 905974 01 6

British Library Cataloguing-in-Publication Data
A catalogue record for this book is available from the British Library

Typeset by Brinnoven, Livingston
Printed and bound by Antony Rowe Ltd, Chippenham

A LIGHT IN THE WILDERNESS

FOR RACHEL

CONTENTS

CHAPTER I

INTRODUCTION TO THE FAR NORTH WEST

Geology, Terminology,
History, Habitation

There's little on the peninsula of Cape Wrath
A lighthouse, buses, bullets and a wall
It's a wilderness, a place of isolation
A thousand miles due east of bugger all

The Cape Wrath peninsula in the very far north west of the County
of Sutherland, between the Kyle of Durness in the east and the
cliffs in the west stretching northwards from Sandwood Bay to
the tip of Cape Wrath, is an area of 207 square kilometres (51,150
acres, or 20,700 hectares) of uninhabited wild, windswept moor and
mountain land. It is the last true wilderness within the British Isles.
The tip of Cape Wrath is nearer to the Arctic Circle than it is to
London and, at latitude 58 degrees 37.5 minutes, is further north
than both Moscow and Vladivostok.

In this narrative the terms 'Parph,' 'the Cape' and 'Capeside' will
be used repeatedly, since each is interchangeable with the others.
'Parph' is a word derived from Old Norse, meaning 'turning point.'
It was at this very far north-western tip of the British mainland
that the Viking adventurers knew that they must alter course to the
south on outward voyages or to the east on their return if they were
to reach their objective in these harsh northern seas.

'The Parph' originally referred to the cliffs at the very tip of Cape Wrath itself, 'Wrath' being a mistranslation of the Norse word 'Hvarth.' This gradually evolved into 'Parph,' a word which over the passage of time came to be applied to the whole of the Cape peninsula; the word may be seen on old maps, including early series Ordnance Survey maps of the area. These old maps show just how remote and inaccessible the whole of north west Sutherland really was until relatively recent times.

'Cape Wrath' can be used to mean the peninsula as a whole, but I have tried to use it in the context of the headland in the immediate vicinity of the lighthouse at the very far north-westernmost tip of the British mainland. 'The Cape' and 'Capeside' tend to be colloquial descriptions of the Cape Wrath peninsula, which equates nowadays with the former 'Parph' description. Thus language develops.

And on some days 'Wrath' seems entirely appropriate, for the weather conditions make it a fearsome place. On these (mercifully rare) days, Cape Wrath is well-named, notwithstanding that the name is founded on a linguistic error. 'Wrath' in this context has no derivation from rage or fury or anger. Gales can howl in from the Arctic with nothing to impede their savagery. But there are many, many more quiet, still, clear days at Cape Wrath: days when it is possible to glimpse remote islets beyond the horizon (in addition to the substantial land masses of Lewis and Orkney, forty or more miles away) and hear nothing at all other than birdsong, and waves gently lapping the bases of the cliffs a hundred feet or more below – out of sight, but always within the consciousness.

Cape Wrath and Cape Cornwall are the only coastal geographical features in the whole of Great Britain with the word 'Cape' in the name. It seems appropriate that each should define an extremity of its own country.

What is now the main A838 road that approaches Durness from the south was not built until 1832. Until 1828 there was no road at all west of the Kyle of Durness and north of Kinlochbervie, and there is still no road or track (or even footpath) direct to Cape Wrath from the south. There was not, and indeed is not, any need to construct one. The only road that crossed the Cape Wrath peninsula was built to service the need for a lighthouse at this most desolate of coastal locations. Proposals in the 1960s and 70s to replace the Kyle of Durness ferry with a road connection to the A838 remain unfulfilled dreams.

The Ministry of Defence does not own the Cape Wrath road, despite notices issued by it which refer to 'permitting' access over it. The road is an ordinary public highway, maintained at the public expense. It has enjoyed that status since 1833, for over one hundred and seventy years in total, and in excess of one hundred years prior to the time when the military authorities cast their covetous eyes upon it. What the military does is deny access to it, which is the direct opposite of the position it seeks to portray. Sounds familiar?

The Cape comprises some of the oldest geology in the British Isles and, indeed, the whole of the earth. The underlying rocks are principally Lewisian gneiss and Torridonian sandstone, with Lower- and Pre-Cambrian formations brought by faulting into close proximity with later Palaeozoic sedimentary limestone. Torridonian sandstone was laid down between 1,000 and 750 million years ago, whereas the Lewisian gneiss is between 2900 and 1100 million years old. The former can be identified by its reddish colouration and sometimes smooth, rounded, form; the latter is easily recognisable by its narrow bands of grey and white strata.

Other distinctive rocks easily identifiable in this far north-western corner of the British mainland are the Moinian series (1100–413 million years old, displaying grey and pink bands within the rock), Limestone (490 million years old, generally whitish in colour and containing fossilised sea shells), and Basal Quartzite (570–550 million years old, recognisably pink in colour). The most spectacular limestone feature in the immediate area is revealed at Smoo Cave, a mile or so to the east of Durness. Smoo is a show cave open to the public; in summer there are conducted tours with subterranean boat trips, in favourable weather conditions.

This is a favourite area in which to study the wide diversity of rock formations; many national and international universities and geological institutes send students to the far north west on practical field courses. There is an excellent display of all the rocks of north west Sutherland at the Tourist Information Centre in Durness.

The area of stunning natural beauty stretching from Coigach, north of Ullapool, to Loch Eriboll on Sutherland's far north coast, has now been awarded Geopark status, the first designation in Scotland by the European Geopark Network. Geopark status is a European accolade recognised by UNESCO, and is based principally on the area's special, diverse geology and landscapes.

This two thousand square kilometre area encompasses some of Britain's finest mountains and coastal landscape, and covers a wealth of classical geological localities. It includes the iconic mountains of Suilven, Arkle, Foinaven, Quinaig and Stac Pollaidh; the pristine isolated beaches of Sandwood, Balnakeil, Sangobeg and Ceannabeinne; dramatic coastal cliffs such as those at Clo Mor and Whiten Head, and Cape Wrath itself.

Within the designated Geopark area are the Assynt-Coigach and North West Sutherland National Scenic Areas, two National Nature Reserves, fifty-four Geological Conservation Review Sites, numerous geological sites of Special Scientific Importance, Special Protection Areas and Special Areas of Conservation. There are also significant numbers of historical and archaeological sites, including scheduled ancient monuments and listed buildings.

The north west Highlands has a unique landscape which includes the craggy peaks of Torridonian sandstone and Cambrian quarzite, shaped by the action of glaciers during the Quaternary Period, as well as secluded glens, some of which are floored by the largest areas of limestone in Scotland. Caves in the limestone, of which that at

Smoo is a prime and notable example, have provided evidence of Pleistocene ice-age fauna and reindeer, polar bears, and wolves.

Renowned geology scholars of the nineteenth century, such as Roderick Murchison (who made an early visit to Cape Wrath in 1840 – see 'Victorian Visitations'), Archibald Geikie, Benjamin Peach and John Horne studied the rock formations of north west Sutherland; on the basis of the evidence found hereabouts the theories of continental drift and the horizontal thrusting of older rocks over younger ones was developed. Early geologists came to understand how mountain ranges like the Alps and the Himalayas were formed. Modern-day students continue the work pioneered by their Victorian forbears.

There is evidence of thousands of years of continuous occupation. From the pre-historic period through the Norse settlements and the Lordship of the Isles to the Clearances, crofting and land reform of more recent years, the human story in this unique landscape can be traced back over nine thousand years.

Unlike a National Park, the award of Geopark status places no additional restrictions on land management and therefore no new planning or land use policies will be introduced. The European Geopark Network consists of seventeen members in nine European countries; the network has no formal connection with the European Union. In 2004 the European Geopark Network was integrated into the UNESCO-endorsed Global Geoparks Network.

The North West Sutherland European Geopark was officially opened in September 2005 by Aubrey Manning, well-known TV presenter, geologist, zoologist, author and Emeritus Professor of Natural History at Edinburgh University.

In the narrative which follows I have taken local place names from the current issue of the 1:25,000-scale Ordnance Survey Explorer Map number 446. The spellings of Gaelic place names are also taken from that source. Gaelic spelling can be notoriously flexible, and pronunciation can assume the proportions of an esoteric art. I have, on rare occasions, attempted both, with varying degrees of embarrassment. Gaelic is a mellifluous language quite beyond my meagre abilities. It is best left to local-born Highlanders, when the language takes on musical qualities of distinctly pleasurable aspect.

There are no recognisable sites of antiquity anywhere on Cape Wrath, but a quick glimpse of the Ordnance Survey map will reveal that Durness over the Kyle has more than its fair share. It is assumed from its etymological derivation from Old Norse that Kearvaig Bay was a favoured landing place of the Viking seafarers; the name translates as 'Bay of the Longships.' But they left no tangible trace of their presence. There are nineteenth-century headstones referring to the place as 'Kerwig' in the old cemetery at Balnakeil; until recent times 'Kerwick' was the preferred spelling.

There are traces of old sheilings, or seasonal dwellings, at the head of the shallow valley leading to Clais Charnach (map reference NC263727, Allt na Clais Leobairnich) but these structures are unlikely to date to much earlier than the nineteenth century.

The surviving stone buildings easily visible from the lighthouse road are nineteenth-century constructions. These settlements comprise four farmsteads, and one dwelling that accommodated the Northern Lighthouse Board's ferryman. The two early nineteenth-century lighthouse storehouses survive: one complete and intact, the other now roofless but otherwise substantially as it was erected. And the Cape Wrath Lighthouse continues to serve the purpose for which it was built in 1828. The lighthouse tower with its associated domestic accommodation and offices are listed buildings, though now unoccupied and closed to the public. Those with an interest in industrial archaeology will be impressed by the nineteenth-century remains at Clais Charnach.

There are further buildings at the very end of Cape Wrath, erected during the early days of the development of radio communication. As radio range and reliability increased, so these installations expanded. They formed a vital watch station in two world wars, but the need for them diminished with the advent of electronic eavesdropping and they are quite derelict now. With the manned lighthouse and radio receiving station at Cape Wrath, there was a sizeable community for over fifty years in this most isolated of places. Life on the very edge, indeed. But as radio power, range and reliability developed, the need for numerous manned coastal stations diminished to the point where the lighthouse keepers resumed their former position as sole occupants of Britain's north-western-most tip. And developing lighthouse automation technology inevitably brought the departure of the keepers, which finally took place in 1998. Cape Wrath is once again the sole property of the seals, the seabirds, the deer, the foxes and the badgers.

A century ago there was probably something of the order of twenty-five or thirty people permanently resident on the Cape. Certainly there was a small school (known colloquially as 'The Cape Wrath Academy') overlooking the Kyle of Durness, near to where the Daill river flows into the tidal estuary. This Side School operated under the auspices of the school in Durness, educating up to ten pre-twelve year-olds from lighthouse, signal station and farming families. The site of the old Side School, which closed in 1947, may (in 2008) be easily identified. After 1947, children were educated in Durness through the week; they returned across the Kyle at weekends. Prior to 1947, Cape-resident youngsters were obliged to make the journey to Durness for tests, examinations and special seasonal school functions. The Achiemore Side School was outlived by a second at Kearvaig, which itself was closed in 1950.

Even today there are no mains electricity, water, or sewerage provisions anywhere on the Cape. Occasionally-occupied houses rely on generators for power and on the resources of the land for their water. There is a telephone land-line to the lighthouse, supported by radio and satellite communications. Diesel generators provide electrical power for the lighthouse – unusual, though not unique, in a shore station.

The road to the lighthouse from the ferry landing stage at West Keoldale was built entirely with muscle- and horse-power. Mechanisation amounted to no more than pick and shovel. Simple mechanical winches and hoists would have been employed in the construction of the two small and one large bridge along the original course of the road. Each of these bridges – plus two more built when the road was extended to the ferry landing stage later in the nineteenth century – still stands, just about wholly unaltered. The most recent radical alteration to the road was the construction of a 'temporary' timber deck bridge, in 1980, which continues to fulfil its purpose of avoiding the constant inconvenience presented by a capricious ford.

The Cape sees perhaps more than its fair share of explosive excitement. The Cape Wrath Weapons Range was commissioned as long ago as February 1933. Military personnel present on Cape Wrath are now restricted to brief periods during the large inter-service and international exercises; the attraction for the military planners is that there are now no resident civilians to endanger (for that read 'to interfere in our games') nor are there many grazing animals to cause disruption. There are moves to enlarge the area of the military bombing and training ranges, and the frequency of use for military purposes is steadily increasing. The PR battalions seemingly command vast resources.

But, as might be expected, the military targets and bombing ranges are situated immediately adjacent to seabird breeding colonies of acknowledged world importance. The Cape Wrath Site of Special Scientific Interest covers 1014 hectares (2505 acres) of coastal land on the north coast adjacent to the Garvey Island bombardment target and the Clo Mor cliffs, and on the west coast between the Bay of Keisaig and the cliffs immediately to the east of Cape Wrath.

Within the SSSI are coastal, heath and mountain areas providing some of Scotland's most unique examples of this type of wild habitat. There are huge seabird breeding colonies, and the whole area is home to long-established herds of red deer roaming unmanaged over the whole of this desolated landscape. Somehow the needs of the military have to be carefully balanced with both sheep grazing and the special requirements of the indigenous wildlife.

The Cape and the Capeside in general was and is a special place. It has now returned to its essentially primeval character – if you ignore the technological requirements of modern defence and warfare. It is not a place to be treated with complacency. That bane of the modern world, the mobile telephone, will work only within sight of the Kyle of Durness and sporadically for approximately six hundred metres beyond Inshore House five miles along the road towards the lighthouse. You will be able to advise others of your achievement in reaching Cape Wrath only when you return to that species of civilisation known in these parts as the Kyle of Durness.

The Cape Wrath peninsula is no environment in which to be alone. You need precise planning, specialist equipment, experience of remote and isolated areas and sufficient food to sustain you for the whole of your time there. The unwary, or ill-prepared, have died there in recent years, victims of the severe weather or unfortunate circumstances, or both. The absolute isolation of the place can be very unforgiving, especially in winter.

Even during the months of spring and summer, visitors enjoying Cape Wrath's peculiar delights must exercise particular care when venturing near to the cliff edges. The tussocky grass can be slippery, especially after sustained dry periods. Photographers must resist the temptation to become so enveloped in their subject that they forget, momentarily, just where they are.

As you savour the unique memories of a visit to the British mainland's far north-western-most tip (and, arguably, Europe's most north-western extremity, if you discount Greenland), rest safe in the knowledge that the wild Cape and its wilder cliffs might just survive much as they have since the dawn of time.

CHAPTER 2

ACROSS THE EMPTY QUARTER

The Wilderness Road to
Cape Wrath Lighthouse

The journey to the lighthouse is undoubtedly one of the few remaining true wilderness experiences left in Great Britain. This really is a wild place; it must be so, since the Euro-bureaucrats have decreed it to be 'The Last Great Wilderness.' But we always knew that, without being told.

Any number of life's awkward little annoyances might conspire against the trip; foul weather, exceptionally low or high tides, tide and wind in the wrong conjunction, use of the bombardment range through which the road passes, etc. Completing the journey by ferry across the Kyle of Durness – which can present more than five metres' difference between high and low water – and minibus along eleven miles of what is essentially an unmade single track road built when the sole means of motive power was the horse, is itself something of an achievement. A sea-crossing at the start of any trip immediately brings the prospect of an expedition, to a greater or lesser degree. A successful completion really will give you a day to remember and a sense of achievement.

The Kyle of Durness ferry is the smallest passenger ferry service in Great Britain. The service has been operated continuously since 1984 by John Morrison: a native-born Highlander with a stare of a thousand yards, a chin of chiselled granite, and with an ability, seemingly, to extrude a beard at will. He has a wicked wit and a scurrilous talent for mimicry just occasionally beyond restraint.

Ferry rights were established by the Northern Lighthouse Board in the nineteenth century and the Board retained the right to operate the ferry across the Kyle until the 1980s. The lighthouse road was adopted as a County road maintainable at the public expense within a few years of it being built, although as beneficial users the Board always defrayed the majority of the maintenance and repair costs. Increased traffic generated by wartime conditions and the establishment of a watch station at Cape Wrath contributed to much greater motor vehicle use of the road, to its eventual deterioration and to periods of closure. The Highland Regional Council acquired the ferry rights in 1983. Thereafter, the right to operate the ferry connection to the lighthouse road has been leased to the present operator.

The Cape Wrath Hotel celebrated its 80th anniversary in 2007 (it was known as the Keodale Hotel until 1927), and promptly closed. It remains to be seen whether it reopens as arguably the north-west's premier sporting hotel.

The slipway has been improved and extended a number of times during its history: most notably when the NLB established the ferry service, and successively during Sutherland County Council and Highland Regional Council ownership. Prior to the formation of the slipway, a small sheltered cove approximately half a mile northwards was the landing point, at a place still known as 'the well.' Fresh water continues to flow at the well, although now it is delivered by underground pipe; occasionally it is necessary for the ferryman to use this landing place when contrary winds and tides make an approach to the west Keoldale slipway inadvisable.

The slipway on the Cape Wrath side of the Kyle was constructed by the Northern Lighthouse Board to accommodate the ferry service during the nineteenth century. It, too, has been successively lengthened and improved over time. There are still examples of the original winch and winding gear in place; this equipment was used to draw up the oar-driven wooden ferry boats in the days before small or portable marine engines became widely available. The small parking and turning area at the Capeside landing is a relatively modern introduction; necessary in more recent years, when two buses have been the norm for the Cape Wrath lighthouse service.

The first section of road towards the lighthouse was built by the Northern Lighthouse Board when the ferry rights were established in the second half of the nineteenth century. The first few hundred yards are quite narrow and constricted. Remember: the road was built to accommodate nothing larger than horse and cart transport. Note the first milestone (11) on your right.

The white cottage on your left was developed by the Northern Lighthouse Board as the ferryman's accommodation, on the site of a smaller dwelling. It is still known as Ferry House, is now in private ownership, and continues without benefit of mains water, drainage or electricity (as, indeed, do all the surviving five domestic and other few commercial properties on the Cape).

The road gradient now eases as it skirts the western shore of the Kyle of Durness, gradually gaining height to present stunning views along the estuary towards the north Atlantic. At low water the exposed sandbars make a narrow channel for the river Dionard. There is always a shallow river channel to the sea – whatever the state of the tide; though the sandbars are constantly shifting. It is possible to walk across the Kyle at low water, upstream of Keoldale road end, but the water will be likely to be waist-deep and the ebb and flow currents remain very strong. The sand on the margins of the stream is often very soft and the incoming tide can trap the unwary. An attempt to bypass the ferry on foot does have its significant dangers. It is best left to the shepherds and their sheep – they are well experienced in these waters and they know when and where to go.

As the road reaches the level it crosses two substantial stone arch bridges built over small burns, and meanders towards Achiemore, a substantial stone-built farmhouse to the right. Note the second milestone (10) on the right. Very often it is possible from here to see seals and their pups basking on the sandbars in the Kyle. The driver knows the best viewpoints and will stop at appropriate times.

Just beyond Achiemore, on the left, is the first military bombardment and firing range sentry post, or vidette, strikingly marked in large black and white squares – presumably to make them so much easier for the more assertive of our allies to hit!! When the range is in use, the videttes are in radio and telephone contact with Faraid Head Range Control, visible from this point away over the water to the east. Faraid Head controls all activity on the Cape Wrath Bombardment Range, on the ground, at sea and in the air. The range is used at various times by all the NATO allied forces, principally for aircraft bombing exercises but also occasionally for ship-to-shore shelling and combined exercises using ground troops.

This point marks the beginning of the Cape Wrath Bombardment and Firing Range; from here to the second vidette, some miles along the road, is military land. The range has been used continuously since February 1933. Field guns and artillery have been tested here, although nowadays the use is mainly aerial and naval bombardment training and practice. The Cape Wrath Bombardment and Military Firing Range is the only range in Western Europe where thousand-pound bombs are live-fired. Large combined military exercises are held throughout the year, usually in February, June and October. Only the summer use of the range occasionally adversely affects the minibus service. The military exercises can be observed safely from Balnakeil beach when the Cape Wrath road is closed.

Immediately to the right of the vidette, the foundations of the old Side School remain clearly visible. This was a small single-room Side School. The Side Schools were conducted by a competent (but sometimes unqualified) teacher under the overall supervision of the nearby formal school establishment (in this case that at Durness). The Cape Wrath Side School closed in 1947. It would have accommodated up to a maximum of ten children at its busiest, though at one time there were just one or two pupils. Some historical data concerning the Achiemore Side School is given in the chapter 'Magnificent Isolation.'

From this point it is just possible to make out the original storehouse erected by the Northern Lighthouse Board in the mid-1820s to facilitate the building of the lighthouse at Cape Wrath. This (now roofless) building is situated overlooking the very northern end of the Kyle, almost at sea level, on a level green area at map reference NC363699. The original road to the lighthouse started at this point and rose gently in a south-westerly direction to the top of Daill brae (NC352682). This original section of the road still exists as a footpath. Although it is overgrown, its course remains easily traceable; one of the two original small stone bridges specified in the lighthouse building contract survives at map reference NC358691.

From the first vidette, the road turns sharply left and approaches the river Daill and Daill House down a steep brae. Until relatively recent times the river here was crossed by a ford, which frequently impeded further progress. The small footbridge here is occasionally covered when the river is in spate.

In the early days of the minibus service it was common practise for the driver, along with a willing passenger, to wade out into the river with a rope (or more usually a towel) strung between them marking the width of the bus. If they could keep the river water below knee level, then it was safe to take the bus across! When the bus stalled it was expected that passengers would leap out and push.

The road bridge was built by the Royal Engineers and Royal Marines in 1981 as a 'temporary moveable structure.' The central supporting column and some of the buttresses are constructed using stone robbed from the former school building we have just passed. The cobbled approaches to the former ford are visible when water levels are low. Note the former quarry when crossing the bridge: eagles may sometimes be observed here.

The road now climbs steadily and steeply up Daill brae. Shortly after crossing the temporary Daill Bridge look for milestone 9, on the right, when ascending Daill brae. Look for the point on the right, almost at the summit, where the track of the original road to the NLB storehouse is just visible, marked by two large white rocks. From this point all the way to the lighthouse the road we are following is the original one built to service the lighthouse construction works in 1828. From Daill brae, for the next mile or so, the road is very uneven and soft in places. In 2005 the military succeeded in severely damaging it and it had to be closed for several months.

The peak of Fashven, at four hundred and sixty metres the highest point on this part of the Cape, is visible to the left. Loch Inshore is to the right. On the approach to Inshore House, just as the road takes a dip; note milestone 7 on the right. Inshore House is an early twentieth-century building adjacent to a well-preserved nineteenth-century cottage, now restored by the sponsors of the Cape Wrath Challenge annual running events and used as a bothy, first aid and feeding station. Inshore House was for a time a holiday cottage for members of the armed forces; it has recently been refurbished with the provision of separate shower and toilet facilities as accommodation for civilian and service personnel involved in the conduct of military exercises.

The narrow bridge just beyond Inshore House is the second of the two original small stone bridges provided for in the contract specifications when Cape Wrath lighthouse was built in the 1828. This bridge, together with the rather more impressive bridge over the river Kearvaig some miles further along, determines the maximum size and width of the minibuses able to be used on the lighthouse service.

The road crosses the Allt na Guaille a second time, via a wooden structure, on the gradual climb to the summit between the hills of Maovally on the left and Sgribhis-bheinn on the right. Note milestone 6 on your right shortly after the wooden bridge. This area is littered with unexploded ordnance, as the many warning signs attest. Leave the road here at your own peril. And no souvenirs on the return bus.

As the summit corner is rounded, there are spectacular views towards Kearvaig Bay and Cape Wrath itself. Note milestone 5 on the right on the approach to the black hut at Kearvaig lane end. Walkers having made the coastal journey from the Cape might be picked up here, on either outbound or return runs. The farmhouse on the beach at Kearvaig is now used as basic shelter and accommodation by the Scottish Mountain Bothy Association. The house, less than a kilometre's walk away, is left open for anyone to use. This really is the place to be if you want to get away from it all. A small Side School was established briefly at Kearvaig, most recently just after the Second World War.

Away to the right are the Clo Mor cliffs: at well over nine hundred feet tall, the highest on the British mainland. Clo Mor is renowned for the numbers and diversity of the seabirds that nest on its cliffs.

The road now enters perhaps its most exciting and challenging section. Milestone 4 appears on the right of the road, on the approach to the high stone arch of the Kearvaig bridge. The second vidette marks the end of the military firing range, although there are proposals for the range to be extended towards Cape Wrath. The videttes are manned during military use of the range, and by civilians nowadays. Originally, armed military personnel were stationed at the videttes.

Kearvaig Bridge has stood virtually unaltered since 1828. It was included in the contract specifications for the building of the lighthouse. The main structure appears now exactly as it was built, and it is perhaps the most awkward over which to take the buses. At its narrowest part it allows just four inches' clearance either side. Note the complete absence of white automotive paint anywhere on the bridge parapets. Skill, or what?

Shortly after crossing the bridge over the Kearvaig river, there is a spectacular view to the right into Kearvaig Bay. The beach here is one example of the many absolutely stunning, secluded, perfect beaches around the north coast of Scotland – which very few people ever see and fewer still get to walk on. It could be argued that it is far better than the more widely publicised beach at Sandwood Bay; you are unlikely to meet anyone else at Kearvaig, something which cannot be said for Sandwood. Kearvaig Bay's isolation is its greatest charm.

The sea stack in Kearvaig Bay is called Stac Clo Kearvaig. In more recent years it has been named 'The Cathedral' because of the twin spires with the natural window between; truly an awe-inspiring sight.

The road now avoids the worst of the severe gradients, meandering towards the very tip of the Cape Wrath peninsula. On the next level section, note milestone 3 to the right. In this area we are most likely to spot some of the hundreds of red deer (stags, hinds and calves) which populate this wild remote region. Look out also for rare water birds on the small lochans, and eagles, buzzards, grouse and skuas (great and arctic) overhead.

Notice how the road carefully follows the contours of the land, avoiding the necessity to ascend steep hills or cross geographical features by further bridges and cuttings. Constructing the road in this way made the engineering simpler, and eased gradients for the horse-drawn heavy loads during the early days of the lighthouse construction. Traces of the many localised rock outcrops used as quarry sources may also be seen. As milestone 2 is approached, we get a spectacular view of the eastern cliffs of Cape Wrath.

Milestone 2 on the right is followed by a steep gradient and a series of corners to the junction with the road from Clais Charnach. The second of the two Northern Lighthouse Board storehouses – built to facilitate the delivery of equipment and building materials during the construction of the Cape Wrath lighthouse – still exists here, exactly as it was erected almost two hundred years ago.

There is a very well-engineered slipway at Clais Charnach, complete with the remains of rope wire haulage winches dating from the very earliest days of the Northern Lighthouse Board's involvement with Cape Wrath. At one time, there was considerable oil-storage capacity here. All the supplies were delivered by sea to Clais Charnach and hauled to the lighthouse two miles away by road. In recent years, helicopters have made the process much quicker and easier. Cape Wrath was the first shore-based light in Scotland to be relieved and re-supplied by helicopter, in January 1977.

Traces of the peat-cutting beds may still be seen in the shallow valley to the west of Clais Charnach. Peat would have been cut and dried here by the families resident at Cape Wrath, before being hauled away for domestic heating and cooking. There have been no trees on the Cape within living memory, and therefore no wood for burning. The lighthouse personnel were provided with coal; peat would be a welcome additional fuel source.

The remaining wooden poles seen alongside the road in various places are the few survivors of the overhead telephone line installed to service the war signalling station in 1939. The Post Office Engineering Department erected four hundred poles and eleven miles of double wire at the behest of the naval authorities. When the overhead line was replaced with a buried connection the poles were left in situ; most of the more easily accessible ones were scavenged for firewood. The more remote ones survive, and some are used as territorial markers by the indigenous red deer. Many posts are heavily marked at their bases, where the deer have rubbed against them. Hinds (and stags towards the end of September) are often encountered between milestones three and two. The ceramic insulators still attached to the surviving telephone posts also attract collectors.

As we approach milestone 1, on the left, we catch a glimpse of Sandwood Bay away to the left, about six miles away as the bonxie flies. Also visible in Sandwood Bay is the sea stack known as Am Buachaille, or The Herdsman. After passing the last milepost we enter perhaps the most gripping section of the road to Cape Wrath. The road is carved out of the valley side, high above a vertiginous drop which would do a large measure of no good at all to either bus or passengers should there be any momentary loss of concentration. This is the 'Wall of Death.' It would, perhaps, be unwise to engage the driver in deep conversation here.

Shortly, we see an impressive view of the sea and the horizon of the North Atlantic Ocean. Directly northwards from here there is no land at all until the North Pole is reached; westwards there is no land until the coast of Canada. Away to the south-west the Butt of Lewis in the Outer Hebrides can often be seen, perhaps forty miles distant, and from the tip of Cape Wrath itself it is often possible to see Hoy, one of the Orkney Islands, a similar distance to the east.

Rounding a corner, we get our first sight of the lighthouse. After the eleven-mile journey across the Parph we can appreciate just how isolated it is, and how vital the need for it on this exposed headland.

The large regular rectangular buildings on the left as we approach are the compressor and machine rooms built at the beginning of the twentieth century to power the newly-developed fog warning apparatus. The similar buildings on the hill top to the right were established by Lloyd's of London as a radio signalling and receiving station. The small square building adjacent to the compressor rooms is a pump house, built to raise water from a spring a hundred or so feet down the nearby cliff-face. This is the only natural water supply at Cape Wrath. Lighthouse men, their families and the signallers who were stationed here relied mainly for their everyday needs on rainwater, which was stored in the many large tanks to be seen dotted around, and on a system of underground cisterns installed as part of the lighthouse construction scheme.

The original fog horn survives at Cape Wrath, although it is no longer used. There is a substantial stone wall at the fog horn house which provides a safe viewing gallery for those who want to be right at the very tip of the Cape. From here, the very north-western-most point of Cape Wrath, it is sometimes possible to see dolphins and porpoises. Seals also appear in the cove at the Cape; they bask on the exposed rocks at low water. Fulmars, kittiwakes, shags, gannets, cormorants and puffins may also been seen in season, soaring around the cliffs.

Small fishing vessels and huge cruise ships pass Cape Wrath. Frequently, warships of many nations pass very close inshore, and occasionally an enormous oil-drilling rig can be watched being towed either to the Shetland drilling fields or to storage in the Cromarty Firth near Invergordon.

Incidentally, the mile markers along the road were carved and erected by the lighthouse keepers stationed at Cape Wrath. That is why they number southwards from the Cape rather than northwards from the ferry. The lighthouse was the centre of their world.

Allegedly there are fifty-two passing places along the road between the ferry and the lighthouse. Most are overgrown, many are soft and at least one is unstable and dangerous. There are probably no more than five or six places along the whole of the route where it is possible to turn the bus. Trust your driver. They know the route and trust their colleagues.

Throughout the whole of its length, the road to Cape Wrath is an ordinary public highway maintained by the Highland Regional Council at the public expense. It forms part of the national road network, although it is not connected to any road other than by the ferry. The road was built in 1828, purely so that the lighthouse could be erected and supplied. It has been a public road since 1833.

The closest other public road on the Cape is the unclassified single track road running from Kinlochbervie to Sheigra at Blairmore, probably over ten miles to the south in a direct line. The walk from there via Sandwood Bay and the west coast is spectacular indeed, but severe. It is always wise to make specific arrangements to be collected at the lighthouse, although tide and weather can still upset plans. Wisdom would suggest commencing any west coast walk starting from the lighthouse. In that way, transport arrangements at the extremity of Cape Wrath can be guaranteed.

In the days when all the farmsteads were occupied, when the lighthouse was permanently manned and when there was a contingent living at the Lloyd's radio station, there would perhaps have been a maximum of thirty residents on Cape Wrath. The lighthouse lorry delivered supplies to resident families every week, and the postman made a three times-weekly delivery, as far as the lighthouse, by bicycle! The past really is another country.

The lighthouse was the last Scottish shore station to be automated, in 1998, and the Lloyd's station was abandoned many years before that. The lighthouse keepers were the last permanent residents on the Cape. No-one lives on Cape Wrath now. Shepherds occasionally stay over on the Capeside, but not for longer than a night or two. Armed Services personnel on exercise leave this least favourite posting as soon as they are permitted.

All civilian vehicles on the Cape are floated over the Kyle of Durness on a specially-built pontoon barge powered by outboard motors. The minibuses are taken across in April and returned to Durness in October. A calm wind-free day has to be selected, and the slack water period either side of high tide presents the fewest problems – no-one really wants an unscheduled trip, backwards and at some speed, in the direction of Norway. Minibuses on a flat pontoon barge act just like a huge sail. The minibuses stay during the season at the Capeside slipway overnight, safe in the knowledge that there is (usually) no-one to take them, and nowhere to go anyway.

Diesel fuel has to be ferried across in twenty-five-litre drums, and pumped into the vehicles via the luxury of a fixed electric pump powered from the vehicle battery. Usually, though, the drivers eschew this unnecessary modern intervention; they rely on the tried and tested use of jug, funnel and gravity. Should you be present when this determined exhibition of manual dexterity is being carried out, then the entertainment is provided at no additional charge.

CHAPTER 3

NORTHERN LIGHTS

*The Creation and Formal Incorporation of
the Northern Lighthouse Board 1786 – 1804,
and Its Work to the Present Date*

After concerted lobbying and pressure from ship owners and merchants who were alarmed at the dangers to shipping in the seas around the Scottish coast, a Bill 'for the Security of Navigation and the Fishermen in the Northern Parts of Great Britain' was presented to the House of Commons on 31st May 1786, largely at the instigation of Angus M.P. Mr. George Dempster. The Royal Assent was granted, for 'An Act for Erecting Certain Light-Houses in the Northern Parts of Great Britain,' on 27 June of the same year.

The Act established an independent board of Trustees, or Commissioners, charged with the duty of erecting four lighthouses, and authorised the Trustees on completion of the structures to levy passing vessels, by which means the lights were to be funded. By this method the initial building costs and subsequent maintenance expenses would be defrayed. The four lights sanctioned by the 1786 Act were those at Kinnaird Head near Fraserburgh (completed December 1787), Mull of Kintyre (April 1788), North Ronaldsay, Orkney (October 1789), and Eilean Glas, Scalpay, Outer Hebrides (December 1789).

The 1786 Act also stipulated the levies payable by passing shipping for the benefit provided by the four lights. One penny per ton was to be charged on British vessels, and two pennies per ton on foreign ships passing any light, with the exception of whaling ships and those on passage to northern Russia.

This was not, of course, by any means the first attempt at establishing lights for navigational assistance around the coast of Scotland. With steadily increasing coastal trade from the early seventeenth century – coal mining and transportation, salt exports, fishing and fish trading for example – the need for warning devices to assist navigation became all the more apparent. In the early days, merchants and ship owners resisted the mandatory provision of fixed navigation lights, since they would be the ones expected to pay the heavy tolls required to fund establishment of the lights.

But increased trade meant busier seaways, and dangers thereby increased: larger vessels meant greater loss of life and cargo when a tragedy occurred. Informal talks continued with no great incentive to improve matters, for there was no consensus in the north. Things were rather different south of the border. There the (private) English lighthouse service had been founded in 1514 as 'The Most Glorious and Undivided Trinity of St. Clement in the Parish of Deptford Strond in the County of Kent.' Trinity House, as it came to be known, established itself as the only body responsible for the provision and maintenance of lights and lighthouses protecting the English Coast, and that remains so to this day. But the authority of Trinity House did not extend to Scottish waters.

In 1636 a permanent light was established on the Isle of May, marking the Inchcape and Carr rocks in the Firth of Forth. May, too, had a fearsome reputation for shipwreck and destruction. Three of the favoured Scottish courtiers of King Charles I were authorised by the Scottish Privy Council to design, build and maintain the light. It may well be that their concern placed profit in equal measure with safety. A stone tower forty feet high and twenty-five feet square was built, supporting an iron brazier in which a coal fire burned. It has been recorded that in 1799 this light burned as much as four hundred tons of coal in a year, and that it could consume three tons in one night during stormy conditions. In 1810 *HMS Nymphen* and *HMS Pallas* foundered with significant loss of life when they mistook a nearby lime kiln for the navigation light, and steered ashore. A substantial part of this, arguably the first formal lighthouse tower in Scotland, still exists.

Following the establishment of the Isle of May Light, local bodies and worthies elsewhere in Scotland began to appreciate the benefits to their local trading positions of safer coastlines. Moves therefore began in the estuaries of the Tay, Solway and Clyde to provide navigation aids with the prime intention of creating safe, reliable access to their port facilities. In 1687, ship owners and masters in Dundee erected lights to help navigation through the constantly shifting sandbars of the Tay.

In 1756, the world's first public body with lighthouse provision and maintenance as its prime function – originally the Cumray Lighthouse Trust, later the Clyde Lighthouses Trust – was empowered to erect a coal-fired light tower on Little Cumbrae, protecting the navigation in the Firth and lower reaches of the Clyde. Glasgow Town Council prepared a bill for presentation to parliament in January 1755 that also permitted the removal of obstacles and shoals in the course of the lower Clyde, and allowed dredging of the channel to maintain sufficient depth for trading ships. Its Private Act received the Royal Assent in April 1756.

1782 was the worst in living memory for the intensity, frequency and ferocity of its winter storms, and great damage and loss of life resulted throughout the whole of the coastal British Isles. This was the catalyst for George Dempster's determination to rectify matters, and he was the prime mover in bringing to Parliament the bill which became the 1786 Act for the Establishment of the Scottish Lights, and the inception of the Commissioners of the Northern Lighthouses.

The new body held its inaugural meeting on 1 August 1786. The Commissioners comprised the Lord Advocate and the Solicitor General for Scotland, the Lord Provost of Edinburgh and the First Bailie of Glasgow, The Provosts of Aberdeen, Inverness and

Campbeltown, and the Sheriffs of Edinburgh, Lanark, Renfrew, Bute, Argyll, Inverness, Ross, Orkney, Caithness and Aberdeen.

Their initial decisions at that first meeting were directed to finding an engineer to design and build the four lights authorised by the Act, and the raising of loans for the work, since the Commissioners obviously could not charge light dues until the lights were built and operating satisfactorily. Robert Louis Stevenson relates in his *Records of a Family of Engineers*, published in 1896, that 'the funds of the Board were at first laughably inadequate. They embarked on their career on a loan of twelve hundred pounds, and their income in 1789, after relief by a fresh Act of Parliament, amounted to less than three hundred.'

The Board's first Engineer, Thomas Smith, was appointed with effect from 22 January 1787; with him an unbroken Stevenson family connection of Engineers to the Northern Lighthouse Board stretched forward to 1938. For more details of this unique part of Scotland's lighthouse heritage, see the separate chapter describing five consecutive generations of the Stevenson family's collaboration of internationally-renowned civil engineers with the Northern Lighthouse Board.

The scope but not the purpose of the Board has changed, of course, over the years since its creation. In 1789, the Board's responsibilities were extended to cover the whole of the Scottish coast. In 1804 'the Commissioners of the Northern Lighthouses' were formally incorporated by Act of Parliament, and in 1815 their powers were further extended to include the provision and maintenance of lights protecting the coast of the Isle of Man. By 1819, the Commissioners were responsible for sixteen major lighthouses, constructed in the most exposed and inaccessible coastal and island locations.

In 1836, it was suggested that overall responsibility for the Scottish and Manx lights might be transferred to Trinity House. Something of an internecine war then developed, such was the resentment at this perceived compromising of the Northern Lighthouse Board's independence. The Board did maintain its independence, although any proposals for new lighthouses had to be submitted to Trinity House: no scheme could proceed until formal approval had been granted by the Board of Trade. This was the situation until 1894.

By 1894, there were sixty-nine lights under the jurisdiction of the Commissioners, designed, erected and maintained by successive Engineers Thomas Smith and Robert, Alan, David, Thomas and David A. Stevenson.

Currently, the Northern Lighthouse Board consists of the Lord Advocate, the Solicitor General for Scotland, the six Sheriffs-Principal of Scotland (viz Glasgow; Tayside, Central & Fife; North Strathclyde; South Strathclyde, Dumfries & Galloway; Lothian & Borders; and Grampian, Highland and Islands), the Lords Provost of Edinburgh, Glasgow and Aberdeen, the Convenor of the Highland Regional Council, the Convenor of the Council of Argyll and Bute, a Department for Transport nominee representing the interests of the Isle of Man, and up to five co-opted Commissioners each serving a term of three years and elected by the Commissioners.

The Northern Lighthouse Board is one of three General Lighthouse Authorities established under the authority of the Merchant Shipping Acts 1894 & 1995. It covers the entire United Kingdom and Ireland. The others are the Commissioners of Irish Lights, and Trinity House in London.

The Commissioners of the Northern Lighthouses, under Section 195 of the Merchant Shipping Act, 1995, now manage all lighthouses, buoys and beacons throughout Scotland and its adjoining seas and islands, including the Isle of Man. The Board is vested with responsibility for 212 major and minor lighthouses (all now automated), 160 buoys, 37 unlit radar beacons, 25 Racon stations and 4 DGPS stations. There are no longer any operational fog signal stations, the last – Skerryvore – having been discontinued in 2005. The Commissioners also have responsibility for the removal of wrecks which might pose a hazard to shipping in Scottish waters.

The Board operates sea-going vessels for the delivery of stores and supplies to lighthouse establishments, buoy-working and the statutory inspections of navigational aids on oil rigs in the Scottish sector, in the form of *NLV Pharos* and *MV Pole Star*.

The current *MV Pharos* is the tenth of the NLB's vessels to bear the name. The first sloop *Pharos* was purchased by Thomas Smith in 1799, fitted out at the Elie shipyard in Fife, and gifted to the Northern Lighthouse Board as a mark of generous appreciation by their Engineer. *Pharos* was used extensively in the early years of the NLB for tours of inspection of the Board's ongoing programme of major lighthouse building.

The second vessel to bear the name *Pharos* was a prize taken by the Navy in 1806 during the North Sea skirmishes of the Napoleonic war. The vessel was a captured Prussian fishing dogger, purchased by the Board as a floating lightship for use during the erection of the Bell Rock lighthouse. By July 1807, this notoriously unstable 'purgatorial' vessel had been renamed, overhauled, rigged for her new purpose and moored in the lee of the Bell Rock.

In 2004, the Board announced its intention to acquire a new seagoing lighthouse supply vessel. The order was placed in November 2004 with the Gdansk Stoczina Remontowa SA shipyard in Poland, and the following year it was announced that the new vessel would be named *NLV Pharos*, thereby continuing the Board's association with the name. The new ship was launched by HRH the Princess Royal on 3 February 2006, and took up station at the Oban base a year later. The previous *MV Pharos* (1986 gross tons, commissioned 1993) left the Commissioners' service in September 2006. She has now been renamed the *Pharos SG* and operates as a fishery patrol and logistics vessel for the South Georgia government.

The new *NLV Pharos* is 84.20 metres in length and has accommodation for seven officers and eleven PO/crew members; she is equipped with the very latest hydrographic surveying and wreck-finding capability, in addition to a thirty-tonne crane and forward helideck.

The move towards automation began as long ago as 1894. This first manned lighthouse to lose its permanent crew was Oxcars (built 1885) off Granton in the river Forth. It was converted to gas operation, and town gas was delivered weekly by boat, with the boatman winding the clockwork timer.

The comprehensive programme of lighthouse automation began in earnest in the mid 1950's, and was completed by 1998; Fair Isle South (built 1892) was the last manned station in Scotland. Fladda light in the Inner Hebrides (built 1860) was the first Scottish lighthouse to be automated in the planned programme of de-manning, in 1956. Between 1960 and 1980, approximately twenty-five major lights were automated and converted to gas operation. Gas pressure performed the dual purpose of turning the reflectors and illuminating the mantles to produce an extremely intense light.

The final phase of the automation programme took place between 1980 and 1998. Generators, batteries and solar power were now the norm; all previous gas-powered establishments were converted to solar power with battery emergency back-up. Strathy Point (1958) was the last manned lighthouse built by the Northern Lighthouse Board; it was automated in 1997.

Cape Wrath light enjoyed a manned life of one hundred and seventy years until it was automated in 1998. North Rona (just visible from Cape Wrath on a very clear day) was built in 1984 as an automatic station, and Sule Skerry, built 1895/automated 1982, away to the east towards Orkney and occasionally visible from the Cape when the weather is particularly clear, is another isolated rock light. (N.B. North Rona is not to be confused with the light at Rona north of Raasay in the Inner Hebrides between Skye and Wester Ross, also built by the Stevenson family). North Rona and Sule Skerry are visible with the aid of binoculars, on the horizon, each some degrees either side of due north from Cape Wrath.

The minor light on the eastern shore of Loch Eriboll was erected in 1894 as a gas-powered automatic installation (the white mark on the cliff below the light is the residue of spent calcium carbide) and updated in 1937; it was fully rebuilt in 2004.

The Board completed its programme of converting all of its statutory lit buoyage to solar power in 1997, and an on-going programme of modernisation and overhaul will continue well into the twenty-first century.

Operational costs are met from the 'General Lighthouse Fund,' financed by the collection of Light Dues levied on all commercial ships and fishing vessels exceeding ten metres in length that call at ports with the Board's jurisdiction. The Board has an annual expenditure in excess of £10 million, not including major projects. Although the Fund is administered by the Department of Transport, the three Lighthouse Authorities are entirely independent and self-financing; they receive no contribution from the national exchequer.

The Northern Lighthouse Board has operated from offices at 84 George Street in Edinburgh since 1832. All the Board's administrative, engineering, ship and helicopter support, personnel, finance, procurement and information technology capacity is at this address, together with the centre which remotely monitors all major and minor lighthouse establishments, by land line and radio link, continually day and night. There is, in addition, a shore base at Oban in the west of Scotland, which provides facilities for the NLB supply vessels, the landing and refuelling of helicopters, maintaining, painting and repairing navigational buoys, battery charging, and the conditioning, servicing and construction of buoys.

The prime concern of the Northern Lighthouse Board and the Commissioners has always been – in the words of its Latin motto –

'IN SALUTEM OMNIUM'
(FOR THE SAFETY OF ALL)

There can be no finer testament than this.

CHAPTER 4

THE LEADING LIGHTHOUSE FAMILY

The Stevenson Connection: Five Generations
of Lighthouse Engineers 1786–1938

For more than two centuries, from the birth of Thomas Smith in 1752 to the death in 1971 of his great-great-grandson David Alan Stevenson, Scotland's foremost family of internationally-celebrated civil engineers designed, constructed and developed lighthouse technology – principally in Scottish waters, but they also undertook major civil engineering schemes throughout the world.

Thomas Smith was born on 6 December 1752 in Ferryport-on-Craig, a small village on the south bank of the river Tay, at a time when the need to expand and improve the nation's capital was beginning to be appreciated. The necessity to drain Edinburgh's north loch, develop the New Town and connect it via an impressive new bridge were the foundations on which Scotland's modernising capital city was built. The New Town also needed street lighting, and this necessity coincided with the need for lights as navigational aids around Scotland's treacherous coastal waters.

Thomas Smith's father was drowned in a shipwreck; young Thomas was raised by his mother and apprenticed at the age of twelve to a Dundee metal-worker. In 1770, when James Craig's plans for the development of Edinburgh's New Town were well-established, Thomas Smith arrived in the capital and took employment in the metal trade. By 1781, he was established on his own account as a tinsmith manufacturing oil lamps, brass fittings and fenders – goods much in demand by the newly-arrived middle classes.

In 1787, Thomas Smith was awarded a contract by the Edinburgh Town Council to provide street lighting, at a rate of six pence per lamp, in the Old Town and part of the New Town. His own design for a revolutionary oil lamp, complete with a polished metal parabolic reflector, was no doubt decisive in his successful tender. By the end of the eighteenth century he was contracted to provide street lights in Glasgow, and by 1810 he was lighting the streets of Perth, Stirling, Ayr, Haddington, Aberdeen and Leith – thus becoming the leading expert in the field.

Throughout the last quarter of the eighteenth century the Industrial Revolution enhanced trade by sea, and increased trade meant more wrecks, given the almost non-existent aids to navigation. Thomas Smith's reputation on the leading edge of lighting technology led, in no small part, to his appointment as the first Engineer to the newly-established (1786) Commissioners of the Northern Lighthouses (later the Northern Lighthouse Board). Smith was not, however, the Board's first choice as Engineer. In September 1786, the Board approached Ezekiel Walker of King's Lynn, who had developed a reputation as one of the foremost lighthouse engineers in the country. Walker declined the post, but offered to pass on his expertise to the engineer appointed. Thomas Smith was appointed as Engineer to the Board with effect from January 1787 and was reported, by the following March, to be fully acquainted with the principles involved, and the Board was satisfied with his abilities. Four lighthouses were sanctioned under the enabling legislation, with the requirement that they be completed and lit within four years. Thomas Smith managed the project and had the lights working satisfactorily within three.

By 1791, Thomas Smith had been married twice, only to see of both of his wives die soon after marriage. He was left with three surviving small children at a time when he was fully engaged in building more lighthouses for the Board and the Glasgow Lighthouse Trustees, in addition to developing his public street lighting commitments. Pladda (Inner Hebrides), Little Cumbrae (Clyde estuary), the Tay Lights (Firth of Tay), Leith Pier lights, Portpatrick (Wigtownshire) and the Pentland Skerries light (Orkney) had all been newly-built or fully modernised under Thomas Smith's management by the early 1790s.

Into Thomas Smith's desperate situation entered a close family friend and neighbour, who had known both his former wives. Jean Stevenson, although widowed herself and bringing up her own offspring, offered to care for Thomas Smith's young family during his unavoidable long absences. Jean Stevenson had been widowed in 1774, when her son Robert was aged just two. A subsequent unsuccessful marriage to one James Hogg left her with a further two children; her husband deserted her and disappeared to England.

Thomas Smith proposed marriage to Jean Stevenson after a decent interval following their meeting, but the problem remained that Jean was still officially married to James Hogg. He was eventually traced to Westmoreland and a divorce was arranged. Thomas and Jean were married on 14 November 1792. There was one child of the marriage, a girl, Betsy, who died aged seven. But the child of Jean Stevenson's first marriage, Robert, now aged twenty, prospered and developed into a skilled young engineer. Thomas Smith took his stepson into his business and it is clear that both men came to rely on and appreciate each other's talents.

Robert Stevenson was first apprenticed to a gunsmith and later to his stepfather, with whom he became a business partner in 1797. Throughout the 1790s, Robert assisted him in his lighthouse projects. Robert Stevenson and Thomas Smith's daughter Jane ('Jeannie') knew each other well, from the time of Robert's arrival in Edinburgh at the age of six; for seven years they had been stepbrother and stepsister when, in 1799, they married. The early years of the Stevenson family tree can be very confusing, given that successive generations relied on repeated Christian names for both male and female children, and that Robert's father-in-law and stepfather was one and the same man.

Robert Stevenson succeeded Thomas Smith as Engineer to the Commissioners of the Northern Lights in July 1808, though from 1797 he had been delegated almost complete autonomy in lighthouse matters. Robert had gained an excellent grounding in lighthouse design but had no formal educational qualifications, having accompanied Thomas Smith for many years during his professional association with the Commissioners for Northern Lights. Thomas Smith continued a close involvement with the design and development of lamp manufacture, and was able to devote more time to his street lighting interests. He died in June 1815.

There can be no doubt that the lighthouse which established and confirmed Robert's reputation as a civil engineer specialising in lighthouse construction was that built under extreme circumstances on the Bell Rock, at the entrance to the Firth of Forth off Arbroath. Bell Rock was the culmination of a rise to prominence extending over fourteen years, which included Robert's supervision of the building of a further three exposed and isolated lighthouses for the Lighthouse Commissioners.

The erection of the Bell Rock light was an overwhelming achievement for the time. Robert was instrumental in making the case for a light on the Bell Rock from as early as 1799. He proposed the erection of a light supported on cast iron pillars, but almost immediately amended this to a stone tower light, as the Bell Rock was submerged to a depth of twelve feet by each tide.

A Bill to sanction the building of the Bell Rock light failed in the 1803 parliamentary session. Because of the hazardous nature of the project, Robert suggested to the Commissioners for Northern Lights that they secure the services of John Rennie as Consulting Engineer. A second application to Parliament secured an Enabling Act in 1806; thereafter a quiet dispute rumbled along between the

Rennie and Stevenson families for many decades into the future as to who made the major contribution to the project.

After Bell Rock was first lit on 1st February 1811, Robert Stevenson developed his own civil engineering practice which became one of the three leading firms in Great Britain. It practised continuously, always with Stevenson managing partners, until 1952.

Robert held the position of Engineer to, and Chief Executive of, the Northern Lighthouse Board from 1808 until his resignation in 1843, during which time he undertook the building of a further twenty-three lights. There can be no doubt that the entire Stevenson lighthouse dynasty was firmly anchored on the foundations laid by Robert. He died in July 1850, leaving one daughter and three sons; each of the sons entered the family civil engineering practice and each, in turn, became Engineer to the Northern Lighthouse Board.

Robert's first son was named Alan, and this is where the confusion starts: Robert's father was also an Alan, and the name occurs again in future generations. Robert's son Alan was born in April 1807, and he became articled to his father in the family practice in October 1822. In 1830, he was appointed clerk of works to the Northern Lighthouse Board under his father, who he succeeded as Engineer on Robert's retirement in January 1843. For much of his professional life, Alan suffered increasing ill-health. His greatest professional achievement was the erection of the Skerryvore lighthouse on a vicious rock outcrop twelve miles south west of the Inner Hebridean island of Tiree, facing the full force of the Atlantic gales.

Planning for the Skerryvore light began jointly between Robert and Alan in December 1837; the light was completed in 1844. Robert Louis Stevenson considered it to be 'the noblest of all extant deep-sea lights.' During his service as Engineer to the Northern Lighthouse Board, Alan oversaw the building of eight major lights and three minor lights. Eventually, illness forced his early retirement in 1853. On his death, the Commissioners for the North Lights recorded 'their deep and abiding regrets for the loss of a man whose services had been to them invaluable and whose works combined profound service and practical skill and conferred lasting honour and benefit on his county.'

On his retirement, Alan transferred his Northern Lighthouse Board work to his brothers David (born January 1815) and Thomas (born July 1818). He died in December 1865.

David entered the family partnership on the completion of his professional training in May 1838, and immediately assumed sole responsibility for the firm's general business management, a responsibility he retained for the next forty-three years. In March 1853 he succeeded his brother Alan as Engineer to the Northern Lighthouse Board. Just two years later, he resigned as sole Engineer and was succeeded in turn by the family firm of D & T Stevenson; this meant that he effectively succeeded himself, though now in partnership with his brother Thomas.

David and Thomas acted as joint Engineers to the Board until 1884, when David's retirement was forced by ill-health. Their most renowned achievements were the building of the lighthouses at Muckle Flugga, Shetland (temporary 1854, permanent 1857), Dubh Artach, Argyllshire (1867–72) and Chicken Rock, Isle of Man (1874–5). They presided over the most intense period of development by the Northern Lighthouse Board, being responsible for the erection of twenty-eight beacons, thirty lighthouses and the improvement of many more.

David died in July 1886. Thomas had suffered deteriorating health for some years, and in 1885 David Alan, born July 1854 eldest son of Thomas's brother David, was appointed as Joint Engineer to the Northern Lighthouse Board along with his uncle Thomas. David Alan assumed increasing lighthouse responsibility until Thomas's death in May 1887.

Robert Louis Stevenson (born 1850) was the only son of Thomas. Although it was intended that Robert Louis would follow the family tradition – and, indeed, he did start formal engineering training and accompanied his father and uncle on several tours of inspection of the northern lighthouses – his wilfulness prevailed and he established himself as one of the foremost literary figures of the Victorian era. Robert Louis always championed the achievements of the Stevenson engineers and wrote a comprehensive family biography entitled *Records of a Family of Engineers.* 'Whenever I smell salt water, I know that I am not far from one of the works of my ancestors,' wrote Robert Louis in 1880. He died in 1894, in Samoa, and is buried there.

David Alan (usually referred to as David A) became a partner in the family firm in 1878. He assumed the sole position as Engineer to the Northern Lighthouse Board on the death of his father David Stevenson in July 1886. David A constantly lobbied the Board for official recognition of his brother Charles Alexander (born January 1855), but it was never forthcoming. David A and Charles A worked together on the majority of the late nineteenth and early twentieth century northern light projects, although it was only David A who ever held an official position with the Board. In 1886, Charles A was taken into the family firm as a partner.

David A worked jointly with his uncle Thomas on the erection of lights at Fidra, off North Berwick (1885), Oxcars, Midlothian (1886) and Ailsa Craig, Ayrshire (also 1886). In his own right and almost always assisted by his brother Charles A, he presided over the design and construction of twenty-four lighthouses, forty-eight fog signal stations, five light ships, seventy-five minor lights and numerous beacons and navigation buoys. Amongst these, the most notable were Sule Skerry (1892–95), at forty miles north of Cape Wrath Britain's most remote lighthouse, Flannan Isles (1897–99), Bass Rock (1900–02), Hyskeir, Inverness-shire (1904) and Duncansby Head, Caithness (1924).

During David A's period of office with the Northern Lighthouse Board, the brightness and reliability of lights increased markedly. In 1875 the most powerful Scottish coastal light shone at 44,500 candlepower. By 1901 there were several in excess of 100,000 cp and the Isle of May light had been upgraded to an electric candle-power equivalent of three million. All this was achieved largely with the unrecognised contribution of Charles A.

Although only five lighthouses were built by the Northern Lighthouse Board after 1914, during David A's last twenty-four years in office great improvements in lighting technology and the modernisation of existing lights, major and minor, presented a heavy workload.

The last generation of the lighthouse Stevensons began in February 1891 with the birth of yet another David Alan (usually referred to as 'D Alan'). He was the eldest child and only son of Charles A. D Alan followed the family tradition of a sound education followed by formal engineering qualification and absorption into the family civil engineering business, in 1917. As time progressed, he was able increasingly to assist his father and uncle in lighthouse inspection tours, although his specialisation and principal interests were illumination and radio beacon technology.

During the 1930s, the Northern Lighthouse Board became increasingly reluctant to confirm the Stevenson family succession as its Engineer. David A had, by 1936, been the Board's Engineer for fifty years and, although over eighty years of age, appeared content to remain in the post and capable of carrying out the duties. David A had no children to carry on the dynastic tradition, but he did have a suitably qualified and experienced brother in Charles A. David A and Charles A are remembered mainly for their refinements to existing systems and for their dedicated commitment to the Northern Lighthouse Board.

But times were changing. By 1936, family disputes had forced the dissolution of the family firm of D & C (i.e. David and Charles) Stevenson, and they were obliged to vacate the offices they had occupied at 84 George Street, Edinburgh (the headquarters of the Northern Lighthouse Board) for almost a hundred and fifty years. A new partnership named A & C (i.e. Alan and Charles – son and father) continued at 90A George Street until the retirement of Charles in 1940, but by then the die had been irrevocably cast.

David A retired as Engineer to the Northern Lighthouse Board on 31 March 1938 at the age of eighty-three, after fifty-two years continuous loyal service. With his retirement the Board severed its formal hundred and thirty-year connection with the Stevenson engineering dynasty; John Oswald was appointed Engineer.

Charles A died in May 1950. D Alan served as Engineer to the Clyde Lighthouses Trust until 1952: he died in December 1971.

Between 1790 and 1938, eight members of the Stevenson dynasty planned, designed and constructed over one hundred manned major lighthouses and a huge number of minor lights, beacons, buoys, fog warnings and radio installations around the inhospitable coast of northern Britain. Thomas Smith and four consecutive Stevenson generations held the post of Engineer (or its equivalent) to the Northern Lighthouse Board during the eighteenth, nineteenth and twentieth centuries. The title might have changed along the way, but there can be no doubt that the Stevenson commitment to the family tradition strengthened the primacy of the Northern Lighthouse Board to the benefit of seafarers in the harsh northern waters. Britain, and all seafaring nations, owes them an incalculable debt of gratitude.

CHAPTER 5

LIGHTING THE VERY EDGE

*Building The Lighthouse and
Associated Works at Cape Wrath*

The need for an effective reliable light at Cape Wrath was recognised as early as the mid-eighteenth century; successive shipping disasters in the vicinity of this wild exposed headland devoid of all human habitation served only to further emphasise the dangers. Violent storms in 1782 and again in the 1790s made the situation quite unacceptable; in the storms of October 1797 three ships were lost at Cape Wrath on one night with just two survivors, and two years later widespread winter gales around the whole of the northern coast made the situation intolerable for mariners and shipowners alike. And piracy and press gangs posed additional problems.

Robert Louis Stevenson (great-grandson of Thomas Smith and grandson of Robert Stevenson) relates in his *Records of a Family of Engineers* that

> In 1794 Smith came 'very near to be taken' by a French squadron. In 1813 Robert Stevenson was cruising about the neighbourhood of Cape Wrath in the immediate fear of Commodore Rogers. The men, and especially the sailors, of the lighthouse service must be protected by a medal and ticket from the brutal activity of the press gang. And the zeal of volunteer patriots was at time embarrassing.

Modern day cynicism springs to mind. With friends like that, who needs enemies?

In his Report on the Island of Lewis to the Right Honourable Lord Seaforth written in 1800, the Reverend Mr. Headrick states:

> They (the Government) should also have a sloop-of-war or stout gun-boat stationed at Stornoway, to cruise occasionally between the Butt of Lewis and the Orkneys. Since convoys were appointed, privateers commonly nestle about the Faro Isles, and run down between the Butt and Cape Wrath, where they find the trade defenceless, as the convoy commonly leaves it at the east entrance of the Pentland Firth.

From this it is clear that occasional piracy was not unknown in these far northern waters. It also seems evident that measures to protect commercial shipping in the North Sea and around the north eastern tip of Scotland by the implementation of a protective convoy system had merely transferred the problem to the waters of the Minch and the inner north-western approaches.

Doubtless also there would have been increasing lobbying and pressure for the provision of a lighthouse at Cape Wrath as the eighteenth century progressed towards its end, following the establishment in 1786 of the Commissioners of the Northern Lights (later the Northern Lighthouse Board). But the inaccessibility of the far north-western tip of Sutherland, the fact that there were no roads in the area at all (which meant, therefore, that even the survey required prior to the formulation of a scheme of proposal could only be undertaken after a hazardous sea voyage and a dangerous landing on these inhospitable northern shores), and the pressing need for lighthouses in other equally dangerous locations, meant that Cape Wrath did not receive the priority it truly warranted.

The 'First' (or 'Old') Statistical Account of Scotland prepared between 1791 and 1799 verifies the official concern felt at the time for the safety of mariners at Cape Wrath. The treacherous nature of the Cape itself and the rocks lying just offshore are clearly spelled out. It is, perhaps, more than coincidental that the petitions of concerned shipowners (and, within a year or so, of the principal local landowner) immediately followed publication of this first detailed national survey of every Parish in Scotland.

There are surviving documents from the very early years of the nineteenth century which graphically illustrate the fears of maritime traders regarding the dangers of Cape Wrath and its waters. They had seen and experienced the benefits that the lights erected and operated by the Commissioners of the Northern Lights had brought to sailing vessels trading around the hazardous north coast of the British Isles. They demanded the protection a light could bring and began a campaign, whole-heartedly supported by Lord Reay, the principal landowner in north west Sutherland, for the provision of an aid to navigation at Cape Wrath.

Following the successful construction and implementation of the first four lighthouses sanctioned by the legislation that enabled the creation of the Commissioners of the Northern Lights in 1786, authority was almost immediately sought for the erection of further lights at acknowledged dangerous coastal locations. These first lights in the second phase of Northern Lighthouse Board expansion were erected at Pladda, Arran, Isle of Bute in 1790 and Pentland Skerries to the east of the Pentland Firth in 1794. This latter light protected the eastern approach to the North channel passing around the north of Scotland; doubtless the Commissioners and their Engineer were only too aware of the need to light the Pentland Firth's western approaches, at Cape Wrath.

Lights erected or improved for other lighthouse authorities by Thomas Smith and Robert Stevenson in the period immediately following the first four NLB lights, were at the River Tay off Dundee (modernised 1789), Leith Pier (modernised 1790), Portpatrick, Wigtownshire (1790), Little Cumbrae, Bute (1793) and Cloch, Renfrewshire (new major light, 1797). All this frantic activity in surveying, designing, contracting and supervising an extensive lighthouse programme inevitably meant that some suggestions for light provision received a lower priority than their promoters would have wished.

At the close of the eighteenth century a concerted campaign began for the placing of a lighthouse at Cape Wrath. Prolonged violent gales lasting for weeks from December 1799 caused the total loss of over seventy ships, including HMS York, around the northern Scottish coast. Evidently a group of shipowners representing the major English ports determined to present a petition to the Commissioners for Northern Lights, to make tangible their demand for a light at Cape Wrath. They engaged an Advocate in Edinburgh to prepare the groundwork and to draw up their petition. And their Advocate, in making his preparatory arrangements, did the obvious thing by immediately approaching Robert Stevenson for his support and technical knowledge.

Now, this was a very cute move. Robert Stevenson was a partner in the foremost firm of lighthouse, lighting and civil engineers in Scotland with a rising reputation, and his stepfather was Engineer to the Northern Lighthouse Board. Who better to approach for advice? Should the petition succeed, then who would be one of the major beneficiaries for the lighthouse construction and design work? Why, none other than Robert Stevenson and his engineering practice, via Thomas Smith, Engineer to the Northern Lighthouse Board, and his joint partner.

Early in 1802, these leading English merchants, unfortunately un-named, approached John Tait, Advocate and Writer to the Signet, to prepare and present their petition to the Commissioners for Northern Lights. Tait's first action was to contact Robert Stevenson for background, historical and technical information likely to be of use in the preparation of the petition.

Robert Stevenson's response, dated 31 March 1802, describes the location of Cape Wrath and the dangers to be encountered on passage around it; he further mentions that there is no safe anchorage when eastbound other than in Loch Eribol, and none at all for westbound vessels. He also refers to a recently-discovered sunken rock approximately twelve miles north west of Cape Wrath which, he suggests, has claimed many ships passing around the Cape. Robert Stevenson refers to the soon-to-be-commenced work on the erection of a new light at Sanda in the Orkneys by the Commissioners (Start Point, begun in 1802 and in operation from 1806); he suggests that a light at Cape Wrath and a second on or near Tiree in the Hebrides would effectively eradicate the most significant dangers to shipping passing around the north west coast. Furthermore, he expresses the opinion that all that would be required for this to be accomplished would be for the 'Mercantile Interest to apply to the Commissioners.'

John Tait then prepared a 'Memorial relative to the erection of a Light House at Cape Wrath' for submission to the Commissioners. He includes all of the points made by Robert Stevenson in his observations of 31 March, and in much the same terminology, but reinforces his case with examples of recent shipwrecks in the area which resulted in great loss of life. Tait quotes the loss, during a great storm on 18 October 1797, of three merchant ships passing from Orkney to the west coast, carrying mixed commercial cargoes. There were a mere two survivors from all ships' complements. Tait also refers to 'many, many other wrecks which might be mentioned, all which a Light house at Cape Wrath would most certainly have prevented.'

Before submitting the petition in its final form to the Commissioners, John Tait forwarded it to Robert Stevenson for appraisal. Evidently Stevenson was quite satisfied with the document; he returned it to John Tait under cover of a letter dated 16 July 1802.

The committee of three maritime trading merchants representing London, Bristol and Liverpool interests ('The Subscribers') then authorised John Tait to sign and submit their petition to the Commissioners for Northern Lights, and to report back as necessary.

That the petition insufficiently impressed the Commissioners is evidenced by a continuing correspondence between Lord Reay and the Commissioners during 1805. On 21 November in that year, Lord Reay wrote supporting the case for a light at Cape Wrath; he repeated the basics of the previous submission, and referred in detail to 'the dread arising from a sunk rock lately discovered.' That hazard obviously caused great concern at the time, as it is referred to continuously throughout the ensuing correspondence.

By the end of 1805 (a time of great turmoil remember, with the then current Napoleonic Wars) the Commissioners of the Northern Lights had completed major lights at Inchkeith, Fife and Start Point, Sanday, Orkney. And they were additionally exercised by demands for and the technical difficulties of a lighthouse at Bell Rock in the Firth of Forth. This massive project was eventually completed in 1811 after five years of continuous struggle. Bell Rock made Robert Stevenson's reputation; he assumed the position of Engineer to the Northern Lighthouse Board in 1808, continuing the work commenced by his step-father Thomas Smith in 1786. Robert Stevenson remained Engineer until his retirement in 1843; during his tenure as Engineer he presided over the design and erection of twenty-three major Scottish lighthouses in addition to the upgrading of many of the early lights.

In 1814, the Commissioners of the Northern Lights gained parliamentary approval to plan and erect further lights without reference to any official body other than the Board of Trade (i.e. they did not have to seek individual parliamentary sanction via a separate Private Act for every proposed new lighthouse). And in that year, Sir Walter Scott accompanied Robert Stevenson on his tour of inspection of the northern lighthouses. His experience at Cape Wrath greatly affected him. In 1814 he wrote in his *The Voyage of the Pharos – Walter Scott's Cruise Around Scotland* (published in 1838):

This dread Cape, so fatal to mariners, is a high promontory, whose steep sides go down to the breakers which lash its feet. There is no landing, except in a small creek, about a mile and a half to the eastward. The foam of the sea plays 'longbowls' with a huge collection of large stones, some of them a ton in weight but which these fearful billows chuck up and down as a child tosses a ball. Cape Wrath is a striking point, both from the dignity of its own appearance, and from the mental association of its being the extreme Cape of Scotland with reference to the north-west. There is no land in the direct line between this point and America. I saw a pair of large eagles, and if I had had the rifle-gun might have had a shot, for the birds, when I first saw them, were perched on a rock within sixty or seventy yards. They are, I suppose, little disturbed here, for they showed no great alarm. After the Commissioners and Mr. Stevenson had examined the headland, with reference to the site of a lighthouse, we strolled to our boat and set sail for Lewis with light winds and a great swell of tide. The country behind Cape Wrath swells in high sweeping elevations but without any picturesque or dignified mountainous scenery.

A further twenty years were to elapse between the efforts of the English merchants supported by Lord Reay for the erection of a light at Cape Wrath and serious consideration leading to its eventual successful completion. In 1826 the case became irresistible and serious planning commenced. By this time, there had developed an almost 'standard' design for the Scottish lighthouses, easily recognisable as Stevenson establishments, which were appearing around the coast.

The Specification of a Light House to be Erected Upon Cape Wrath' is dated 12 May 1826, though work did not commence formally until the following year. The specification, running to over eleven thousand words, provided, in the schedule of Preliminary Works, for the construction of a 'Harbour and Road.' The boat harbour was to be constructed at Clais Charnach, approximately a mile and a half eastwards of the Cape Wrath lighthouse site, at the only place on that part of the wild northern coast suitable for the provision of a landing place. Civil engineering works of a considerable nature were envisaged, the specification requiring that the existing creek 'be deepened and improved by the removal of the boulder stones, and blasting, or otherwise excavating the rock in a manner, and to an extent, calculated to afford shelter and passage for boats drawing not less than two feet water to float landward to low-water mark of Spring-tides.' It was further required that the entire boat harbour works be 'executed in a manner calculated to give the greatest possible facility to the landing of materials for the immediate works and ultimate use of the Lighthouse.' Clearly, the new harbour was seen as the principal lighthouse servicing point after completion of the construction works.

The road between Clais Charnach and the lighthouse construction site was specified as having to be fourteen feet wide overall including the side drains, ten feet wide on the carriageway and six inches deep and metalled or laid with 'broken stones from rock or gravel of approved quality,' found locally. 'The line of draught is to be made as easy as the natural difficulties of the ground will admit; but, nevertheless, so as nowhere to be of greater acclivity that at the rate of one perpendicular to ten horizontal.' There was clear concern that the new road should not be so steep in parts that horse-drawn traffic would encounter too great a difficulty in delivering the heavy materials landed at Clais Charnach.

When the boat harbour and road to the lighthouse building site had been completed to the satisfaction of Robert Stevenson the Engineer, it was provided that the sum of £952.12s.0d (£952.60p) would be paid to the Contractor in full and final settlement of that part of the contract.

The specification of May 1826 also included detailed descriptions of the two storehouses to be constructed for the greater lighthouse scheme, one at the tip of the Kyle of Durness (approximately nine miles from the lighthouse site) and the second at the Clais Charnach landing place. Each store house was to be twenty-six feet in length by eighteen feet in width and nine feet in height; each was to be provided with one door and two windows, a fireplace and a chimney.

The storehouses were required to be completed 'during the course of the summer of 1827.' When completed to the satisfaction of the Engineer the Contractor was 'to receive the sum of £333.12s.6d (£333.62p) as the full and complete price of the Storehouse works.'

The specification for the Lighthouse Works included precise dimensions of the light tower and the dwelling-house and offices, and other necessary buildings. The tower was to be forty-three feet seven inches in height 'from the level of the bottom of the basement course to the upper surface of the balcony course;' beneath the tower there was to be a vaulted oil cellar nine feet four inches in height. The tower was to be eighteen feet in diameter at its base at ground level, diminishing to sixteen feet six inches at the balcony floor. A tower storehouse was to be constructed, semi-circular in aspect and concentric with the tower, and nineteen feet six inches in radius.

The main body of the dwelling-house and offices block was to be seventy feet six inches in length, thirty-one feet six inches in width and thirteen feet nine inches in height; the offices, formed as wings to the main dwelling-house, were to be fifteen feet in length by twenty-four feet nine inches in width, with a height of twelve feet. An open court between the dwelling-house and the light tower was to be fifty-nine feet six inches by thirty-two feet three inches, protected by high stone walls.

Other constructions completing the lighthouse works were ash-pits, privies and drains. As there was no natural water at Cape Wrath, a system of underground water cisterns was built so that rainfall could be collected from the roofs of all the buildings and stored for later use for all domestic purposes.

The specification covered every aspect of the project. Every item in the masonry works was described in precise detail, from excavation of the groundwork and foundations to the corbelled tower cornice and the Light Room parapet wall, the stones for which were to be provided by the Lighthouse Board ready for laying, the Contractor being responsible only for the provision of mortar and labour for their installation. Stone for the tower stair and other specified purposes was to be taken from named quarries in Forfarshire. All the pavement stone was to be 'taken from the best quarries of Mr. Traill of Castlehill, in Caithness-shire.' All other stone used in the construction including, apparently, that for the external aspect of the light tower itself, was to be 'taken from such Quarries, within one mile of the Lighthouse, as shall be approved of and pointed out by the Engineer, or Clerk of Works: the same not being nearer than 200 yards from the Lighthouse Tower. The lime for the use of the lighthouse works is to be taken from the Limestone Quarries in the Parish of Durness.'

Carpenter and joiner work was specified in similar minute detail: roofs, lintels, joists, laths, windows, doors, shutters and shelving each commanded precise descriptions. The best crown timber, American pitch pine or American yellow pine was specified throughout. Specifications for the glaziers' work set out the composition of the putty to be used and required that 'two coats of white lead paint' be applied to the outsides of the windows prior to glazing. Plumbers work was required to be undertaken using 'the best cast sheet lead of the weight of not less than 8lbs to the superficial foot.' Smith work specified the types and sizes of all the locks, hinges, sash-pulleys and window fasteners to be used.

The scheme for the lighthouse at Cape Wrath was technically no more difficult than many other mainland lights built during the first half of the nineteenth century; what added considerably to the difficulties was its total isolation devoid of road access and its height above sheer sea cliffs, making a sea-borne approach hazardous at best and impossible at worst.

During July 1826 Robert Stevenson ordered his surveyor Mr. Slight to select the route of the access road to be constructed, and he planned the landing place on the western shore of the Kyle of Durness from which a new road was to strike westwards. A storehouse was built there, which still exists, though it is nowadays without its roof.

The route of this original road is still traceable and one of the two small bridges (i.e. that crossing the un-named burn near to Geodh Chreamha at map reference NC358691) included in the lighthouse specification survives on this early section of road.

The principal storehouse was to be built at Clais Charnach (NC271735) together with a slipway, oil storage facilities and materials handling winches, as described in the specification referred to above. Clais Charnach was to be the landing point for building materials and equipment delivered by sea; Clais Charnach is the 'small creek, about a mile and a half to the eastward' referred to by Sir Walter Scott in his 1814 diary entry. Winches and cranes were also built immediately adjacent to the lighthouse site at Geodha an Fhuarain (NC260747). This is the precipitous cove just east of the lighthouse wall which provided the only landing place prior to the construction of the facilities at Clais Charnach; a view down it from behind the safety of the lighthouse boundary wall provides a graphic realization of just how dangerous access by this means really was.

John Gibb, Architect of Aberdeen, and his son Alexander, who had long experience of constructing Robert Stevenson's lighthouses, were contracted to carry out all the building work. Stones for the balcony-course of the light tower itself were fashioned in Aberdeen of local granite, dovetailed and interlocked on their inner surfaces following the practise found to be beyond improvement in Stevenson's previously successful projects. Stone for the Cape Wrath lighthouse tower, the dwelling-houses and offices etc and the boundary walls was quarried on the Cape, much of it at Clais Charnach. Road stone was quarried along the route of the road or within five hundred yards of it; many of these small quarries of outcropping rock are still recognisable today. Turf on which road gravel was laid was required to be cleared of all stones 'of the size of a hen's egg or upwards;' the ditches and cross-drains (culverts) are also specified in similar close detail.

John Reid, who acted as keeper and master of the floating

light throughout Robert Stevenson's Bell Rock lighthouse works fifteen or so years earlier, and who became principal light keeper there when the light was completed, was transferred to the Cape Wrath project during 1827, in a supervisory or overseeing capacity. He suggested the initial specifications for the wall to enclose the Cape Wrath ground. The full specification and requirements for the excavation and building of the stone walls and turf dikes formed a separate contract.

Attention was given to the living conditions of the keepers and their families. Land was provided within the walls for the cultivation of root vegetables and the keeping of livestock. Milking goats were tried initially, but their depredations amongst the gardens were so damaging that they were replaced by cows. Thereafter cheese of a 'very excellent' quality was produced.

John Gibb and his son Alexander drew up the sketches and specifications for the bridges required on the road extension from Clais Charnach to the Kyle of Durness storehouse. Bridges of thirty foot and ten foot span were required: the larger necessary to cross the Kearvaig river (referred to in the documentation as 'Kerwick water') and the smaller near to Inshore House. It was later found necessary to erect a similar smaller bridge approximately one kilometre south of the Kyle of Durness storehouse.

The bridge spanning the Kearvaig river was estimated to cost £125.4s.2d (£125.21p) and each smaller bridge £30.16s.4d (£30.82p). The sketches, specifications and estimates for the bridges are dated March 1828.

Alexander Gibb wrote to Robert Stevenson on 28 March 1828 submitting the sketches, specification and estimates for the bridges, indicating that the price was based on those included in the tender for the lighthouse construction contract. He also pointed out that as the track connecting Clais Charnach with the sites of the bridges was too narrow to permit the passage of a cart, then the building materials other than the stone would have to be taken on horseback;

presumably the stone was quarried adjacent to the bridge sites, and evidence remains in the immediate vicinity of these bridges that quarrying operations were undertaken there.

The formal building contract for the whole of the lighthouse works, the two storehouses, the harbour at Clais Charnach and the road connecting it with the lighthouse construction site, was drawn up and signed during the summer of 1827. Parties to the contract were Charles Cunningham 'Clerk and Cashier to and having the authority of the Honourable Commissioners of Northern Lighthouses' and John Gibb 'Architect in Aberdeen as principal and Alexander Low, Timber Merchant in Aberdeen and Donaldson Rose, Merchant there' acting as sureties for John Gibb.

The contract went into the same precise detail as the specification for the works (and, indeed, embodied the whole of the written specification as part of the contract) setting out the financial penalties to be imposed should John Gibb fail in his obligations to the Commissioners. John Gibb's son Alexander was specifically named as responsible, jointly with his father, for personal supervision of the works. The Gibbs were not at liberty to sub-let any part of the contract other than the plumber works, or works previously approved by Robert Stevenson as Engineer to the Commissioners. Any dispute as to quality or completeness of any work was to be referred to Robert Stevenson for arbitration, as was any question as to the intent, meaning or spirit of the contract terms. His decision was to be final and binding on all parties.

Construction work was to commence immediately on the signing of the contract and to proceed to the state where all foundation excavations and building work to the level of the basement-course of the lighthouse tower and the associated buildings was to be completed. Work was to be suspended on the first of December 1827 until March 1828, unless required to the contrary by Robert Stevenson. John Gibb was obliged by the terms of the contract to have all the masonry work to the level of the Light-room parapet completed by the first of August 1828; the Commissioners were obliged to provide the finished stones for the lamp room in such time so as not to delay the August completion date.

The whole of the lighthouse scheme construction works were to be 'completely finished and ready for being inhabited by the term of Martinmas 1828'. The term at that time ran from 11 November (the Martinmas Quarter day) through to 2 February the following year.

For the whole of these works, John Gibb was to receive a total of £5756.1s.10d (£5756.9p), which included the sums previously identified as being payment for the harbour and storehouse works (£952.60p and £333.62p respectively). The contract provided for stage payments to be made to the Contractor by the Commissioners throughout the progress of the building operations. The first instalment of £446.19s.9d (£446.98p) was to be paid on the signing of the contract in order that work could commence without delay. Eight further payments of an equal amount became payable as the works progressed towards completion. The final instalment became due within three months after 'the whole of the works are certified to have been completely finished and approved of by the Engineer.' A pencil calculation in the margin of the contract confirms the ten instalment payments and the total contract price – (£446.19s.9d x 10 = £4469.17s.4d + £952.12s.0d + £333.12s.6d = £5756.1s.10d).

The cost of the bridges (£125.21p for that crossing Kearvaig water and two smaller bridges along the road each costing £30.82) was clearly additional to the work specified in the main contract, since at the time of the signing of the contract the bridge works had been neither finalised not costed.

It has been quoted elsewhere (notably on the information panel recently erected at the lighthouse) that the total cost of the Cape Wrath light was of the order of £14,000. But the documentary evidence referred to above suggests that by far the vast majority of the project involved expenditure of no more than £5,900. In addition to this sum would be the cost of the completion of the lamp room and installation of the lamp array and reflectors (and their manufacturing costs), the oil storage tanks in the oil-cellar (questionable, since the Colza oil used at the time would in all likelihood remain in the barrels in which it was delivered), equipment for the offices, walls enclosing the lighthouse ground at the Cape and the construction of the road linking Clais Charnach with the Kyle of Durness storehouse.

This additional expenditure certainly could not have amounted to costs in excess of £8000, or 133 per cent more than that already committed. An Admiralty document dated 1919 states that the cost of building the road had been £3520. (See Appendix XVIII.) This expenditure included the cost of the 1870s road realignment between Daill brae and the Capeside pier, in addition to the line of the original road from the lighthouse to the Kyle storehouse.

I have considerable doubt as to the accuracy of the construction cost of £14,000, although I am willing to be corrected. Could it be that that figure represented the construction and first year's running costs for the Cape Wrath light?

David Stevenson, at the age of thirteen, records in his diary the voyage he shared with Lighthouse Board personnel and others on a tour of some of the northern lighthouses:

August 1828. Monday eighteenth. Embarked at Newhaven (i.e. Edinburgh) in the Regent tender boat at six PM . . . with my father being on his annual voyage to the Lighthouse. Our gallant ship being under the command of Captain Soutar. Her cargo consisting of the apparatus for the Lighthouse now building at Cape Wrath.

The journal entry records nothing further of relevance to the Cape Wrath project, although these brief comments are useful in confirming other relevant facts. Firstly, the vessel 'Regent' and her master Captain Soutar is the same combination which conducted the surveyor Mr Slight at the direction of Robert Stevenson on his (i.e. Slight's) survey of the north coast of Sutherland preparatory to the commencement of the Cape Wrath lighthouse project, two years earlier, in July 1826. The 'Regent' was, between 1820 and 1846, the Northern Lighthouse Commissioners' own schooner of one hundred and seven registered tonnes used as the tender for all lighthouse inspection tours.

And secondly, the language used by young David Stevenson (he became Engineer to the Northern Lighthouse Board in 1853) confirms that in mid-August 1828 the Cape Wrath light was incomplete. This is precisely what one would expect given that the building contract provided for the light tower to be finished only to balcony parapet level by August 1 in that year. Clearly the purpose of the voyage of Captain Soutar and the 'Regent' with Robert Stevenson and his son David, so far as the Cape Wrath project then nearing completion was concerned, was to deliver the lamp array and other lighting equipment in order to complete the works. The word 'apparatus' in this context can have no other meaning.

Some sources quote the Cape Wrath lighthouse as operating from 1 February 1828. In view of David Stevenson's comments, and of the terms of John Gibb's construction contract, this cannot be so. The Cape Wrath lighthouse was required to be ready for occupation only from 11 November 1828, in time for the ensuing winter.

But the unarguable proof is the publication by the Commissioners for the Northern Lights of the usual Notice to Mariners, concerning the inauguration of the light at Cape Wrath. The Inverness Journal of 14 November 1828 gave notice that the Cape Wrath light would be functioning with effect from 25 December 1828; furthermore the Notice published details of the precise location, character and signature of the light.

That the light was so very vital to the safety of seafarers in these dangerous northern waters is emphasised by a separate report in that same newspaper. At noon on 30 October the welled smack the 'Freeling' of Greenwich with a cargo of live fish for London was wrecked and lost on the Stag Rock, although the crew of twelve were all saved. Presumably, personnel working at Cape Wrath engaged in the final commissioning of the light assisted in the rescue. ('Stag Rock' or 'The Staigs' is nowadays called 'Duslic,' and is readily visible from the lighthouse.)

The lighthouse at Cape Wrath remained in the state in which it was originally built for the next seventy-five years. Not until the very early years of the twentieth century were alterations and additions found necessary; these developments were required largely as a result of the progress of technology and refinements in safety equipment available to mariners, although serious thought was given to the effectiveness of the light in its established position immediately prior to World War I.

Enhanced safety provision for mariners rounding Cape Wrath included the provision of a fog signal in 1905 and a radio receiving station established by Lloyd's in 1908. The signalling station was closed in October 1932 but reactivated for the war years; in 1943 it was reduced to a coast watching station with the building of the major wartime radar establishments in the immediate Durness area. The fog signal remained operative until 23 September 2001, by which time ship design developments requiring enclosed bridges and the rapidly expanding GPS and satellite technologies rendered it obsolete.

Cape Wrath lighthouse was re-designated as a Rock Station in December 1975, and the light-keepers' families were relocated to Golspie. The light was automated in March 1998, the last shore station in Scotland to lose its manned complement.

Cape Wrath was, and is, a special place. Long may it remain so.

CHAPTER 6

SCRATCHING A LINE IN THE WILDERNESS

*Perennial Problems with
the Road Across the Parph*

Maintenance and Repair Practices Over the Years

The private road to the Cape Wrath lighthouse, built by the Northern Lighthouse Board in 1828, was adopted as a public county highway in 1833. Throughout much of the nineteenth century responsibility for the repair and maintenance of public highways rested with local Road Trusts. Cape Wrath fell into the area covered by the Eddrachillis and Durness Trust. Highway responsibility was transferred to new County Councils (in this case Sutherland) under the Local Government Act 1889: Sutherland C.C. was abolished in 1975 to be superseded by the Highland Regional authority.

Within the archives of the National Library of Scotland there are surviving documents from the mid-1830s which provide fascinating insights into road maintenance practices and social conditions from the years immediately following the adoption of the lighthouse road. Bi-monthly returns of labourers' hours were delivered to John Baigrie, Alexander Stewart and latterly John McIntosh at Scourie House, Scourie, by George Campbell, described as 'Overseer' on the Cape Wrath road. Campbell addressed his returns from Achiemore, Kerwig and Daill. In the annual summary for 1835 his address is given as Balvolich and in 1837 as Sangomore. Labourers identified as employed on the road were:

Hugh McKay, Durine; Angus Whyte, Durine; John McLeod, Daill;
McKay Campbell, Balvolich

January is excluded from each annual return, an indication that
maintenance was not undertaken in that winter month. Labourers
were paid between 1s 6d (7.5p) and 1s 8d (8.3p) per day. Overseer
George Campbell was paid two shillings, or ten new pence, per day,
increased to 2s 6d (12.5p) by 1837. From these wages were deducted
the costs of meal and tools provided. The total cost of repairs to the
road for the year 1835 was tabulated as £19.17s. 0d. (£19.85p).

With each return, George Campbell was required to describe the
work that had been undertaken during that period. The following
are selected extracts:

> ... the bank has fallen down near the Lighthouse. We have build 12
> feet in height with stones and feal and 59 yards in length and nine feet
> in breadth.
>
> (15 February 1837)

> I have finished this bank upon the 2nd. It is in need of looking to in
> different places.
>
> It was one flag was brock upon the cross drain in the middle of this
> bank that turned the water the wrong way until it carried away the
> whole bank what was very easy to do when it happened.
>
> (16 March 1837)

> ... 69 yards gravelled three and a half miles from the Lighthouse in a
> steep place   where the water carried away the gravel. There is a great
> deal of snow upon this road and it is melting through the day and
> carrying away the gravel in different parts.
>
> (31 March 1837)

> ... one piece gravelled near Lochinchour Bridge and cleaning drains
> near Daill.
>
> (30 April 1837)

. . . cleaning drains between Carrvag and the lighthouse and one bank built 4 miles from the lighthouse and I commence to build banks above Daill water.

(16 June 11837)

. . . cutting grass of the surface and cleaning drains and fulling tracks between the Lighthouse and Clashcarnach Storehouse.

(14 October 1837)

As principal user, the Northern Lighthouse Board always contributed the major portion of road maintenance expenses, notwithstanding that the local and county Road Trustees were responsible in law. In 1912 the lighthouse Commissioners agreed to contribute a sum of £25 annually towards the cost of road maintenance, and in 1922 the agreed annual contribution was increased to £50. This level of road maintenance subsidy continued beyond the outbreak of the Second World War out of a total annual cost usually between £78 and £100. It was not re-negotiated until 1946.

There are repeated references in the minutes of the former Sutherland County Council throughout the twentieth century which cast some light on the difficulties presented by inclusion of the Cape Wrath road in the list of public highways. It is clear that for many years (certainly after the formation of the Sutherland County Council) the practice was for private contractors to be appointed to take responsibility for the repair and maintenance of sections of county highway. Using the early years of the twentieth century as a purely arbitrary starting point, we find that the County Road Board at its meeting of 6 May 1910 awarded the road repair and maintenance contract to John Mackay of Durine West, Durness, at the agreed rate of £2.8s.0d (£2.40p) per mile per year for the period 25 May 1910 to 25 May 1913.

For the next three-year perio,d the repair contract was awarded to Peter Whyte of Sangomore at the price of £2.12s.0d (£2.60p) per mile per annum. But the County Road Board at its meeting of 5 August 1915 heard from their Surveyor that the contractor had 'done practically no work on his Section since January last, and although repeatedly warned he refused to carry out his Contract; that, in consequence, he (the Surveyor) has made arrangements for the repair of the Section out of the instalments retained from the Contractor amounting to £19.10s.7d (£19.53p).' The Board approved the Surveyor's actions.

It is probable that the road repair and maintenance programme was continued on an *ad hoc* basis for the remainder of the First World War years, as the formal tender and contract process did not recommence until 1920. John Campbell and Son, of Sangomore were awarded the Cape Wrath contract for the period 25 May 1920 to 25 May 1923, at the annual rate of £5.10s.0d (£5.50p) per mile, and the ensuing three-year contract was awarded to Angus Sutherland & Son, Capeside at the rate of £6 per mile per annum.

The Board, at its meeting of 7 May 1926, awarded the road repair and maintenance contract to Murdoch Mackenzie of Grudie, at the unchanged annual rate per mile of £6, for the period 25 May 1926 to 25 May 1929. This marked the start of a continuous period of nineteen years during which Murdo Mackenzie took responsibility for the care of the lighthouse road.

The contract was retained by Murdo Mackenzie, now of Kerwig (Kearvaig), Capeside for the period 1929 to 1932 at the annual rate per mile of £6.10s.0d (£6.50p), and for the periods 25 May 1932 to 30 April 1935 and 1 May 1935 to 30 April 1938 the contract terms remained unaltered.

The minutes for the meeting held on 25 June 1937 record that a letter dated 18 February 1937 was received from The Northern Lighthouse Board complaining of 'the condition of the road leading to Cape Wrath Lighthouse, and suggesting that the Council take the matter up with the Ministry of Transport with a view to obtaining a grant to be devoted to placing the road in a really serviceable condition.' The County Road Surveyor was authorised to deal with the matter.

This record is significant on a number of points. It confirms that the prime responsibility for the maintenance of the road remained with the Sutherland County Council. And 1937 marks the commencement of a protracted argument between the local highway authority and central government aimed at securing financial contributions sufficient for the proper upkeep of the road. It was to take more than ten years and another global conflict to finally bring the matter to a satisfactory conclusion.

During 1937 and 1938, the County Council pursued claims against the Admiralty for compensation arising out of their use of the Cape Wrath range. I met crofter Billy Bremner, then in his late seventies, on a return visit to Cape Wrath in the summer of 2004. He went, at the age of two, with his family to occupy Inshore House in 1934, and he clearly recalled sitting on the front step there watching shells fired from naval vessels beyond Garvie Island landing in the family peat banks to the south of the road and Loch Inshore. The actual target was, apparently, Lochan nam Breac Buidhe, which is nowadays noted for the quality of its angling. Were these incidents partially responsible for prompting the County Council claims of 1937/38?

County Road Surveyor Mr. J. Robertson reported to the County Road Board meeting held on 15 April 1938 that Mr. Murdoch Mackenzie of Kerwick, Cape Wrath had tendered for the repair and maintenance contract for the Cape Wrath road in the sum of £6.10s.0d. (£6.50) per mile, per annum. The contract was to extend for the three-year period 1 May 1938 to 30 April 1941. The Board was pleased to accept the offer, for it was the only one received for that section within the County.

Three years later, Murdoch Mackenzie again sought to renew his repair and maintenance contract, and again he was successful. The terms remained unaltered (i.e. £6.10s.0d. per mile per year). The contract was to extend from 1 May 1941 to 30 April 1944.

Sutherland's new County Road Surveyor, Mr. Walter Sutherland (Mr. Robertson retired in June 1943 to be succeeded on a temporary basis until the end of the war by his Assistant) reported to the Board on 30 June 1944 that Murdoch Mackenzie had again offered to repair and maintain the road for a period of three years ending 30 April 1947 at a fixed price of £10 per mile, per annum. The County Council had judged this offer as too high, and after further negotiations Mr. Mackenzie agreed to reduce the price to £9 per mile per annum, which the Board found acceptable. We shall hear more of this road maintenance arrangement later.

On 16 March 1945, the County Road Board considered a letter from Mr. D.J. Macaskill of Daill, Secretary for Durness S.F.S.S., making application for the construction of a road from the Cape Wrath Motor Road to the end of the Kyle and for the replacement of the bridge at Daill by a traffic bridge. This proposal is interesting for two reasons. Firstly, it would appear to propose upgrading the existing but unused section of the original lighthouse supply road built in 1828 between the top of Daill brae and the original landing place/storehouse at the head of the Kyle of Durness. This road remained, though much overgrown and impassable to any wheeled traffic. And secondly, it suggests constant problems for vehicular traffic at the ford across the river Daill. The 'Daill Bridge' referred to was simply a narrow pedestrian bridge serving the farmhouse; it still exists, after several reconstructions.

After discussion, the Board referred Mr. Macaskill's proposed road and bridge upgrading to Major the Hon. Robert Bruce of the Scottish Council on Industry for his attention and further consideration, and nothing further was heard. The road never was upgraded and it remains today as it was built in 1828. It would be another thirty-five years before a vehicle-carrying bridge replaced the ford at Daill.

The County Road Surveyor reported to the County's Finance and General Purposes Committee on 27 July 1945 that Murdoch

Mackenzie had relinquished his contract early in May and that efforts to find a replacement had failed. Four men from the Kinlochbervie road crew had been instructed to go to Cape Wrath for a period of one month in order to carry out the necessary remedial works. (There would appear to have been some simmering discontent at this order, as the committee minutes record 'the foreman's reply for information' without stating quite what that reply was).

Murdoch Mackenzie cancelled his final three-year contract with the County Council after only one year. From this we must assume that the road was in a very parlous state, and quite beyond his ability to keep in good repair. Heavy use of the road for additional military supplies traffic during the final year of the war must have inflicted almost terminal damage. The committee therefore recommended to the County Road Board that they take the necessary steps to have the road deleted from the list of county highways.

A Roadman's Dismissal

The County Road Surveyor next reported to the County Road Board on 15 October 1945. He described an incident which perhaps highlights the reluctance of some of the men employed on highways maintenance duties in the Durness area to work on the Capeside.

Surveyor Sutherland intimated that, whilst inspecting roads in the Durness area, he observed that Sectionman James Gunn of Sangomore, Durness was absent from duty, and that on being questioned Gunn admitted that he had been gathering sheep without permission for absence from duty. Surveyor Sutherland instructed Gunn to proceed immediately to the Capeside on urgent repair work, and that Gunn refused. Surveyor Sutherland then summarily dismissed Sectionman Gunn.

The County Road Board considered the matter on 15 February 1946, and unanimously approved their Surveyor's actions after being advised that another man had been employed in Gunn's place.

Road Damage In The War And Immediate Post-war Years

The winter of 1945–46 saw some urgent discussions between Sutherland County Council and the Commissioners of the Northern Lighthouses concerning the state of the road. There had been a committee recommendation in July 1945 for the road to be removed from the list of County highways, and constant difficulties had been experienced in meeting the cost of repairs and in persuading men to work on the Capeside.

The matter came to a head at the County Council meeting of 17 April 1946. The County Road Surveyor reported that he had visited the offices of the Northern Lighthouse Board on 15 November 1945 when he described in detail all of the difficulties in maintaining the Cape Wrath road to an acceptable standard, and confirmed the Council was considering removing the road from the list of county highways.

The Northern Lighthouse Board agreed that with effect from 26th November 1945, it would . . . increase their annual Grant towards upkeep of the road . . . from £50 to £150.'

The County Council resolved that the Surveyor and the Committee Convener should visit the Lighthouse Commissioners to apply for further increases in the annual grant and a contribution towards repairing the road. They were also authorised to approach central government, but it appears the Lighthouse Commissioners undertook this themselves, according to correspondence between the NLB and the Ministry of War Transport held in the National Archives at Kew.

In 1946, the Northern Lighthouse Board began a two-year correspondence with the Ministry of Transport aimed at securing funds for repairs to the lighthouse road that were deemed to be necessary because of continual use by the military authorities servicing the signal station and observation point throughout the war years. The voluminous file of correspondence and reports in the National

Archives at Kew mirrors the minutes of the Sutherland County council but, of course, from the central government perspective. An analysis of all the points at issue was prepared by R.J. Samuel of the Engineering (Highways) Division, Ministry of Transport, dated 5 December 1947, which brought the matter to a mutually satisfactory conclusion. This analysis is transcribed at Appendix XIX.

The minutes of the County Road Board for 8 May 1947 record a report by the County Road Surveyor of his joint inspection of the road with Mr. Joss of the Department of Agriculture and Mr. Cadger representing the Lighthouse Commissioners. The badly rutted state of the road was noted. Surveyor Sutherland stated that £1250 had been spent on repairs already in the current financial year and expressed the opinion that the road would continue to be a heavy liability to the Council. Mr. Cadger agreed that more extensive repairs were required. Mr. Joss kept his counsel.

The County Road Board meeting noted a letter dated 1 May 1947 from the Northern Lighthouse Board advising that they (i.e. NLB) estimated the cost of repairs at £7,000 with future annual maintenance at £600, and proposing a meeting with County Council representatives in Edinburgh. The Road Board, after consideration, resolved that they should meet the Commissioners, but at the office of the Clerk to the County Council.

The same meeting further resolved that 'the prospective liability of this road was an impossible proposition for the County Council to undertake and that the repair and maintenance of it should be completely taken over by the Northern Lighthouse Commissioners'. Matters were approaching the point where one party had to blink first, and it was clear that although the Ministry representatives had hitherto maintained a studied silence, they would be unlikely to remain entirely detached for very much longer. Something had to be done to solve once and for all the perennial problem of funding for the repair and maintenance of Robert Stevenson's 120 year-old road to the Cape Wrath lighthouse.

Towards the end of 1947, the road had further deteriorated so as to be dangerous. Storm damage, heavy continuous rains and the severe winter weather, allied to sustained wear and the minimal maintenance programme of the war years, led to its closure by the County Road Surveyor. He reported to the County Road Board on 14 October that heavy rains had recently destroyed sections of road, cutting off the lighthouse from the West Keoldale ferry stage; that he had attempted to get men from Kinlochbervie and Durness to carry out repairs to the road but that only two were available; and that it would take a considerable time to make the road passable again, at a cost estimated to be in excess of £1000.

He reported again on 30 October, confirming that the road was in a 'very dangerous condition and in order to safeguard the Council he has closed the road while repairs are carried out' – adding that the estimated cost of immediate repairs was now over £2000. This was a huge sum at the time. On 12 November 1947, the Board confirmed the actions of the Surveyor and invited all interested parties to a meeting.

Sutherland County Council met on 21 November with representatives of the Northern Lighthouse Board (Mr. Simpson), the Ministry of Transport (Mr. Dakers) and the Department of Agriculture for Scotland (Mr. Henderson and Mr. Joss). Convenor W. Morley Hames gave a brief resume of matters relevant to the Cape Wrath road. He described the road as extending eleven miles from Keoldale Ferry to the Lighthouse and Signal Station at the sea end; that there were four shepherd's houses and the adjoining lands carried two thousand sheep; that during the war the road had been damaged by Admiralty traffic; that an application had been made to the Ministry of Transport for a repair grant of £1500; and that the estimated cost of making good all of the road damage including that attributable to recent storms and flooding was now £2,000.

The County Road Surveyor stated that annual road repair costs in the war years had risen to £300 or £400 and that the Northern

Lighthouse Board had recently agreed to treble their annual contribution to £150; but the application to the Ministry of Transport for a grant of £1500 for repairing the damage done to the road by wartime Admiralty traffic had so far produced no reponse.

At this stage, the County Council decided that in future it would limit its Cape Wrath road repair and maintenance contribution to an annual £50 and it further determined that 'no further contribution should be made by the Council towards making good the damage caused by extraordinary traffic and by flooding.' Mr Simpson of the Northern Lighthouse Board indicated that the decisions taken by the Council were not entirely unexpected and that he thought, in the circumstances, that they were not unreasonable. He would report to his Board accordingly. Government department representatives Messrs Dakers, Henderson and Joss 'noted the position but could give no indication whether their particular Departments would assist or not,' perhaps a not-unexpected civil servant response when a decision beyond their pay grade was required.

The County Council minute of 21 November 1947 ends with the comment that: 'The Council left it to the Northern Lighthouse Board to make what arrangements it could with the Ministry of Transport and the Department of Agriculture and, thereafter, to send a report of the Board's final decision to the County Council.' This decision by the County Council was obviously designed to assist the Northern Lighthouse Board in bringing to a satisfactory conclusion its long-running dispute concerning road repair funding with government departments in London.

At a County Council meeting held on 16 December 1947, it was reported that a letter had been received from the Northern Lighthouse Board confirming that 'the Commissioners are prepared to bear the expense estimated at £2000 which will be incurred by the County Council in repairing the road to enable it to be reopened,' and further that they (the NLB) understood 'from the Ministry of Transport that a contribution of £1227 is being made by the

Ministry on account of damage done by Government traffic during the war, provided the County Council retain the road on their List of County Highways' and agreeing to continue contributing £50 per year towards the upkeep of the road. The County Clerk also reported that the Ministry of Transport had submitted a letter in much the same terms. Game, set and match to Sutherland County Council, no?

The Council then voted unanimously to accept the offer of £2000 from the Northern Lighthouse Board and a further £1227 from the Ministry of Transport; agreed to continue their own annual maintenance contribution of £50, and to retain the road across Cape Wrath on their list of public highways. This exercise in brinkmanship established the precedent of much larger annual road maintenance contributions from those bodies for whom the Cape Wrath road provided most benefit.

At that same 16 December 1947 meeting, the County Council further resolved to instruct the County Clerk to 'urge upon the Department of Agriculture for Scotland the need for repairing the Ferryman's house at Keoldale Ferry, and also for the erection of a shelter at the Ferry.'

From the minutes of the council and committee meetings held between February 1948 and May 1949, it would seem that the County Council took the opportunity presented by funds made available from central government and the Northern Lighthouse Board to upgrade the road once and for all. During the period 1948 to 1951 the road was reconstructed and top-dressed with a surface coat of Tarmacadam for the first time.

The Northern Lighthouse Board provided a series of motor vehicles for the use of the light keepers at Cape Wrath, including a Morris Commercial one-tonne truck from the 1930s and a Commer 25cwt lorry of circa 1947. From the 1950s, Land Rovers were stationed at Cape Wrath to deliver supplies from the Clais Charnach pier to the light, and to collect groceries and mail. In the early 1960s an Austin

Champ was used by the light keepers. Its remains (cruciform chassis, axles with wheels and tyres, engine and gearbox) were to be seen well into this century, parked in the lee of the former Lloyd's building.

A photograph of the Commer truck clearly shows it negotiating the ford at Daill. This feature was perhaps the most likely to cause disruption on any motorised journey along the road. The river rises and falls with notorious rapidity; water levels could rise (either by heavy rain or a high tide with onshore winds) so as to make the ford impassable during the time it took to collect supplies or a relief lighthouse crew at the west Keoldale pier. The keeper complement remaining at the lighthouse would be able to perform their required duties in the absence of their colleagues, but would clearly be hard-pressed. Relatively long periods of absence from the station, whether due to accident or adverse weather conditions, were to be avoided wherever possible.

Improvement To Modern Traffic Standards

After the contracting-out of the maintenance work came to an end, County Council highway repair crews were assigned to the Capeside. Crews were required to remain on Cape Wrath throughout the repair programme. They stayed in bothies or huts near to the section of road being repaired, or with local Capeside families. A semi-permanent camp was established near to the southern end of the Daill ford. The foundations of this building still survive. Nearby are the remains of the Bean lorry used on the post-war road reconstruction programme. In 2006 the engine, gearbox, steering column and wheel and rear quarter-bumpers of the vehicle were evident but have since been buried.

In 1948, with the programme to surface the whole of the road across Cape Wrath well underway, something of a minor revolt developed amongst the resident repair crews. They began to feel their isolation on the Cape and to flex, gently, their industrial muscle. Complaints about the 'lack of recreational facilities' and threats 'to leave their employment' were made to their County Council employers. The County Surveyor reported that the men wished to be provided with a radio.

The Council's Finance and General Purposes Committee on 22 September 1948 requested the Northern Lighthouse Board to pay for the cost of providing radio receivers for the men, 'as the road was mainly serving the functions of the Northern Lighthouse Commissioners.' The Committee noted at its meeting of 8 December 1948 that 'two *Invicta* Wireless Receivers' had been installed.

The minutes of the County Council make clear just how difficult the immediate post-war conditions really were in the isolated reaches of the far north west. The scheme to repair, upgrade and improve the Cape Wrath road was adversely affected during 1950 by what is termed 'labour difficulties.' The Surveyor submitted a letter dated 5 May 1950 to the County Council meeting held on 12 May. In it, he described the 'great difficulties he was experiencing in procuring labour for the (Rhiconich-Loch Clash) and (Cape Wrath) roads.'

A tender for the resurfacing of the Rhiconich to Loch Clash road had recently been accepted, at a price of £11,725.00. The County Road Surveyor had inspected these works on 3 May and found only three men on duty out of a squad of eighteen.

The situation was perhaps even more extreme on Cape Wrath. The County Surveyor reported that he had been obliged to request the Labour Exchange at Thurso 'to let him employ every available man in the Melness and Durness areas; the men, up to thirty in number, were to report for duty on 1st May, but he was informed that only two men appeared; he reported again to the Labour Exchange but the position was still unchanged. Mr Elliot, Factor, Achfary, was prepared to support the County Road Surveyor in his endeavours to get labour.'

The Surveyor had promised the Northern Lighthouse Commissioners that he would do all in his power to complete the levelling and resurfacing of the Cape Wrath road by September of 1950. He was being pressed to expedite the work. The County Council directed the County Road Surveyor to approach the Labour Exchange yet again. If a satisfactory response was not forthcoming he was directed to transfer roadmen from other parts of the County to work on the Cape Wrath road reconstruction.

The minutes of the Roads Committee of Sutherland County Council held on 22 June 1950 record that estimated expenditure on the Cape Wrath road for the financial year May 1950 to May 1951 would be £10,050 to which the County Council would contribute £50, the balance being funded by the Ministry of Transport.

That the major reconstruction of the Cape Wrath road was undertaken over a period of years either side of 1950 (with winter breaks to avoid the worst of the weather) is evidenced by the Roads Committee minutes of 3 April 1951. The Surveyor reported on 27 March 1951 that reconstruction works on the road had been recommenced. He asked if the 'old' Kylescu ferryboat could be transferred to the Capeside and used for the conveyance of plant, tar, vehicles, etc. over the ferry.

The Surveyor suggested that the Lighthouse Commissioners be made responsible for the delivery of the boat to the Cape, and that the Council be freed from all responsibility in connection with the ferrying of plant etc. to be transported by this boat. The Committee accepted this suggestion. The delivery of the former Kylescu ferry boat to the Kyle of Durness and the ferrying services to be undertaken by it whilst engaged on the road reconstruction works were expected to be the responsibility of the Northern Lighthouse Board. The County Council as Highway Authority were clearly determined to preserve their expenditure on maintenance of the Cape Wrath road to as minimal a level as possible.

The Military And The Lighthouse Road (1)

In 1953 proposals to enlarge the Cape Wrath Firing Range again caused concerns locally. The Planning Committee at its meeting held on 27 May received a letter and plan from the Department of Health giving details of a proposed enlargement. The letter also intimated that the range would in future be used for aerial bombardment and air to ground firing as well as 'normal sea bombardment.' It went on to state that 'though it would not be possible to pinpoint specific targets there would be no risk of injury or damage outside the area and all suitable precautions would be taken against fire risks.' The Council's observations were requested.

The Planning Officer, in a report dated 20 April 1953, noted that:

(1) The public highway formed the southern boundary of the range. During bombardments the road was closed to all traffic, which inconvenienced the sheep farmers.

(2) In past years, shells had fallen outside the bombardment area on to Keoldale Farm land and that the structure of the shepherd's house at Inshore had developed cracks due to vibration during bombardments. Inshore House was to be rebuilt under a Hill Farming Scheme by the Department of Agriculture; it was felt that it might be difficult to get shepherds to stay in the property owing to possible danger to themselves and their families (not to mention the grazing stock) especially as there were now proposals to use the range for aerial bombardment.

The Planning Officer therefore suggested that the southern boundary of the danger area be adjusted to ensure the safety of the occupants of Inshore House, and that the Admiralty be asked to give an undertaking that no ordnance would fall outside the boundaries of the identified danger area.

The County Clerk reported that he had forwarded a copy of the Planning Officer's report to the Department of Health for Scotland and that the Department 'have asked the Admiralty for their urgent observations on the points raised.'

After considerable discussion it was resolved that on receipt of a reply from the Department of Health, senior council officials would consult in order to 'make such protest as might be advisable.' Clearly the Council was expecting the military authorities to formally insist on implementing their proposals.

But matters moved rather more rapidly than the County Council expected. Minutes of the meeting held on 26 June 1953 record the very recent receipt of a telephone message from the Department of Health indicating that the Admiralty would conduct a naval exercise within the bombardment range in early July, and it was hoped that 'the Council would withdraw the objections submitted by them.'

Councillor W. Morley Hames recounted the incidents involving the use of the bombardment range in 1937/38 when life and property had been endangered. The Council then resolved 'to instruct the County Clerk to insist upon their representations receiving full consideration and to submit to the Department evidence furnished by Councillor W. Morley Hames regarding claims for compensation made against the Admiralty in 1937 arising out of their use of the range at that time.'

And there the matter rested. Claims for compensation went quiet, unlike the bombardment range on the Cape Wrath peninsula.

The Bridge Over the River Daill

In 1980 an agreement was made between the Highland Regional Council (successor body to the Sutherland County Council) and the military authorities for the provision of a road bridge over the ford at Daill. During the winter of 1980 Sergeant Mark Hugill surveyed the site at Daill and reported to Lt. Col. D.A. MacLean R.E., Commander, Royal Engineers Scotland. It was agreed that the bridge building could be undertaken as part of the Military Aid to the Civilian Community (MACC) scheme, which provides Service personnel and equipment in both emergencies and routine situations to assist the community at large. In this way, community projects are completed for the cost of the materials only, and the military benefits from practical training without any material cost.

The Northern Lighthouse Board and the Highland Regional Council jointly ordered the bridge sectional steelwork from a civilian contractor and, after months of planning and preparation, all the required elements of the scheme were brought together at a temporary base at Keoldale, on the eastern side of the Kyle of Durness. Exercise Condor Wrath was ready for implementation.

The scheme involved the building of a 'temporary moveable structure' bridge 110 feet long, in a double span supported on a central pier with landward approaches sited well above the expected high water levels of the Daill River. Staff Sergeant Pete Ellis accompanied Condor Troop, 59 Independent Commando Squadron, Royal Engineers to the temporary site at Keoldale from where construction was co-ordinated.

Large steel sections, timber decking and other ancillary construction materiel were quite beyond the combined capacity of the small outboard motor-driven ferry boat and the rudimentary barge available in the Kyle. It was necessary therefore to bring in an APB (Air-Portable Bridge), which also functioned as a floating raft. Even then, the services of two Sea King naval helicopters were required in order to deliver pre-fabricated bridge sections direct to the construction site.

For projects of this nature it was usual to launch the bridge deck from one bank, but the confined approaches at Daill made this impossible. The bridge was therefore constructed from the centre supporting pier outwards towards each bank simultaneously. The centre pier was built with large-section timber baulks supported on a masonry base, some of which was removed from the site of the old Achiemore Side School overlooking Daill and the river.

The whole project was accomplished in a matter of days without celebration or ceremony. When the bridge was deemed complete, a long wheelbase military Land Rover was unceremoniously driven across it. The military personnel collected their equipment and departed for their base near Arbroath.

A plaque was left attached to the new bridge simply inscribed 'Condor Bridge, erected by Condor Troop, 59 Independent Commando Squadron, Royal Engineers.' This simple undated recording of what really was a monumental event in Cape Wrath's quiet history was swiftly stolen.

The Military And The Lighthouse Road (2)

In the early 1980s, there was further considerable local disquiet at the use and expansion of the Cape Wrath Military Firing Range. The Northern Times of 9 January 1981 reported that the Ministry of Defence was adamant that they had no intention of either vacating the bombing and practice range or reducing its use, which local opinion had sought to achieve. The military authorities went so far as to admit that should it become necessary they would have no hesitation in seeking a compulsory purchase order for all the Capeside land they currently used under lease agreements. Aerial practice using live 1,000lb bombs and shore bombardment from ships at sea would continue. The Highland Council and the local elected members were obliged to accept the situation, notwithstanding the quantifiable adverse effects the military firing range had on the local tourist infrastructure.

As recently as 2005 the Cape Wrath road was again closed to the public. But on this occasion the cause was not the extremes of weather, but abuse by the military authorities. The combined winter exercise held in February involved the use of large tracked vehicles flown in by lifting helicopter. Some of these military vehicles were simply far too heavy and wide for the single track road, a fact which should have been quite obvious to those senior supervisory personnel in positions of authority. The inevitable happened, and the road surface was severely damaged in many places. The worst damage was inflicted approximately a half-mile beyond the top of

Daill Brae, where side-drains, cross-culverts and the full width of the road surface were damaged to the extent that the road was rendered impassable to traffic of any description.

After much negotiation and argument it was arranged that the Highland Regional Council would carry out the necessary reinstatements to the road and the Ministry of Defence would reimburse the cost of repairs attributable to the actions of their personnel. The road was reopened only on 25 April, just in time for the commencement of the 2005 tourist season.

At its meeting on that date, the Sutherland County Committee of the Highland Regional Council determined that negotiations should be initiated with the Ministry of Defence with a view to obtaining an agreement limiting the type of military vehicles to be used on the Cape Wrath road. It was recognised that should an agreement in these terms not be forthcoming, then a mandatory weight or width restriction might have to be imposed under existing highway legislation.

The same Council committee, at its meeting held on 15 August 2005, noted that attempts to secure the agreement with the military authorities referred to earlier in the year had been unsuccessful, and further noted that a second large combined military exercise was scheduled for the coming October/ November. Accordingly, the committee agreed to the immediate preparation and implementation of a statutory weight and width restriction order applicable to the Cape Wrath road.

Copies of the Order were posted at the Keoldale road and at the Capeside pier at the end of August 2005, and formal public notice was given in the Northern Times published on 9 September. The effect of the Order was to prohibit vehicles over seven feet wide from using the whole length of the Cape Wrath Lighthouse Road, and to prohibit vehicles over 7.5 tonnes gross weight from crossing the bridge at Diall (a temporary structure, which had been installed over twenty years previously, it will be recalled) and Inshore bridge

No. 2 (i.e. the wooden bridge half a mile or so beyond Inshore). The full text of the width and weight restriction Order can be found in the Appendices.

These provisions permitted continuation of the existing tourist minibus service and the unrestricted passage of farm and other vehicles necessary for the conduct of everyday business on Cape Wrath. But larger and heavier vehicles were effectively excluded. The temporary width and weight restriction order was made permanent in the spring of 2006.

Whilst the whole of the eleven-mile road between the pier and the lighthouse was protected by the width and weight restrictions, who was to police them? Although the Ministry of Defence by no means owns the whole of the Cape Wrath peninsula, the military authorities effectively exclude all non-military personnel by the application of byelaws during the larger military exercises. Are they likely to confess their own unseen transgressions or report themselves to the civilian authorities?

CHAPTER 7

MAGNIFICENT ISOLATION

LIFE AND THE COMMUNITY ON CAPE WRATH

The world forgetting by the world forgot
(Anonymous visitor to Cape Wrath, 1876)

With the commencement of the lighthouse construction works and, to a lesser extent, the making of the road from the Kyle of Durness nine miles away, the Cape Wrath peninsula began to be opened up for permanent habitation by the men posted to the lighthouse and their families. And with a road across the Parph, the area became more attractive for the development of permanent farm dwellings where previously only the most basic of temporary seasonal shelters had existed.

The Parph Prior to the Lighthouse

Intensive commercial sheep farming has been associated in the far north west with the clearances of the early nineteenth century. But the Parph and the Cape Wrath peninsula was an established sheep-rearing area throughout much of the previous century. For most of the eighteenth century, the Reay Estate included the areas of the modern parishes of Tongue, Durness and Eddrachillis; George Mackay, Lord Reay acceded to the title and the estate on attaining his majority in 1699, and steadily became involved in agricultural improvements. He conducted experiments at both Tongue and Balnakeil, which included fine grazing land at Faraid Head, in close proximity to the 'sheep rooms' of the Parph on the largely uninhabited tract of land between the Kyle of Durness and the tip of Cape Wrath.

George, Lord Reay died in 1748; examination of transactions described in his correspondence suggests that Black Face or Tweeddale sheep had been introduced to the Parph and, whilst their numbers may have been small, they did steadily increase. George, Lord Reay's grandson (also named George), took possession of the estate Mains farms in 1764 and continued sheep development around Faraid and Balnakeil. In April 1767 the agent at Balnakeil warned that the shepherd on the Parph had been taken ill and that the sheep may have suffered, especially with the storms. In the second half of March provender was short, and many sheep had died.

Between 1768 and 1797 the Reay estate was managed by Factors, and grazing on the Parph continued to support the rearing of sheep. In 1789 the Sheep Rooms at Cape Wrath had been let on an annual tenancy to James Anderson, manager for the merchant partnership at the fishing station at Rispond, who required meat to feed workers processing the herring there.

The Highland Clearances thus did not affect life on Cape Wrath; sheep farming was well established there before, during and after the clearances that disrupted Durness in the first quarter of the nineteenth century. At the time, sheep were feared as the 'white tide.' Even today they are referred to, occasionally, as white vermin.

It is clear that right from the very start of the lighthouse-building project, men were stationed permanently at Cape Wrath. The majority of these new residents were building and road navigation workers housed in temporary camps near to the work sites. There would be a more-or-less permanent camp at the main construction site at the lighthouse, although work was suspended between December 1827 and March 1828. Robert Stevenson had his own trusted personnel on site, responsible for the supervision of the works.

One such was John Reid, who had been employed in a similar capacity at the Bell Rock light. Reid continued in Stevenson's employ and was transferred from the Bell Rock light to the new Cape Wrath project during the late summer of 1827. A letter surviving from him to James Hall, Merchant of Lerwick, dated Cape Wrath January 7 1828, states in part:

> I have been here preparing for a Lighthouse this season; and hopes we will built it this year; it is a very dreary place; and not near any house or houses; we need to have a store house the nearest in a creek among precipices two miles from the Cape which only in fine days of summer we can land, the other store house fifteen miles off (sic) in a dock or Bay called Daunch-coil (?), and through a very marshy, and hilly ground to pass between these places by land – and not a house but one shepherds hut by the way. I have had to encounter some little difficulties in our first settling or landing here for the ground would not carry up a horse here, and the Contractor had not much experience. I am lead to trouble you with this letter from a wish to inform you that you may warn any of your ship masters of a dangerous Rock that has been doubted off the Cape – on which the storms this winter I have seen the sea brake very high, so that the best ship that ever was built would she be in its way would be foundered – and as it lyes in the Track of ships from Shetland bound through the Minch…situated five leagues N.E. by N1/6E from Cape Wrath and from the sea breaking at half tide on it must be very little water upon it.

From this we must assume that John Reid remained at the Cape Wrath construction site throughout the winter of 1827/8, perhaps in a supervisory or watchman capacity. This is surprising, since the construction contract between John Gibb as the principal builder of the lighthouse and the Commissioners for Northern Lights specifically provided for all construction work to cease between the first day of December 1827 and March 1828. As it is likely that John Reid was in the employ of Robert Stevenson as Engineer rather than that of John Gibb as Contractor, then perhaps the anomaly is partially explained.

And note also that the notorious sunken rock is still causing concern and alarm. Here there must be some confusion. The original references to this hazard to seafarers (contained within the original Statistical Account of Scotland gathered in the 1790s and repeated in correspondence in the very early years of the nineteenth century making the case for a light at Cape Wrath – see Appendices I, II, V and XV) placed the recently-identified 'sunk rock' at approximately twelve miles out to sea from Cape Wrath itself. John Reid, in his letter quoted above, places it at fifteen miles. This cannot be seen from either the Cape Wrath cliff top or the balcony of the light tower. I suspect that John Reid's reference is to the rock now known as Duslic, but then called the Stag or the Staigs, which is barely submerged at high water and easily identifiable at low water, just a mile or so directly offshore from the lighthouse.

The New Statistical Account of Scotland

The 'Second' or 'New' Statistical Account of Scotland undertaken between 1834 and 1845 (that for the parish of Durness is dated September 1834) manifests obvious pride in the recent completion of the Cape Wrath lighthouse. But it also makes clear that access to Cape Wrath, even with the new landing facilities at Clais Charnach, could be troublesome and interrupted or denied altogether by adverse sea and weather conditions. See Appendix XVI.

Access Difficulties

A clear illustration of just how difficult access to Cape Wrath could be in the early days of the lighthouse, even for experienced Northern Lighthouse Board personnel, may be gleaned from an entry by Alan Stevenson in his day to day diary of August 1844, part of which records his tour of the northern lighthouses in that year. The Cape Wrath reference states:

> 8th August: Land at Cape Wrath at 6 – in very heavy surf. I fall on the slippery quay and am nearly drawn back by the backdraft of the surf

which wet me to the skin with some risk of injury and I got dried at the lighthouse.

By way of explanation it should be pointed out that, in recording this incident, Alan Stevenson was referring to a landing at the small harbour at Clais Charnach created prior to the building operations at the Cape Wrath light. Clais Charnach is approximately one and a half miles from the lighthouse; the road from the harbour to the light crosses very exposed ground, and the journey to the warmth and safety of the lighthouse, probably on foot but possibly by pony, whilst clearly soaked through, cannot have been pleasant. But each member of the several Stevenson lighthouse generations would have been prepared for these occurrences, and equally would not have been strangers to many similar incidents.

Four years later, Alan Stevenson again records his tour of the northern lighthouses, and of his landing below Cape Wrath and climbing

up the cliff below the lighthouse. A path (dyke?) is required (at the top) for the cattle to keep them from the cliffs over which they fall.

Balnakeil Cemetery Records of Cape Wrath Residents

There are just a few headstones in the old cemetery at Balnakeil church that briefly record the lives and deaths of nineteenth century Cape Wrath residents.

Catherine McLeod died 3 October 1860 at Kerwick, aged 27. Her husband Donald McLeod, shepherd of Kerwick died on 9 December 1909, aged 65.

Catherine Williamson, wife of Neil Morrison, Principal Light Keeper, died at Cape Wrath lighthouse on 3 March 1886, aged 44. Her epitaph HER END WAS IN PEACE surely reflects the serenity of her surroundings as much as the circumstances of her demise.

The Cape Wrath Academy

The educational needs of the Capeside children were addressed in a uniquely Scottish way, by the establishment of Side Schools. The school at Achiemore is well recorded and there is evidence that a similar though smaller and less permanent example operated at Kearvaig. Both schools were under the overall authority of the Higher Grade school at Durine, Durness. In this widespread and sparsely populated area of north west Sutherland, Side Schools were a common feature. In the immediate area there were similar establishments at Eriboll, Strathbeg, Gualin, Rhigolter and Grudie at one time or another. There were also more permanent public schools at Hope and Laid.

The Side School at Achiemore often enjoyed the title 'The Cape Wrath Academy' by locals. The school must have originated after 1834, when the Second Statistical Account for the Parish of Durness was compiled (and in which it was not mentioned), and it closed in 1947. Some records have survived, which provide fascinating insights into ordinary life in the isolated far north west.

The provision of adequate heating for these small schoolrooms appears to have been a constant annual concern for the education authorities. The Eddrachilles and Durness School Management Committee at its meeting at the Rhiconich Hotel held on 31 July 1930 recorded arrangements for the supply of coal for all of the Durness schools. Richard Mackay & Son, Merchants of Durness agreed to supply seventeen and a half tons of Best English coal at Port-na-Con, Loch Eribollside, at 45 shillings (£2.25p) per ton; Mr. Morrison of the Post Office, Durness agreed to cart the coal from Port-na-Con to various Durness schools for the overall sum of £11.1s.0d.(£11.05p).

Coal was provided as follows:

Durine Higher Grade Public School	8 tons
Hope Public School	2 tons
CAPE SIDE	1 ½ tons
Laid Public School	3 tons
Eriboll	1 ½ tons
Strathbeg	1 ½ tons

The Committee, at its meeting in Durness School held on 7 October 1931, recorded that Murdo Mackenzie of Kearvaig had offered to cart the Achiemore School coal supply (presumably from the Capeside slipway) for an inclusive charge of £2.00.

There are repeated references to coal supplies for schools. Harsh winters often caused coal stocks to be exhausted before the end of the school year, and there are repeated references to the necessity for additional supplies at short notice.

Repairs were frequently needed to the fabric of school premises, and the Cape Wrath Academy at Achiemore was no exception. The S.M.C. at its meeting held at Scourie on 6 July 1932 authorised the payment of £11.5s.0d (£11.25p) to G. Mackay of Midvilla for property repairs to the school.

In 1934 a rather more serious matter arose. The Committee at its meeting held 'at the Rhiconich office' on 24 January 1934 debated an item identified as 'Removal of Achiemore School.' A letter from the Secretary of the Keoldale Sheep Stock Club (proprietors of Keoldale farm) was read requesting 'the removal of Achiemore School nearer to Inshore as the children from Inshore (who are the only pupils attending that school) have to travel a long distance over an exposed road and also have to cross a river before reaching the School.' The Committee considered this to be a reasonable request and instructed the Clerk to forward the letter to the Director of Education with its support.

The Director of Education replied on 9 February 1934, stating that 'the question of the removal of the Cape Wrath Side School was under consideration and that the Education Committee resolved to obtain a report from the Architect on the matter.'

Nothing more was heard of the proposal, and it must therefore be concluded that the education authorities felt unable to support the local view. The Cape Wrath Academy continued to occupy its spectacular site overlooking the Kyle of Durness and Balnakeil Bay until its demise thirteen years later.

The Committee returned to its coal concerns in 1937. At its meeting of 3 February a letter from Mrs. Corbett, teacher at Achiemore Side School, was considered requesting the provision of a coal storage box. It was resolved to forward the request to the Director of Education together with the Committee's recommendation for approval.

At its next meeting, held on 23 March 1937, the Committee was advised that the Architect, Mr. E.W. Brannen, had been asked by the Director of Education to make arrangements for the erection of a coal bin at Cape Wrath Side School as recommended.

It took over a year for hopes for the adequate storage of school coal on the Capeside to be dashed. The Committee at its meeting in Rhiconich on 15 June 1938 was advised that the Director of Education had concluded that expense involved in the provision of a coal bin could not be justified. The estimated cost of a suitable bunker 6' by 6' was £15.00, and the Education Committee was of the opinion that in view of all the circumstances such expenditure was not possible. It was suggested that the coal be left in bags at the school.

The Cape Wrath Academy survived the war with a minimum of pupils, and in the final year of the war there were local concerns at falling numbers. The local management committee at its meeting on 14 June 1945 resolved that: 'It was agreed to recommend to the Director of Education that Achiemore Side School be kept open as there is a possibility of children coming to Achiemore in the near future.'

That indicator of the wellbeing of the Side School, the annual coal supply contract, shows that the Committee's plea was effective, since Achiemore was included in the annual contract awarded on 17 October 1945. However, it was not included in the coal supply listed on 8 May 1946. Perhaps the school operated at the barest minimum throughout the preceding winter months, and coal stocks were sufficient for the time being.

Two months later, more pressing concerns affected the Cape Wrath Academy. The Committee at its meeting of 5 July 1946 recorded that: 'It was agreed to ask the Director of Education to send a teacher to Achiemore Side School.' The County Council Education Committee minutes of the meeting of 31 July state that 'Mr. Charles Mackenzie was appointed teacher for the children of Mr. Morrison of Achiemore.'

Later that year, the Committee returned to its coal supply concerns, which confirms that at that time the school continued to function. The minutes of the meeting held on 12 December record that the Director of Education had agreed that coal should be delivered to the Cape Side School. The Clerk had written to Messrs Burr of Tongue concerning this supply, and reported that the coal had been delivered.

School Management Committees were abolished with effect from 1 October 1947; thereafter school matters at a local level were administered by sub-committees of the County Council Education Committee.

Examination of the Sutherland County Council Education Committee minutes reveals further references to educational matters on Cape Wrath. The local school closure concerns towards the end of the war would appear to be founded on a decision of the County Education Committee held on 27 September 1944, which resolved '(1) that David Morrison, one of the two pupils on roll at Cape Wrath Side School, be granted lodging allowance of ten shillings (50 pence) per week to enable him to attend Durine (i.e. Durness) Public School, and (2) that Cape Wrath S.S. be continued for the winter months and that thereafter, should there be only one pupil on roll the school be closed down.'

Just a year later, on 26 September 1945, the Education Committee decided that 'In view of the fact that there is only one pupil in Cape Wrath S.S. and that he is over ten years of age, that the School be closed down and that the pupil be granted lodging allowance of ten shillings (50 pence) per week to attend a Public School. The Medical Officer of Health agreed that the boy might now go into lodgings.'

We have seen above that a teacher for the Cape Wrath Academy was appointed in July 1946; Mr William Morrison of Achiemore was clearly doing his best to assure the future of the Side School there, for the Education Committee minutes of 5 June record he made application for the provision of a teacher for his (further) two children. The Committee granted his request 'when the second child is old enough to attend school.'

By the end of 1947 the Morrison family had moved from Achiemore to take up residence at Kearvaig, and this prompted the resignation of teacher Mackenzie and the closure of the Cape Wrath Academy. The Education Committee minutes for the meeting held on 28 January 1948 record that Miss M.E. Monro of Sangomore, Durness had been appointed teacher to take up her duties 'as soon as a suitable room is prepared for use as a schoolroom at Kerwick (i.e. Kearvaig)' for the children of Mr. William Morrison. But by November of the same year Miss Munro had also resigned.

The Morrison family had by then left Kearvaig, for the Education Committee at its meeting held on 7 June 1950 records receiving a letter from Mrs. Clarke of Kerwick requesting the provision of a Side School teacher for her child Elizabeth (born 9 November 1943). The Committee resolved, not for the first time, to appoint Miss Marion Munro to the post. However, she must have declined the appointment, as at its meeting of 8 September 1950 the Committee noted 'The Director of Education had been unable to find a teacher for Kerwick Side School.'

On 27 September 1950, the Committee noted that Mr William Clarke of Kerwick had accepted the offer of a boarding allowance of thirty shillings (£1.50p) weekly for his daughter to attend the school in Durness, and that he subsequently made application for an additional allowance to enable her to travel home and back at weekends. Mr Clarke was informed that the cost of travel at weekends was a parental responsibility.

From this it is clear that the Achiemore Side School closed in

1947 with the departure of the Morrison family for Kearvaig, and that the brief later existence of the Kearvaig Side School ended just three years later, when Elizabeth Clarke lodged in Durness and was educated there.

Mr Clarke made an application for the provision of a home teacher in January 1951. He stated that his daughter had returned home to Kearvaig from school in Durness because of illness, for a period of three months. He was politely advised that no teacher would be provided and that the lodging allowance would continue to be available to his daughter on her recovery. The era of the Cape Wrath Side Schools had well and truly ended.

County Council Education Committees were required to advise the government Department of Education, by 28 February 1951, of their intentions as to those Side Schools remaining within their areas. In Sutherland at that time there were thirteen such establishments still operating; Achiemore and Kearvaig were not included in the list. It was proposed to close the eleven remaining Sutherland Side Schools and either upgrade or improve just two: those at Achfary and Assynt.

Inter-War Lighthouse Excursions

Private excursions to and across Cape Wrath continued with increasing regularity between the war years of the twentieth century. The Cape Wrath Hotel established motorised tours to the lighthouse (probably incorporating shooting and fishing trips) during the 1920s. The hotel transported a large Argyle motor car across the Kyle of Durness for the purpose of taking guests and passengers into the empty quarter of the Parph. The Argyle Motor Car Company started in 1899 in Glasgow and continued until 1914, when the magnificent Alexandria works were turned over to munitions manufacture. The company was resurrected in 1917 although few private motor cars were manufactured during the 1920s. By 1932 the company had folded again, this time irretrievably. It seems likely that the Cape Wrath Argyle motor car was a rarity in Scotland and possibly unique in north-west Sutherland.

The tourist excursions were held responsible for damage caused to the road. In the late 1930s Principal Keeper John Mitchell wrote to the NLB complaining that

> The Hotel car is on the road nearly every day . . . which is the cause of cutting up the weak parts. During the summer months tourists arrive at the Cape Wrath Hotel (and) hire the Hotel car at a cost of 25 shillings. Last summer 240 persons visited Cape Wrath.

Mitchell believed that the tourist traffic was damaging the ford across the Daill river, and that consequently the higher water level there adversely affected the brakes of the lighthouse truck.

> It is only when we reach the ferry we find the brakes will not hold

was his laconic but nevertheless alarming comment.

The Cape Wrath Hotel venture pre-empted the current minibus trips. I am sure that whilst their Argyle motor car probably did spend a good deal of time over on the Capeside, it was retrieved at the end of the summer (or shooting?) season. Then, as now, there was no other road access; the Argyle must have been taken across by raft and brought back by the same method.

The venerable old Argyle survived until about 1940, and as late as the early 1950s its remains were still to be seen adjacent to the Capeside pier. It is said that the rolling chassis, devoid of all bodywork, was later pushed over the cliff opposite Ferry House.

Wartime Developments at Cape Wrath

The Second World War years saw an increased level of activity at Cape Wrath, with the re-establishment of the former Lloyd's radio station as a vital link in the coastal watch and defence system. Not only were personnel stationed at the Cape to watch and listen for enemy shipping passing along the North Channel, but they were also expected to be alert to the possibility of enemy landings on this far outpost of the British mainland and to be aware of any reports of suspicious activity.

German U-boats were a constant presence in the shipping lanes off the north Scottish coast, and it was always assumed that spies would be landed in order to watch shipping and report on British naval movements. Norwegian skippers frequently attempted to infiltrate security in Lerwick, in the Shetlands. They embarked German agents and returned them to Norway, where Gestapo personnel awaited their return. It was a natural concern that attempts would be made to infiltrate enemy agents onto the British mainland; where better than in the isolated far north west, where the chance of detection was much reduced?

No spies were ever apprehended on Cape Wrath, but there was evidence of them operating in the area. The discovery of several radio transmitters and other communications equipment of German origin on Cape Wrath supported the theory that enemy spies were landed (either by parachute or submarine) and that they did observe the movements of British shipping. This equipment was handed over to the local military authorities. There were also reports of shepherds occasionally observing lone strangers who, when seen, swiftly hid themselves. Articles of clothing and food remnants were also discovered on several occasions.

The war Signal Station was hurriedly reactivated during the summer of 1939. Its main shortcoming at that time was a telephone link by which the observation personnel there could contact the Radar Defence Network. Prior to 1936 there were no telephones in north west Sutherland; there was a single Omnibus telegraph circuit, from Thurso along the north coast, with spurs off to each post office. This would have been an earth return circuit, with messages transmitted in Morse code. In 1936 Durness was equipped with a UAX12 (Unit Automatic Exchange) and thereafter a private wire extended to the lighthouse with hand generators for ringing and Leclanche cell batteries for speaking. Before the outbreak of the war there were only ninety or so subscribers to the local Durness telephone service. This basic telecommunications technology was insufficient for the wartime demands.

In September 1939 the Post Office Engineering Department erected four hundred poles and laid eleven miles of double wire on Cape Wrath. The telephone connection was with the post office in Durness rather than direct to the exchange. This upgraded system allowed the military personnel at Cape Wrath some indirect communication with the military authorities until the new Durness radar installation became fully operational in 1941.

Blackout regulations were strictly enforced in and around Durness, and the lighthouse was no exception. Now the Cape Wrath light was vital to shipping, especially to the Atlantic and Russian convoys. And any convoy needing a navigational fix when steaming out of UK waters around Cape Wrath would need the light to be illuminated. Apparently the practice was for the naval authorities to telephone the Durness Postmaster with the request that he in turn request the Cape Wrath light-keeper to display the light for X number of seconds at a specific time. On such tenuous connections was the war conducted in the far north west.

The Cape Wrath War Signal Station was downgraded to the status of Coast Watch Station during 1941 to 1943 as the Durness radio and radar facility became fully operational.

The Third Statistical Account of Scotland

The Third Statistical Account of Scotland was proposed in 1944, almost exactly a hundred years after completion of the Second or New Statistical Account. The task was complete by the mid-1950s, that for the Parish of Durness being dated June 1955; an update was added in March 1985. The only reference to Cape Wrath is in the addendum, where it is stated that:

Housing: . . On the Capeside where there were until recently nine occupied houses, there are now only three. These are occupied by lighthouse keepers whose families live on the East Coast.

It is surely an unfortunate omission that no mention of the Achiemore and Kearvaig Side Schools was included in the allegedly detailed 1955 survey, when they had so recently ceased educating the Capeside children.

The Last Casualty

The seas around Cape Wrath and the rocks and shoals within them have always been dangerous to shipping. Indeed, the very fact that the Cape is marked by a lighthouse is testament to the need for absolute care in these waters. There are very many wrecks all around the north-western tip of the Scottish mainland which provide sport for divers. The two World Wars added significantly to the numbers of maritime casualties, both warships and freight vessels, consigned to the deep.

The last recorded incident at Cape Wrath resulting in the total loss of a vessel occurred in December 1962, and involved the fishing vessel 'Scottish Maid.' The boat was deploying nets off Cape Wrath, when a combination of wind and tide dragged the boat and its gear onto the Duslic Rock. The vessel struck the rock and heavy damage was inflicted on the hull below the water line, although not sufficiently to prompt an immediate sinking.

The skipper being aware of the seriousness of his situation instantly cut his gear free and, with the vessel taking on water and rapidly settling, made haste for the cove at Clais Charnach. He managed to come alongside the pier without injury to his crew, and all were landed safely with the assistance of the lighthouse complement and their lifesaving equipment. The vessel settled on the shingle beach and was made secure for the night. But a strong northerly blew up, with the result that, by the time repair crews had arrived the following day, the boat had been smashed to pieces.

Some gear was saved, but the Scottish Maid was a total loss. The boat's Gardner diesel engine still remains at Clais Charnach, the only tangible reminder of this most unfortunate incident, but it is gradually being covered by pebbles as a result of incessant wave action.

CHAPTER 8

FOR THOSE IN PERIL ON THE SEA

*Later Developments and Improvements
for Mariners at Cape Wrath*

On Christmas Day 1828 the lighthouse at Cape Wrath was commissioned; it provided the first fixed point of reference for and protection to mariners rounding the dangerous north-western tip of the British Isles. The establishment of a light here had taken almost thirty years of pressure and planning, and the lighthouse and its permanent personnel settled into a long period of quiet calm punctuated only by the vagaries of the weather and, no doubt, the gentle panic engendered by the periodic visits of the Engineer and representatives of the Commissioners of Northern Lights.

Originally the flame was provided by an oil-burner, the light-beam of which was intensified by Robert Stevenson's system of polished reflectors. The oil used in the earliest days was refined rapeseed oil, otherwise called Colza oil.

The central core of the lighthouse tower housed the weights and winding mechanism for the clockwork motor by which the lamp array rotated continually through the hours of darkness. It required rewinding every one and a half hours through the night. It would have been perfectly possible to have had a clockwork mechanism capable of operating for days. But in order to ensure that the light keepers remained awake and alert throughout the whole of their shift, it was made a requirement that the mechanism be manually rewound every ninety minutes.

In the early years, the Commissioners and their Engineer made no attempt to produce beams or recognisable characteristics in their lights. Once oil was introduced as the illuminant, this process began. As the number and, in some instances, the close proximity of lighthouses in some locations (the Pentland Firth on the north east tip of Scotland, for instance) increased, there arose the need for identifying features. It was important that seafarers should not only be able to see the light warning of dangerous rocks, reefs or coastlines, but that they should also be able to pinpoint their position with reference to a particular light.

Experiments were conducted in which light towers were painted with coloured differentiating characteristics to enable them to be distinguished during the daytime; some towers were painted with red and white bands, and some were painted with solid identifying colours. And light rays were collected and concentrated by reflectors, lenses and mirrors into directed beams.

The next stage was the revolving light which, with the use of colour and timing, allowed each light to have its own identity. All these varying identifying markers became somewhat confusing, and eventually it became standard practice for a unique pattern of light flash signature to be assigned to each light. These individual light characteristics were and are published in the Northern Lighthouse Board's Notices to Mariners, which not only specify the signature of every light under the Board's jurisdiction, but also advertise interruptions in, and temporary changes to, the signature at any light.

The first revolving light was set up at Start Point, Orkney, in 1806; an alternate red sector was introduced at the Bell Rock light in 1811; flashing lights were installed at Buchan Ness in 1827.

The Cape Wrath light was inaugurated with a pattern of red and white flashing lights

> exhibiting from one and the same Lantern a light of natural appearance, alternating or changing with one tinged red; which two kinds of light successively attain their most luminous effect every two minutes.

The original public notice advertising all the relevant location and characteristics data of the new light is given in Appendix XIV.

This unique light signature remained unaltered throughout the remainder of the nineteenth century and much of the twentieth. Within the archives of Royal Commission on the Ancient and Historic Monuments of Scotland there is lodged an original scale drawing, dated 30 May 1895 over the signature of D.A. Stevenson, of a plan, elevation and section through the Lantern Room at Cape Wrath, which refers to:

... Red and White Panels of Optic.

The small harbour, materials handling facility, and storehouse at Clais Charnach were improved during 1863–64, the redevelopment centring on the landing place, which was always subject to ferocious seas. Even after the improvement works, it could safely be used only during higher tides on relatively calm days.

The slipway was rebuilt and consolidated. It was probably at this time that the steam winding gear was installed to assist in hauling materials landed from the supply vessels. The discarded winching and winding gear is still visible at Clais Charnach, along with the iron band let into the pier and its approaches used in conjunction with the wire rope hawsers. The pier was further extended during the 1950s.

In the third quarter of the nineteenth century, the road between the Kyle of Durness and the top of Daill Brae was realigned. As originally built, the road left the Kyle storehouse north of Geodh na Leodhassich (map reference NC363699) and approached the Daill river at NC352682. The new road extension left the existing road at this point and headed eastwards, gradually descending the northern side of the valley until it reached the valley floor at map reference NC358682.

Here a ford was built crossing the Daill river; the new road then ascended the southern side of the Daill valley to a height of approximately one hundred feet, and turned southwards to follow the western shore of the Kyle of Durness. It remained at a level high above the Kyle of Durness until its final half mile or so, where the approach to the new ferry landing was built.

This approach is extremely steep and constricted, even for horse-drawn traffic, and the route is walled on its seaward side; two passing places only were provided between the ferry slipway and the first mile marker.

The three homesteads along this new section of road (i.e. those at Daill House, Achiemore and Ferry House) each date from this period, or a little later. Ferry House was built and later remodelled by the Northern Lighthouse Board as accommodation for its ferryman. From this point, the ferry landings at The Well (map reference NC374666) and Keoldale slipway (NC378661) across the water on the eastern side of the Kyle of Durness could be conveniently observed by the resident ferryman.

Hand winches were provided at the Capeside ferry landing to enable the wooden ferry boats to be drawn up out of the water. The Capeside landing is in a sheltered cove, the obvious spot for it. Over the years the stone slipway here has been extended and widened, as has that on the opposite side.

Generally, the new road extension is constructed to a greater width than the original 1828, and two stone bridges were built wider than the original specification of nine feet between parapets. Nevertheless, they each exhibit a certain 'olde-worlde' charm. This extension was shown on the first edition of the Ordnance Survey six inch map dated 1874 and was described by a visitor just two years later, which provides us with a date by which it was in use.

The mid-1890s were years of development and upgrading of the lamp arrays necessitated by new illumination methods. The Royal Commission on the Ancient and Historic Monuments of Scotland archives house original drawings and plans headed CAPE WRATH LIGHTHOUSE LANTERN depicting the sectional elevation of the lantern, ventilator and parapet generally, each signed 'D.A. Stevenson, Edinburgh, 6th June 1895.'

David A. Stevenson records in his 'Personal Historical Notes 1871–1914' that in 1903 he

> ... introduced the use of incandescent oil burners. I adopted that known as the Chance burner and it was gradually introduced at all lighthouse stations in the service, greatly increasing the power of the lights.

In 1904 the Board of Trade sanctioned expenditure on repairs and refurbishments to the buildings at the lighthouse, and sums of £100 for repairs to the buildings and a further £50 for an extension to the landing slip were authorised, and work began. It soon became apparent that £150 would be insufficient to carry out the necessary work, so on 13 August 1906 the Secretary to the NLB wrote to the Board of Trade explaining why additional funds were necessary. The text of that letter is transcribed at Appendix XVII. The Board of Trade, in a letter dated 26 August 1906, sanctioned the excess expenditure of £133.9s.9d. (£133.49p).

Cape Wrath Fog Signal

In October 1902, plans were well advanced for the provision of fog warning apparatus at Cape Wrath. Three separate drawings in the RCAHMS archives refer to *Cape Wrath Fog Signal* and depict the Engine Room ground levels and plan, various structural details, plans and sections of the Horn House, and front, back, end elevations and cross section of the Machine room. These drawings are each signed *D.A. Stevenson, Edinburgh, October 24th, 1902.*

The Northern Lighthouse Board's Notice to Mariners number 11 of 20 September 1905 gave notice 'that on or about 1st November next, a SIREN FOG SIGNAL will be established at Cape Wrath Lighthouse, which during thick or foggy weather will give ONE BLAST OF SIX SECONDS DURATION EVERY 1 ½ MINUTES.'

The fog signal at Cape Wrath was powered by compressed air. The whole process of installing the fog signal itself and the compressors to power it, erecting a building to house the compressors and laying the pipe-work by which compressed air could be delivered to the fog signal apparatus, was technically straightforward and by this time not innovative. The constraints of the site provided the challenges at this installation.

The only suitable ground on which to build the compressor house was perhaps a hundred yards distant from the cliff-top on which the foghorn house and fog signal could be sited so that it faced due north without any physical obstruction. The machine room could not be erected near to or annexed to the light tower or the adjacent offices; to do so would adversely affect the groundworks already in place on which the lighthouse depended – rainwater cisterns and drainage works, for instance.

The compressors to power the fog signal were housed in a new building erected for the purpose, and this building much later housed new electrical generators to provide lighting and power for the lighthouse offices and domestic accommodation. The compressor building still exists, complete with the original diesel compressors and most of the original electrical generators.

The original engines powering the compressors in 1905 would have been Campbell gas engines, which were in turn superseded by Atlantic engines. Most NLB stations were equipped or re-equipped with Atlantics in the 1920s, which were linked to Alley and MacLellan compressors. During the 1950s the Atlantics were replaced by Kelvin diesels, engines which remain in place in the Cape Wrath machine room.

This same building also provided extra upgraded housing for light keepers' families resident at Cape Wrath. The building now accommodates the visitor interpretation centre and accommodation for occasional residents other than lighthouse personnel at Cape Wrath. It is proposed to establish refreshment facilities here.

Having established the site for the new compressor and generator house, the problem of delivering compressed air to the foghorn house and fog signal had to be addressed. This was solved by the use of wrought iron storage tanks and underground pipes. There are three large wrought iron tanks of circular section standing on substantial masonry plinths directly adjacent to the compressor room, linked to it by a short length of overhead cast iron pipe. Note also the wheel of the control valve which permitted delivery of compressed air from the diesel engines to these first storage tanks in the system.

A further cast iron pipe passes underground from the tanks adjacent to the compressor room to two further storage tanks sited next to the foghorn house itself. This delivery pipe is visible in one or two places as it nears the south west of the light tower. The foghorn house itself housed the final pipework and valvegear by which the fog signal operated.

Notice that the huge horn could be directed manually through an arc of perhaps 180 degrees. The simple application of a large crank handle enabled one or more keepers to wind the horn around a geared track, so that the warning signal could be directed at any fogbank developing off the north west coast in the vicinity of Cape Wrath. Should the entire seascape off the Cape be shrouded in fog, then the horn would be directed due north.

The signal took the form of six blasts every ninety seconds. With the signal sounding and the diesel compressors running to supply the system with compressed air, Cape Wrath would not be entirely the quietest place in north west Scotland.

A further drawing in the RCAHMS archives referring to Cape Wrath Fog Signal depicts the '3 minute clock in Horn House Full Size.' This drawing is signed *D.A. Stevenson, Edinburgh, March 17th 1904.*

By 1913, repairs were required to the fog signal engines. The Secretary to the Northern Lighthouse Board wrote to the Harbour Department of the Board of Trade on 5 March explaining that 'the exhaust pipes of the Fog Signal engines at Cape Wrath Lighthouse are worn out and require renewal.' A tender by Messrs John Shaw & Co, Glasgow for the supply of the necessary pipes etc in the sum of £42.7s.6d. (£42.37.1/2p) was submitted along with the letter. The Board felt the need to point out that 'the pipes required are of a special quality of which Messrs Shaw are the makers.' Approval of the expenditure was agreed a mere six days later.

The compressed air fog signal remained operational until the mid-1970s, when it was superseded by LIE 300 apparatus attached to the lighthouse tower balcony. In this updated system an electromagnetic signal produced by alternating current vibrated steel diaphragms, which in turn generated pressure waves in the resonating horns.

The Northern Lighthouse Board's Notice to Mariners 21 of 2001, dated 24 August 2001, gave notice that: 'On or about 23 September 2001 the Fog Signal service will be PERMANENTLY DISCONTINUED. The navigation light will continue to operate as advertised.' The GPS age had finally arrived at Cape Wrath.

Cape Wrath Radio Signalling Station

The early years of the twentieth century were ones of significant activity at Cape Wrath. In addition to the extensive building works of 1904–05 described above there were also proposals to re-site the light itself and to erect a signal station at the tip of the Cape to accommodate the newly-developed Marconi radio transmitting and receiving apparatus.

Telegraphy by wire was developed in the middle years of the nineteenth century following the experiments of Joseph Henry. Fellow American Samuel F.B. Morse successfully exploited the device in 1844, and from then onwards developments were constant. But this system of communication depended upon a fixed line of contact between sender and recipient; it was fine for use on land, but that is where its application ended.

Theoretical work on wireless telegraphy by the Scottish physicist

James Clerk Maxwell in the 1860s led to further experimentation, principally in Italy and Germany, which culminated in Gugliemo Marconi successfully transmitting messages by radio over a mile or so towards the end of 1895. The Italian government not being sufficiently impressed with these experiments, Marconi travelled to England where, in 1896, he was able to demonstrate his invention to the satisfaction of the Post Office which was at that time responsible for all aspects of telegraphy throughout Great Britain. Marconi's device was awarded a British patent in 1897.

It soon became clear that the marine industry would be the major customer for the new wireless method of communication; radio was the only means by which ships could communicate at sea beyond the line of sight. Developments to 1900 enabled radio communications to be successfully carried out up to twenty-five or thirty miles offshore, where the greatest dangers in the voyage were likely to be encountered. The following year, Marconi communicated radio signals across the Atlantic between Cornwall and Newfoundland.

Marconi's system was soon adopted for use by both the British and Italian navies, and by 1907 had been so much improved that a transatlantic wireless service was established for public use.

Lloyd's of London, marine and commercial insurers, established signal stations as far back as the mid-nineteenth century relying, at that time, on telegraphy by wire, semaphore or heliograph. In 1882 Lloyd's stated that their signal stations were to give notice of vessels in distress and requiring assistance, of the state of the wind and weather, and were to report to ship owners and other persons interested in shipping all passing vessels that made their name known to any station.

Information on the movement of vessels en route from port to port was of direct benefit to Lloyd's' underwriters, but indirectly it was even more important, making Lloyd's the recognised clearing house for global shipping intelligence.

In the early twentieth century, Lloyd's' introduced the use of wireless telegraphy for communication between ship and station. Ship-owners used the signal station network to communicate alterations in orders to ships in UK and foreign waters. By 1891 there were forty station in the UK and one hundred and eighteen abroad, either controlled by or allied to Lloyd's. In 1928 there were twenty-eight stations in Great Britain, the range and reliability of radio communication having improved so much, and one hundred and thirty-four abroad.

Lloyd's of London acquired the Cape Wrath site, leased from the Commissioners of the Northern Lighthouses, in January 1890 following a visit by the Secretary of Lloyd's to northern Scotland in October 1888. The purpose of this exercise was to secure the site whilst Lloyd's decided whether to establish a station at Cape Wrath or at the Butt of Lewis.

Subsequently the Admiralty proposed that Lloyd's should erect buildings for a joint station at Cape Wrath. As a result, the original (undeveloped) site was surrendered in 1903 and a different site location overlooking the lighthouse leased from the Commissioners, who simultaneously leased the adjacent ground to the Admiralty.

David A. Stevenson recorded in his *Personal Historic Notes 1871–1914* for the year 1903:

> Lloyd's wished to establish stations for signalling to passing vessels at Dunnet Head, Cape Wrath, St. Abb's Head and Butt of Lewis and they came to us (i.e. D. & C. Stevenson, Civil Engineers, Edinburgh) to design and carry out the work of establishing them. They each involve the provision of offices and accommodations for four families and owing to the remote positions were works of considerable difficulty, but were successfully carried out.

Lloyd's and the Admiralty agreed in January 1908 that the Cape Wrath signalling station should be taken over by the Admiralty; signalling commenced on t October 1910 by H.M. Coastguard under the agreement, as a day station only.

In July 1932 the Admiralty asked Lloyd's whether they would be willing to close the Cape Wrath station as it was very expensive to operate. Signalling was discontinued from 31 October 1932.

The former Lloyd's buildings were hastily reactivated during the late summer of 1939 as an observation post, listening station and signal station. Cape Wrath provided the principal north Atlantic communications station during the early years of the war. Between 1941 and 1943 permanent listening and radar installations were established in and around Durness and the relevance of the former Lloyd's site at Cape Wrath gradually diminished. In 1943 the Cape Wrath Signalling Station was down-graded to that of Coast Watch Station; the main data-gathering function was transferred to the newly-established Royal Air Force radar, listening and transmitting facilities in Durness.

After the end of the Second World War the buildings were again closed. Gradually they fell into disrepair, and their only use was during military training exercises, when debris was frequently left scattered around. This problem was particularly noticeable during the winter exercise of February 2005, when large amounts of unexploded small arms and machine gun ammunition were discarded across the whole area of the lighthouse ground.

During 2005 the Northern Lighthouse Board indicated that approximately fifty acres of land in their ownership at Cape Wrath, including the former Lloyd's signal station buildings, might be offered for sale. The military authorities expressed an immediate interest in purchasing all of this ground. They proposed to demolish the former Lloyd's signal station buildings and replace them with what was at the time described as a 'tin shed.' It would have been interesting indeed to have seen just how long this suggested replacement structure would have withstood the fierce Atlantic gales which batter this exposed headland.

But the residents of Durness were also interested, and throughout the summer and autumn of 2005 the Durness Development Group formulated a scheme, which was supported by the Highland Regional Council and which eventually attracted funding from the Scottish Executive, for a community buy-out under the Land Reform (Scotland) Act, 2003. In January 2006 confirmation was received of the acceptance by the Scottish Executive of the community's registration of interest, which effectively placed the Durness Development Group in prime position for the sale of the land; it could not be sold or otherwise transferred without the NLB first consulting with or offering it to the Durness community. That is still the situation at the time of going to press.

But the Durness Development Group was unable, because of the terms of their existing constitution, to proceed with their approaches to the Northern Lighthouse Board in June 2005. At that time it was clear that the Board were intending to sell the land at Cape Wrath and the military were intent on buying it. What was needed was the activation of a legal convention unique in Scottish property law, i.e. the recording of an interest in the land by a private individual in order to ensure that a sale/purchase deal was not finalised *in camera*, so to speak. That interest was registered with the Northern Lighthouse Board as a matter of some urgency, and the Development Group gained some latitude to enable them to both amend their constitution and make the necessary administrative approaches prior to the finalisation of their proposals. And who was the private individual responsible for ensuring that the land at Cape Wrath was not disposed of before the local community could formally express their interest? Why, your author, of course!

The substantial stone and concrete former Lloyd's signal station buildings erected by the Stevenson partnership have already been standing for over a hundred years; they are now in a perilous state and they have suffered significantly in recent years during military training exercises. It is genuinely to be hoped that their decline has now been halted and that their future is protected and assured.

Proposal to Re-site Cape Wrath Light

The main problem with the lighthouse from the start was that its light could be obscured by sea haar, mist and fog, due to its position four hundred feet above sea level. At the end of the nineteenth century, following improvements to the light's power and magnitude, it was proposed that the light be rebuilt nearer to sea level.

The Northern Lighthouse Board had formulated a scheme to re-site the light by mid-1911, but it was apparent that the scheme would be very costly and would involve techniques at the limit of the technology then available.

David A. Stevenson recorded in his 'Personal Historic Notes 1871–1914' for the year 1913:

> . . . Also (engaged) with designing a plan for erecting a lighthouse on the outmost reef at Cape Wrath to take the place of the old light which was too high and frequently obscured by fog. This involved some new features in lighthouse construction, the sinking of a vertical shaft down to the level of the reef with a lift in it, the construction of a covered way over the reef, the construction of two bridges, and the erection of a tower and fog horn house on the extreme end of the reef. The work was begun, but the contractor deserted the work, and on account of the Great War coming on it was found impossible to get a contractor to finish the work nor to carry it on by days wages. It is still (1927) unfinished.

By June 1914 blasting and excavation had begun on sinking the lift shaft as the first element in the new lighthouse scheme. Fifty feet of this still exists, although it is now capped by a substantial concrete cover. Stairs descend the internal walls of the shaft which, due to safety considerations, is largely filled with stone rubble.

Some tangible evidence remains of this project: close to the lighthouse ground boundary wall directly adjacent to where the tower was to be relocated, there remain discarded and broken rock drilling and winch machinery castings. Manufacturer's identifications which remain discernible today read:

TAYLOR PALLISTER & CO. LTD
TAYLORS IMPROVED PATENT
DUNSTON-ON-TYNE
and
THE
INGERSOLL-SARGEANT
DRILL CO.
NEW YORK

The scheme to re-site the light foundered for the reasons given by David A. Stevenson in his report quoted above. In October 1914 the light was extinguished for the duration of hostilities, and the scheme to re-site the light tower was never resurrected.

Arrangements for Maintenance of the Ferry

Lodged in the National Archives at Kew is a most interesting document referring to arrangements for the maintenance of the ferry across the Kyle of Durness by which access is gained to the road to the lighthouse and war signal station. Arrangements prior to 1919 are described in some detail, as are the changes consequent upon sale and new ownership of the land at the Capeside ferry landing. This spurred the Admiralty to investigate the legal responsibilities for the maintenance of the ferry (and, to a lesser extent, the Cape Wrath road). The Admiralty's assessment of the situation and proposals for the future can be found in the Appendices.

Cape Wrath Weather Station

With the outbreak of the Second World War, the strategic importance of Cape Wrath's early warning system was recognised, and in 1940 a weather station was established there. The permanent light keepers operated the instruments and recorded the readings; observations were relayed by telephone. The light keepers took the meteorological readings. After the lighthouse was automated a Semi-Automatic Meteorological Observation Station (SAMOS) was established by the Meteorological Office, in Durness, with a local resident appointed to supervise the equipment.

The weather station was inside the boundary wall north of the present tarmac-ed turning area; the concrete bases on which the recording instruments stood remain visible. The recording instruments were located inside louvred wooden boxes (called 'Stevenson Screens') recognisable the world over. Keepers were obliged to make synoptic meteorological reports every three hours, by telephone, to the Met Office at Wick. On one occasion in the 1970s it was reported on the TV weather forecast that Cape Wrath was enjoying the warmest temperatures in the British Isles. Evidently one relatively new keeper, unfamiliar with the intricacies of weather recording, considered that it would be much easier, in view of the stormy weather, to take the instruments inside the lighthouse offices. From there he relayed the readings quite unaware of the effect of his actions. The mistake was never repeated.

Seismic Recording

The small block building directly to the south of the light tower, between it and the former compressor and generator rooms, housed a Single Vertical Instrument, part of the British Geological Survey Seismograph Network. The British Geological Survey is responsible for maintaining and developing a network of earthquake recording instrumentation across the United Kingdom. The instrument at Cape Wrath remotely monitored seismic activity (earthquakes, sonic booms, live bombing etc), recording and relaying data to computers in Edinburgh. It was powered by solar panels and data is transmitted to the collating centre by telephone landline. The instrument was de-commissioned in 2005.

The most recent significant earthquake affecting northern

Scotland occurred on 13 August 1816, when considerable damage to property was experienced in Inverness.

Redesignation as a Rock Station

Although situated on the mainland, Cape Wrath was little different from other offshore rock lighthouses in the oceans around Scotland, due to its isolation and access problems. In December 1975 this was recognised and it was re-designated as a Rock Station. Thereafter only the keepers remained, with their families housed in Golspie.

General Technical Developments from the Early Days

When Thomas Smith first became involved in the design and development of Scottish lighthouses, he was obliged to pioneer a system of illumination by which those establishments were to guide mariners. Given his experience, his first tower navigation lights were inevitably based on refined street lamp practise.

Until the 1820s Smith and Stevenson lighthouses emitted a beam produced by burning oil. The oil used was colza (refined rapeseed) oil, though experiments were conducted with olive and household oil. Smith was convinced that reflectors could be utilised to both increase and direct the light beam, given the great distances over which the coastal lighthouses were required to be effective. His original reflectors were simple arrangements of sheet copper beaten by hand into an approximate parabolic profile. Later developments led to silvered mirrors being welded or soldered into the reflectors, which improved the focus and intensification of the beam.

Light intensity is measured in candela, or candle-power. The first Eddystone light employed twenty-four tallow candles, and was measured at thirty candle power.

From the 1820s technical advancements centred upon the lamp burners, which continued to use oil. The Argand lamp, developed by Swiss inventor Aime Argand, was introduced. Simply explained, the Argand lamp employs a glass chimney placed above the burner to protect and intensify the flame, with a series of lenses arranged round it. Robert, and later Alan, Stevenson worked closely with Parisian brothers Augustin and Leonor Fresnel in pioneering developments of the characteristics and placing of new lens forms incorporating prisms. The use of whale oil was introduced as a preferable alternative to colza, and whilst expensive, was effective; it burned without smoke emissions and gave a much brighter light. Whale oil was the principal light medium until almost the end of the nineteenth century.

In the latter half of the nineteenth century, rotating clockwork mechanisms which permitted unique patterns of flashes were perfected, along with Dioptric lenses, which gradually replaced reflectors. And paraffin became the burner medium, replacing whale oil. Paraffin remained the principal lamp fuel until the second half of the twentieth century; the vast majority of stations were manned, and there was much with which the light-keepers could fill their days.

The automation programme of the twentieth century prompted diesel generator development and electric illumination. Mains electricity, even where it was available, was considered not sufficiently reliable for lighthouse use. The isolated locations of many of the establishments, and all of the rock stations, militated against the use of mains power.

The huge lamp arrays utilised in Scottish lighthouses (and lighthouses generally) were direct descendents of the Dioptric Azimuthal Holophotal lamps developed by Thomas Stevenson. (Dioptrics use Fresnel lenses by means of which a single light source is concentrated forward in one direction) Modern units no longer employ reflectors, but they can produce more than three million candle power from a lamp little larger than a conventional domestic light bulb. The bulb powering the main light at Cape Wrath is of one hundred and fifty watts, whilst the two external emergency lamps operate at a mere five watts each.

At Cape Wrath the paraffin vapour burner was replaced in 1978 by mercury vapour lamps; in January 1980 an additional electrically-operated temporary power beam beacon was installed. In December of that year a completely new electrically controlled gearless pedestal and lamp array system was installed as part of the ongoing programme of renewal and upgrading implemented by the Northern Lighthouse Board.

The current Cape Wrath light statistics are:

Position:

Latitude: 58 degrees 37.6 north
                   4 degrees 59.9 west

Light Character: Flashes four white every 30 seconds

Elevation: 122 metres over sea level

Power: 204,000 candle power

Nominal Range: 22 miles

CHAPTER 9

THE CAPE WRATH
REGISTERS OF KEEPERS

God's Deputies on Earth

(Jan Blankenstein, Occasional Keeper, 1973/4)

The NLB Registers of Keepers are fascinating historical documents containing a wealth of material on life in isolated places from the early years of the nineteenth century. The Board has been unable to store, catalogue and maintain all its early documents, so these unique archives have been entrusted to national collections throughout Scotland.

The National Archives of Scotland hold, on microfilm, Light Keepers Registers for the years 1837 to 1958 inclusive. It must be assumed that prior to 1837 no separate keepers registers were maintained.

Throughout the middle years of the nineteenth century, coinciding with the appointment in 1830 of Robert Stevenson's son Alan as Clerk of Works to the Northern Lighthouse Board, a continuous programme of lighthouse building was implemented, in which both Robert and Alan Stevenson were closely involved. This inevitably meant more new appointments and greater rotation of staff between lighthouses.

The early hand-written keeper registers are not completely comprehensive. The Cape Wrath records contain numerous errors and omissions including recording the arrival but not the departure of keepers and vice versa, as well as some transfer records being missing.

Although the Cape Wrath light was commissioned and in use from December 1828 (and presumably staffed by permanent resident keepers from that time) the earliest date in the keeper registers for this station is July 1842. There is a brief prior entry referring to the Principal Keeper at Cape Wrath which does not quote any specific date of appointment; presumably George Kirk was already in post when the separate keeper registers were initiated. Similarly there is no date of his leaving or indication of his transfer location. The inference is that he left prior to the appointment of Principal Keeper John Morrison in May 1845.

But examination of the early Register of Principal Light-Keepers provides a little more illumination. George Kirk entered the service of the Northern Lighthouse Board on 28 October 1824, at the age of 39. He was appointed Principal Keeper at Cape Wrath in January 1837 and served there until 7 May 1845, when his record shows him as 'Superannuated.' This confirms that he directly preceded John Morrison as Principal Keeper at Cape Wrath. Sadly, of the personnel stationed at Cape Wrath during its first eight operational years, there would appear to be no surviving record.

There are other brief references contained within the registers which really are priceless gems. The earliest Cape Wrath register gives no indication of keepers' salaries, but the second page of the register (commencing 1847) records a Principal Keeper's annual salary as £50.00 and an Assistant's as £40.00. These figures are crossed through and the figures £55.00 and £45.00 respectively entered in their places.

Furthermore the second page states boldly: 'A horse allowed here.' This is in recognition of the fact that, as supplies for both light and personnel could only be landed at Clais Charnach, approximately a mile and a half east of the Cape Wrath lighthouse site, a draught horse would be vital to deliver those supplies from the storehouse at the small harbour there to the light itself.

Page three (commencing 1866) continues the reference to salaries, which remained at that time at £55.00 and £45.00, and to the provision of a horse ('A horse kept at this station'). This page also contains a further nugget, recording - with effect from 1 November 1905 – the establishment of a Fog Signal.

The Scottish Lighthouse Museum at Kinnaird Head, Fraserburgh has the Principal and Assistant Keeper records from the Northern Lighthouse Board for the period 1919 to 1998. These later records are much more complete and meticulous than their nineteenth century counterparts, although there is one instance of a keeper arriving at Cape Wrath and, apparently, never leaving.

The provision of a horse continued at Cape Wrath until well into the twentieth century, and there are pictorial records of motor vehicles provided for the use of the keepers there as early as circa 1930. A replacement Morris Commercial truck was provided just prior to the Second World War. In the late 1950s, Land Rovers became the station vehicles. By this time, the horse had been permanently superseded by motor transport.

The keeper registers record only one other significant item during the remainder of the twentieth century; that is that with effect from December 1975, Cape Wrath was re-designated as a Rock Station. Further details of the re-designation and its effects are given in the chapter 'Magnificent Isolation.'

Much can be gleaned from the bare facts recorded in the keeper registers. Throughout the one hundred and seventy or so years during which the Cape Wrath light was tended by resident keepers, a mere thirteen resigned; dismissal was necessary in one case only, and that as long ago as 1862. In the latter years, when the programme of lighthouse automation was approaching completion, seven keepers were made redundant from Cape Wrath. It appears that keepers posted to Cape Wrath in the few years prior to automation were promoted to Principal. Latterly all the rock stations had two Principals as they were all double-crewed. Cape Wrath does appear to have experienced a high staff turnover in its latter years, as the de-manning programme accelerated the rate of retirements.

The simple pleasure of reading the final column of the following table, which records the lighthouse establishments to which Cape Wrath staff were posted, reveals a wondrous list of the most romantic lights erected under the auspices of the Northern Lighthouse Board. And by far the greatest proportion of these names was designed, built and commissioned by a Stevenson, be it Robert, or Alan, or David, or Thomas, or David A, or Charles A, or D Alan.

The mere mention of lighthouses at Skerryvore, Dubh Artach, Dunnet Head, Ardnamurchan, Chicken Rock, Butt of Lewis and Muckle Flugga conjures up mental pictures of Stevenson sentinels resisting the sea, among the finest achievements of Scotland's pre-eminent civil engineering dynasty.

Cape Wrath lighthouse was the last shore station in Scotland to be automated, on the last day of March 1998. It would appear that each of the four keepers stationed at the light at that time elected to take voluntary redundancy.

Transcribed Principal and Assistant Keeper registers follow:

KEEPERS STATIONED AT CAPE WRATH

Date of Arrival	Name	Principal or Assistant	Time of Service here	Date of leaving	Where Sent
	George Kirk	Principal			
	Wm Heddle	Assistant	7yr	6 Jul 1842	Leave of abscence
1842 Jul 6	John McCracken	Assistant		10 Mar 1847	Lismore
1845 May 7	John Morrison	Principal		16 Oct 1850	Hoy
1847 May 10	Peter Ewing	Assistant	10yr 3m	15 Jul 1857	Promoted
1850 Oct 16	James Sutherland	Principal	9yr 6m	11 Jul 1860	Hoy
1851 Jan 2	A R Wallace	Principal	4yr	16 May 1855	Buchan Ness
1855 May 16	John Soutar	Principal	2yr	25 Feb 1857	Skerryvore
1857 Jul 15	Peter S Beal(?)	Assistant	4yr 9m	8 Mar 1862	Clythness
1860 Jul 11	James Burnett	Principal	3yr 8m	16 Mar 1864	Rhinns of Islay
1862 Mar 8	Thomas Aibloe(?)	Assistant	1yr 9m	2 Dec 1863	Dismissed

Date of Arrival	Name	Principal or Assistant	Time of Service here	Date of leaving	Where Sent
1863 Dec 2	James Edgar	Assistant	2yr 3m	7 Mar 1866	Noss Head
1864 Mar 16	Alex McIntosh	Principal	2yr 3m	20 Jul 1866	Skerryvore
1866 Mar 7	Donald Paterson	Assistant	2yr 4m	15 Jul 1868	Resigned
Jul 20	John Ewing	Principal	3yr 6m	9 Feb 1870	Hoy Sound (Low)
1868 Jul 8	John Currie	Assistant	3yr 6m	18 Jan 1872	Kyleakin
1870 Mar 9	David Waters	Principal	7yr 3m	18 Jun 1877	Lamlash
1872 Jan 18	William Ross	Assistant	4yr 3m	3 May 1876	Rhinns of Islay
1876 May 3	Donald A Sinclair	Assistant	10yr 6m	11 Nov 1886	Montroseness
1877 Jun 18	John McGill	Principal	3yr 10m	21 Apr 1881	Girdleness
1881 Apr 21	William Gutcher	Principal	2yr 5m	11 Oct 1883	(Indistinct) Leave
1884 Feb 8	Neil Morrison	Principal	9yr 5m	11 Jul 1893	Dunnet Head (as ALK)
1886 Nov 19	Alex Gilmour	Assistant	3yr	2 Nov 1889	Monach (as PLK)
1889 Nov 5	John Clyne	Assistant	3yr	7 Nov 1892	St. Abbs Head
1892 Nov 1	William Crow	Assistant	5yr 6m	2 May 1898	Isle of May
1893 Jul 8	Neil McDonald	Principal	7yr 11m	25 Aug 1900	Corran
1898 May 20	Alex I Grant	Assistant	1 yr 3m	18 Aug 1899	Loch Ryan
1899 Aug 18	William Smith	Assistant	4yr 8m	31 May 1904	Fair Isle
1900 Aug 25	Robert MacIntosh	Principal	4yr 9m	30 May 1905	Dunnet Head
1904 May 31	Gino Baigrie	Assistant	6yr 3m	30 Aug 1910	Isle of May
1905 May 30	Wm. A Tulloch	Principal	7yr 6m	3 Dec 1912	Ardnamurchan
Jul 17	Kenneth Paterson	Assistant	4yr 3m	4 Oct 1909	Dhubheartach
1909 Oct 1	David G Coull	Assistant	9yr 11m	1 Sep 1919	Tiumpan Head
1910 Sep 7	James W Milne	Assistant	5yr 10m	4 Jul 1916	Sule Skerry
1912 Dec 9	Wm R Davidson	Principal	6yr 6m	3 May 1919	Holy Island
1916 Jun 23	Alex F Birnie	Assistant	3yr 7m	19 Jan 1920	Resigned
1919 May 5	David A Denoon	Principal	4yr 5m	15 Oct 1923	Mull of Galloway

Date of Arrival	Name	Principal or Assistant	Time of Service here	Date of leaving	Where Sent
Sep 1	John Mowat	Assistant	2yr 5m	16 Feb 1922	Auskerry
1920 Jan 23	John Anderson	Assistant	4yr 7m	11 Aug 1924	Corsewall
1922 Feb 16	Alex Munro	Assistant	5yr 3m	9 May 1927	Corsewall
1923 Oct 15	George Miller	Principal	4yr 6m	4 Apr 1928	Langness
1924 Aug 20	Chas L Gilbertson	Assistant	4yr 7m	15 Mar 1929	Chickens Rock
1927 May 5	Wm A Budge	Assistant	2yr 5m	23 Sep 1929	Whalsay Skerries
1928 Apr 4	Wm JM Gray	Principal	4yr 8m	6 Dec 1932	Dunnet Head
1929 Mar 22	JS Petrie	Assistant	4m	13 Jul 1929	Hoy High
Jul 26	Wm AJ Sinclair	Assistant	4yr 2m	20 Sep 1933	Corsewall
Oct 2	Wm Scott	Assistant	4yr 9m	19 Jun 1934	Holy Island
1932 Dec 5	Sim Baigrie	Principal	2yr 9m	5 Sep 1935	Duncansby Head
1933 Sep 22	Alex Campbell	Assistant	4yr 7m	19 Apr 1938	Ardnamurchan
1934 Jun 12	R MacPherson	Assistant	2yr 10m	20 May 1937	Resigned
1935 Sep 5	John Mitchell	Principal	6yr 7m	26 Mar 1942	Clythness
1937 May 20	Harold Park	Assistant	5yr	25 May 1942	Glas Island
1938 Apr 19	DS McLandy	Assistant	5yr 2m	13 May 1943	Hellyer Holm
1942 Mar 26	Neil Matheson	Principal	3yr 2m	25 May 1945	Auskerry
May 28	Wm SS Smith	Assistant	3yr 3m	21 Aug 1945	Noup Head
1943 May 6	Alex Matheson	Assistant	10 m	31 Mar 1944	Resigned
1944 Apr 23	James McLeod	Assistant	3yr 3m	14 Jul 1947	Rona
1945 May 20	WB McKellar	Principal	5yr 4m	30 Sep 1950	Storekeeper, Oban
Aug 21	Robert Laidlaw	Assistant	1yr 6m	25 Feb 1947	Rhinns of Islay (as PLK)
1947 Feb 25	Murdo Nicholson	Assistant	5yr 1m	8 Apr 1952	Rona
Dec 25	Neil M Thorburn	Assistant	8m	1 Sep 1949	Fladda
1948 Sep 1	TT Russell	Assistant	7yr 8m	9 May 1956	Duncansby Head
1950 Oct 2	J Foubister	Principal	4yr 6m	27 Apr 1955	Corsewall

Date of Arrival	Name	Principal or Assistant	Time of Service here	Date of leaving	Where Sent
1952 Jul 25	JM Hughes	Assistant	3yr 2m	5 Oct 1955	Hyskeir
1955 Apr 29	G Sutherland	Principal	7yr 7m	12 Nov 1962	Mull of Galloway
Oct 5	T Stenhouse	Assistant	1yr	4 Oct 1956	Corsewall
1956 Oct 10	TM Grieve	Assistant	4yr 11m	27 Sep 1961	Resigned
1957 Jul 4	MC Davidson	Assistant	2yr 3m	30 Sep 1959	Resigned
1960 Feb 5	JW Thomson	Assistant	1yr 1m	12 Mar 1962	Whalsay Skerries
1961 Oct 27	JS Hardie	Assistant	4yr	18 Oct 1965	Holy Island
1962 Nov 10	J Budge	Assistant	1yr 8m	19 Nov 1963	Butt of Lewis
Nov 12	G MacKenzie	Principal	3yr	31 Oct 1965	Retired
1963 Nov 20	A Ross	Assistant	1yr 1m	31 Dec 1964	Retired Medically
1964 Dec 2	F Bremner	Assistant	1yr 3m	11 Mar 1966	Holy Island
1965 Oct 20	IE Baislerown	Assistant	8m	29 Jun 1966	Resigned
Oct 29	C Thomson	Principal	3yr 7m	20 May 1969	Duncansby Head
1966 Mar 15	L Middleton	Assistant	4yr 2m	25 May 1970	Rubh Re
Jun 29	WS Smith	Assistant	4yr 9m	2 Apr 1971	Bass Rock
1969 May 19	EL Omand	Principal	2yr 11m	31 Mar 1972	Welfare Officer, HQ
1970 May 25	W Weale	Assistant	3m	3 Sep 1970	Butt of Lewis
Sep 3	B Johnston	Assistant	2yr 10m	10 Jun 1973	Artificer
1971 Apr 12	JM Sinclair	Assistant	1yr 8m	20 Dec 1972	Resigned
1972 May 18	D MacAulay	Principal	2yr	4 Apr 1974	Hyskeir
1973 Jan 9	LM Tulloch	Assistant	2yr 6m	14 Jul 1975	Muckle Flugga
Jun 11	AS Pairman	Assistant	4m	6 Sep 1973	Holy Island
1973 Sep 6	RA Crowe	Assistant	3yr 1m	15 Nov 1976	Ruvaal
1974 Apr 3	A McAulay	Principal	4yr 3m	3 Jul 1978	Neist point
Sep 2	B Kerr	Local ALK	2yr 2m	31 Oct 1976	Resigned
1975 Jul 18	PM Caisley	Assistant	3yr 5m	17 Dec 1978	Resigned

Cape Wrath Redesignated as a Rock Station December 1975

Date of Arrival	Name	Principal or Assistant	Time of Service Here	Date of Leaving	Where Sent
1975 Dec 6	DM Cowie	Principal	2yr 6m	14 Jul 1978	Resigned
Dec 11	L Hendry	Assistant	2yr 8m	7 Aug 1978	Bell Rock
1976 Nov 8	JB Grierson	Local ALK	5m	24 Apr 1977	Resigned
Nov 16	FE Adams	Assistant	3yr 4m	31 Mar 1980	Resigned
1977 May 23	E MacKay	Leading assistant	4yr	31 May 1982	Medical Retirement
1978 Apr 9	J Oliver	Assistant	6yr 5m	22 Jan 1985	Pentland Skerries
Jul 4	EJ Stewart	Principal	4yr 5m	22 Nov 1982	South Rona
Jul 31	GJR Pearson	Principal	4yr 1m	23 Aug 1982	Girdle Ness
1979 Mar 20	AE Law	Assistant	4yr 6m	18 Oct 1983	Stroma
1980 Oct 21	G MacKay	Assistant	4yr 10m	26 Aug 1985	Mull of Kintyre
1982 Aug 25	W Anderson	Principal	4yr 7m	31 Mar 1990	Redundant
Nov 25	D MacLeod	Principal	6yr 4m	31 Mar 1989	Retired
1983 May 31	A Dorricott	Assistant	3yr 6m	17 Nov 1986	Calf of Man
1984 Mar 6	C McKay	Assistant	10m	31 Jan 1985	Medical Retirement
1985 Apr 1	TA Scott	Assistant	4yr 5m	17 Aug 1989	Medical Retirement
May 1	A Rankin	Assistant	6yr 1m	10 Jun 1991	Relieving complement
Aug 27	J Wilson	Assistant	2yr 7m	22 Aug 1988	Relieving complement
1987 Jan 24	J Dickson	Assistant	No other details recorded		
1988 Mar 22	D Morrison	Assistant	3yr 2m	30 May 1991	Relieving complement
1989 Apr 25	J Tytler	Principal	5yr	30 Mar 1994	Retired
Sep 12	AJ Smith	Assistant	5yr 6m	31 Mar 1995	Relieving complement
1990 Apr 10	AT McConnell	Principal	1yr 2m	3 Jul 1991	Rhinns of Islay
1991 May 8	CG McKewan	Assistant	4yr 11m	3 Apr 1996	Relieving complement
May 7	RR Fulton	Assistant	4yr 11m	4 Apr 1996	Hyskeir
Jul 2	TP Budge	Principal	3yr 8m	31 Mar 1995	Retired
1994 Mar 31	CJ Mac Aulay	Principal	4yr	31 Mar 1998	Redundant
1995 Mar 31	J MacKay	Principal	3yr	31 Mar 1998	Redundant
Mar 31	D MacDonald	Assistant	1yr	31 Mar 1996	Redundant

Date of Arrival	Name	Principal or Assistant	Time of Service Here	Date of Leaving	Where Sent
1996 May 1	I Longmuir	Assistant	10m	5 Mar 1997	Relieving complement
Apr 3	Alex Smith	Assistant	2yr	31 Mar 1998	Redundant
Apr 17	R Nixon	Assistant	11m	31 Mar 1997	Redundant
1997 Feb 19	R Weir	Assistant	1yr 1m	31 Mar 1998	Redundant

Station Fully Automated 31 March 1998

Light-keepers' Duties and Conditions

Although from the 1820s it was occasionally the practice to employ two keepers at rock stations, some of the more isolated offshore lights maintained a complement of four. This was certainly the case following the Flannan disaster of December 1899. Initially single-man complements were established as only night watches were kept. In the years either side of the turn of the nineteenth century, the Northern Lighthouse Board employed in excess of six hundred men as keepers, in addition to holding a waiting list of over two hundred hopefuls. Female keepers were never appointed.

The average or expected tour of duty at a particular light was four years, although examination of the Cape Wrath Keepers Registers confirms that men could and did stay considerably longer, presumably at their own request. Light crews worked for a period of three weeks continuously and then took a week's leave. Shifts on duty extended to four hours.

In 1857 the NLB Commissioners stated: 'From the day that a Light-keeper enters the service he possesses a certain income, a free furnished house of a description greatly superior to that occupied by the same class in ordinary life, all repairs and taxes paid, coal, candle, clothing, land for a couple of cows or an equivalent in money. He is provided for in case of age or infirmity; and, lastly a provision is made for his widow or family in case of death. The only thing that can deprive a Light-keeper of these secured benefits is his own misconduct.'

The advent of fog signal stations began a programme of the appointment of Second Assistants. Examination of the staffing register reproduced above will confirm that only with the appointment of keeper Kenneth Paterson in July 1905 was a Second Assistant appointed to Cape Wrath. Fog signals necessitated watches being kept night and day when sounding for fog. On these occasions one man would be on duty in the light room, one in the engine with one off watch.

Even in the years of the late twentieth century automation programme, when men were being recruited in the knowledge that the keeper's career in the lighthouse service could only be curtailed, the NLB required that: 'A light-keeper must be a man of parts, from his study of the sea, he will respect its immense power; he will be a handyman of varying proficiency, he will be a useful cook and a good companion. A light-keeper will not make a fortune but the odds are that he will be at peace with himself and with the world.'

Principal keepers were provided with an annual coal allowance of ten tons; Assistants received eight. Reading matter was provided at all lighthouses by the Board. Keepers, wives and children were catered for in the supply of magazines, instruction books, childcare manuals and approved fiction. Copies of the *Weekly Scotsman* and the *London Illustrated News* were provided to each light, subject to delays in getting the relief boat through.

By the mid-1870s keepers were allowed a daily ration of a pound of butcher's meat, a pound of bread, oatmeal, barley, butter and a quart of beer; vegetables were grown in the lighthouse ground and were assiduously guarded against the depredations of the local wildlife.

By 1850 the list of keepers' duties ran to thirty-seven express rules, but never throughout the whole of the manned lighthouse service did they include instructions on procedures in case of a shipwreck within sight of a light. The Board's view always was that the lights acted as warnings only, and that keepers were therefore expected to do no more than watch for wrecks and enter details in the Wreck

Book when they did occur. Keepers were discouraged from rendering assistance, since to do so would mean them deserting their posts and duties. But conspicuous acts of bravery by light-keepers did occur, and are well recorded. Cape Wrath was a lifesaving station in addition to its principal lighthouse status. Coast Guard Rocket Apparatus was kept and used there, as evidenced by Principal Keeper George MacKenzie's recollections transcribed in the 'Varied Views from Fifty-Eight Degrees North' chapter.

CHAPTER 10

VICTORIAN VISITATIONS

Nineteenth Century Accounts of
Visits to Cape Wrath and the Parph

Introduction

It is clear that with the building of the lighthouse at Cape Wrath and of the road linking it with the relatively sheltered waters of the Kyle of Durness, the Parph came less and less to be regarded as an impossibly difficult area to visit with insuperable problems of access. The new lighthouse at the very far north western tip of Scotland attracted a certain level of novelty interest, and those with the means to visit were no longer dissuaded from attempting it.

The following contemporary accounts are taken largely from newspaper reports of the time, although that describing the visit of the Duke of Sutherland's legal representative has been selected from the Sutherland family archives; I am indebted to Malcolm Bangor-Jones for its appearance here.

Robert Louis Stevenson

The first account following was penned by Robert Louis Stevenson, included in his *Records of a Family of Engineers,* written in 1893 and published posthumously in 1896. (He died on 3 December 1894.) Whilst RLS relied principally upon diaries and notebooks compiled by those illustrious forbears to whom he was referring, it is unsafe to rely wholly on his statements of fact.

For example, he states that his grandfather Robert Stevenson was fifty-eight when he first visited Cape Wrath, which would have

RIGHT: Normal everyday lighthouse maintenance operations in the days before health and safety considerations had assumed their present level of importance. The 'cradle' is slung from the light room parapet and presumably the painter hangs on with one hand. With the other he manipulates the brush. Simple, effective and exciting.
Photo credit: Mr. M.C. Davidson, Peterhead, Keeper at Cape Wrath 1957–1959

BELOW: Everyday maintenance included painting the foghorn, precariously perched directly over a 200ft drop into the north Atlantic. This photograph and that preceding date from the 1950s.
Photo credit: Mr. M.C. Davidson, Peterhead

An image from the archives of the celebrated Victorian photographer George Washington Wilson. Wilson died in 1893, so the date of the image is prior to that. It shows the tower and buildings as originally built, and un-rendered. Notice also the pediments and the high wall enclosing the courtyard. The several figures shown must include some keepers' family members. Keepers and families were resident at the Cape Wrath light until 1975. *Photo credit: George Washington Wilson collection, Aberdeen University*

A postcard photograph of the lighthouse and headland dating from the 1930s. Thousands were printed and sold. Access to the very tip of Cape Wrath was at that time severely restricted – no tourist minibus in those days. Picture postcards satisfied the demands of visitors to the far north-west.
Photo credit: Author's collection

The Cape Wrath Hotel pictured circa 1932, during its heyday when it was perhaps the foremost sporting hotel in the far north-west. The hotel brochure boasted of the fine fishing in the Kyle of Durness, "famous for its large Sea-Trout, and about the only place where Salmon are caught in salt water."
Photo credit: Author's collection

The Kyle of Durness and the road to the lighthouse circa early 1930s. Visible, across the water, is the Cape Wrath Hotel and in the mid-ground is Ferry House, home to the ferryman during the days of NLB operation. Note the precipitous drop immediately over the road retaining wall, and the gravel road surface. A tarmacadam top surface was not provided until the early 1950s. *Photo credit: Author's collection*

An extremely evocative shot of Daill ford from the early 1930s. Daill House is to the left, immediately over the signboard denoting the boundary of the military firing range. Two figures, one on the river bank and another on the footbridge, anxiously watch the tourists' motor car negotiate the water, mercifully low on this occasion. On the skyline towards the top left is the side school, or "The Cape Wrath Academy", in its magnificent position overlooking the estuary and the open sea. *Photo credit: Author's collection*

The Northern Lighthouse Board have purchased a Morris-Commercial 1-ton truck for carrying daily supplies from Durness Ferry to Cape Wrath, in the north of Scotland. The unmounted chassis is here seen being put aboard the ferry at Durness.

The NLB provided trucks for the use of the resident keepers, to enable them to collect and deliver their groceries and other supplies ordered from Durness. This photograph from circa 1929 shows the arrival of a Morris Commercial one-ton vehicle, minus goods body, at the Keoldale slipway and the rudimentary arrangements for its voyage across the water to the Capeside. Horse carriages would be delivered by the same method in Victorian times (the horses being walked round the head of the Kyle) as would visitor's motor vehicles prior to 1940. *Photo credit: Geoff Lumb collection*

"Into the Great Unknown" or "North-westwards, young man." A fine example of the cartoonist's art.
Photo credit: Am Bratach magazine issue 144 October 2003

Around the time that this picture was taken the Keeper at Cape Wrath was complaining to the NLB that visitors' motor cars were having an adverse effect upon the state of the road. Annual visitor numbers were approximately 240 in those inter-war years and very often the brakes of the NLB truck after passing through the ford were found to be defective only when descending the steep and constricted brae approaching the ferry slipway. This postcard view shows an Austin Sixteen or Twenty Open Road Tourer of circa 1929 vintage crossing Kearvaig Bridge heading home towards the ferry during the early 1930s. *Photo credit: Author's collection*

Following the Second World War and the intensive use of the facilities at Cape Wrath and the road servicing them, the NLB provided a 25-cwt forward-control Commer lorry for the keepers' use. This photograph dates from circa 1946, when the road was in a badly damaged state. It was reported that the driver usually had to re-make the road as he went along, using brushwood, heather or anything else handy. The vehicle is pictured here negotiating the ford at Daill. *Photo credit: Geoff Lumb collection*

This photograph is said to record the centenary visit by motor car in 1928. The vehicle appears to be a flat-nosed Morris of the mid-1920s. *Photo credit: Durness Archive c/o Ronnie Lansley*

This old postcard view shows almost all of the buildings and installations at Cape Wrath in the days when the station was manned. From the left, the longer range of buildings was the garages, workshops, storerooms and, at the far end, the 'bothy' occupied by occasional and supernumerary keepers. The small box-like building just over the perimeter wall to the left was the petrol and paint store. In the centre is the 1905 compressor, machine room and, to its left, the new Principal Keeper's accommodation. To the right, behind the 1905 building, is one of the metal communications masts with, to its right, the small block building used in later years to house the British Geological Survey's seismic monitoring equipment. The white building directly in front of the communications tower is the pump house which raised fresh water from a spring down the cliff face. To the right of the pump house is the fresh water storage tank. To the right of the lighthouse tower and offices (note the absence of fuel storage tanks) are the flagstaff, the fog horn and the wrought-iron compressed air receiving tanks. *Photo credit: Author's collection*

The most significant date in the history of the Cape Wrath Minibus service. The picture shows the very first minibus being rafted across the Kyle of Durness in July 1964 at the start of operations. The large whisky incentive is, unfortunately, not visible. But note the undersized outboard motor powering (?) the rather overloaded ferry boat and the application of auxiliary wooden motors as insurance.
Photo credit: Mr. Hugh Powell, Balnakeil

The newly-completed road bridge at Daill ford, pictured in August 1981. *Photo credit: Mr. D. Hulme*

Daill House at its most picturesque, in the days before the ford was superseded by the 'temporary moveable structure' military bridge in 1981. Note the steepness of the road ascending Daill brae heading towards the lighthouse. *Photo credit: Mr. D. Hulme*

This stunning view of the sandbanks of the Kyle of Durness at low water pictures the 10 mile marker on the lighthouse road, located near to Achiemore and the site of the former Cape Wrath Academy. It offers a popular viewpoint from which to observe common seals basking in the Kyle.
Photo credit: Author

Clais Charnach Storehouse. The storehouse built at Clais Charnach as part of the 1828 lighthouse construction scheme was essential for the safe storage of materials and supplies to enable the light to function. This building survives to this day, in exactly the form in which it was built. An identical storehouse was built at the northern end of the Kyle of Durness, which also survives, but minus its roof.
Photo credit: Ronnie Lansley, Durness

The peace and solitude of Kearvaig with its isolated pristine beach is perfectly captured here. The very tip of Cape Wrath is visible in the left background. The former farmhouse is now owned by the military authorities and let to the Scottish Mountain Bothy Association. The ideal place to get away from it all.

Photo credit: Mr. D. Hulme (July 1980)

Lighthouse re-provisioning the modern way. The NLB supply vessel anchors off the cliffs nearby and all necessary items are shuttled to the lighthouse station slung beneath the helicopter. All refuse for recycling or destruction is taken back to the vessel. The operation is usually completed within an afternoon whereas formerly, when everything had to be manhandled, it involved an almost constant effort.
Photo credit: Author

Every lapse in concentration, however slight, will inevitably result in a total loss of street-cred. And there is no benefit to be gained from calling out the national road recovery services. It takes three weeks for them to stop laughing and three months to find you. What you need, as on this occasion, is half a rugby team. *Photo credit: Mr. D. Bowater*

Carbreck the Ferryman ("stare of a thousand yards, chin of chiselled granite and a scurrilous talent for mimicry just occasionally beyond restraint") skilfully pilots the smallest British passenger ferry towards the Capeside landing stage and another compliment of apprehensive customers. *Photo credit: Author*

Lighthouse re-provisioning in pre-helicopter days. The NLB supply vessel *Pole Star* is anchored off the narrow inlet of Clais Charnach; two of the vessel's own lighters are in use ferrying material between the ship and the slipway. An inflatable dingy is also present, at the end of the pier, which could be used only near to high water. Altogether a time-consuming and labour-intensive procedure, not without its hazards. From the storehouse at Clais Charnach every item delivered had to be man-handled the mile and a half to the lighthouse station. *Photo credit: Mr. D. MacLeod, Golspie*

This aerial view of the Cape Wrath headland was taken from the helicopter bringing Principal Keeper Donald MacLeod in to commence a tour of duty in the mid-1980s. It shows how the lighthouse station occupies almost every inch of ground at the very tip of the Cape. *Photo credit: Mr. D. MacLeod, Golspie.*

The abandoned former Lloyds radio station and wartime observation post overlooks the tip of Cape Wrath from the slopes of Dunan Mor. The Durness community have an interest in acquiring this site for a community project. *Photo credit: Ronnie Lansley, Durness*

The secluded pristine beach at Kearvaig, one of a number around the coast of the far north-west of Sutherland, is dominated by Stack Clo Kearvaig, which has in recent times come to be known as 'The Cathedral'. It has twin spires with a natural window between, formed entirely by the erosion forces of wind and water. This is the classic view from the minibus on the return trip to the ferry slipway. *Photo credit: Author*

dated his visit to 1830, over a year after the lighthouse had become fully functional.

I suggest that in 1826, having instructed Mr. Slight to carry out the Cape Wrath survey by way of the 'Regent' captained by Soutar, Robert Stevenson almost immediately decided that he would accompany the party. That is why the vessel anchored in Loch Eriboll rather than at Clais Charnach, the small harbour and landing place serving the lighthouse, which had not been built by 1826 but was complete in 1830. It is probable, therefore, that the difficult journey taken by Robert Stevenson and Messrs Slight and Soutar, and described by Robert Louis Stevenson some seventy years later, took place in the summer of 1826, when Robert Stevenson was fifty-four years of age.

Robert Louis Stevenson wrote:

Up to 1807 my grand-father seems much to have travelled on horseback; but he then gave up the idea – 'such' he writes, with characteristic emphasis and capital letters, 'is the Plague of Baiting.'

He was a good pedestrian; at the age of fifty-eight (sic), I find him covering seventeen miles over the moors of the Mackay country in less than seven hours, and that is not bad travelling for a scramble. The piece of country traversed was already a familiar track, being that between Loch Eriboll and Cape Wrath; and I think I can scarce do better than reproduce from the diary some traits of his first visit.

The tender lay in Loch Eriboll; by five in the morning they sat down to breakfast on board; by six they were ashore – my grandfather, Mr Slight an assistant, and Soutar of the jolly nose, and had been taken in charge by two young gentlemen of the neighbourhood and a pair of ghillies.

About noon they reached the Kyle of Durness and passed the ferry. By half past three they were at Cape Wrath – not yet known by the emphatic abbreviation of 'The Cape' – and beheld upon all sides of them unfrequented shores, an expanse of desert moor, and the high-piled Western Ocean.

The site of the tower was chosen. Perhaps it is by inheritance of blood, but I know few things more inspiriting than this location of a lighthouse in a designated space of heather and air, through which the seabirds are still flying.

By 9 p.m. the return journey had brought them to the shores of the Kyle. The night was dirty, and as the sea was high and the ferry-boat small, Soutar and Mr. Stevenson were left on the far side, while the rest of the party embarked and were received into the darkness. They made, in fact, a safe though an alarming passage; but the ferryman refused to repeat the adventure; and my grand-father and the captain long paced the beach, impatient for their turn to pass, and tormented with rising anxiety as to the fate of their companions.

At length they sought the shelter of a shepherd's house. 'We had miserable up-putting', the diary continues, 'and on both sides of the ferry much anxiety of mind. Our beds were clean straw, and but for the circumstance of the boat, I should have slept as soundly as ever I did after a walk through moss and mire of sixteen hours.

Further verification can be gleaned from this text that the journey occurred before the lighthouse and its associated facilities had been built. That this was Robert Stevenson's first visit to Cape Wrath confirms that it took place before building works commenced; Stevenson visited the construction site in his summer tour of the northern lights of 1828. The statement that: 'The site of the tower was chosen' clearly confirms that construction works were yet to be commenced.

And if the journey had taken place in 1830, the party would not have had to beg shelter in the cottage of a local shepherd; a weatherproof storehouse complete with fireplace and chimney was erected as part of the greater lighthouse scheme approximately a mile from the beach on which Stevenson and Soutar were stranded overnight. In 1830 Stevenson would have known that the storehouse was available as emergency accommodation; he was the one who authorised payment of the builder's account. In 1826 the storehouse did not exist.

It is to be assumed that the stranding took place at the mouth of the Diall river (there is no other Capeside 'beach' accessible to the ferry) and that overnight accommodation was found in the cottage at Diall, which survives to this day. The present Capeside landing place and the first two miles of road linking it to the valley of the Diall river was not built until the 1870s.

George Sutherland Taylor

George Sutherland Taylor of Dornoch, Solicitor for the Sutherland estates, toured the Duke of Sutherland's landholdings in the far north west during August 1831, and recorded the following account:

I visited Cape Wrath and its Lighthouse . . . I returned to Durness by the Road that brought me to the Cape. That Road is miserably narrow throughout but for a Couple of Miles after leaving Durness Ferry it is only three feet wide, a mere Bridle road; and although the remaining seven, or eight, Miles of it appear, from Contrast, to be tolerably broad, a Gig or carriage Could not attempt to pass along it at a quicker pace than a walk, with any degree of safety. The Light House Establishment is particularly well kept, all parts of it, & especially the machinery being in as complete order as if they had never been in use. This Establishment is really worthy of a great Nation: and the practical application of a great many scientific discoveries & principles; and the exact order and discipline with which it is attended to, and rendered effectual, at so very remote and wild a point as Cape Wrath, are proud trophies of the beneficial results that flow from our National Institutions when judiciously attended to and protected. In the garden or enclosed Cultivated ground attached to the Light House, Potatoes, Turnips, Cabbages, and a few patches of corn were in a tolerable state of forwardness, notwithstanding the elevated and exposed situation of the ground; thus affording a satisfactory illustration of the effects of well directed labour, even in the most unpromising situations. The Keeper also produced Butter and Cheese of very excellent quality furnished by the pasture Land attached to the Establishment. He at first kept Goats for the sake of their milk; but he found them to be so intractable and mischievous to his garden, that he was obliged to substitute Cows for them.

At the time, the land on which the Cape Wrath lighthouse was built was leased by the Northern Lighthouse Board; it remained in the ownership of the Sutherland estates until 25 June 1831, when the Marquis of Stafford granted a feu disposition of sixty acres of ground at Cape Wrath to the Commissioners of the Northern Lighthouses. Perhaps Taylor's visit was in connection with this as boundaries would have to be agreed and fences erected. The transaction was not legally registered until 1851.

Accounts Published in John O'Groat Journal

On Friday 11 September 1840 it published two separate accounts recording the visit of the Duke and Duchess of Sutherland to the far north west of their estates, each of which mentions Cape Wrath and the lighthouse.

The first account is a short single paragraph:

CAPE WRATH LIGHT-HOUSE, 1st September - We were truly surprised and delighted by a visit, on Saturday last, from the Duke and Duchess of Sutherland, Marquis of Stafford, and Lady Elizabeth Gower, accompanied by Alexander Stewart, Esquire, their Graces' Factor at Scowrie, and Mr. Scobie, Keoldale. After examining this establishment, and showing kindness to all, they took their departure in the afternoon. They are the first Duke and Duchess, Marquis and Duke's daughter, that ever visited the Light-house.

The second account, alongside on page three, gives a rather more comprehensive description of the whole journey of the ducal party from Dunrobin Castle to the extreme limits of the Sutherland holdings. [Paragraphs have been added in the interests of clarity;

the original is a solid body of text, which is somewhat difficult on the eye]. The account is headed:

TOUR OF THEIR GRACES THE DUKE AND DUCHESS OF SUTHERLAND

A friend has favoured us with the following short account of their Graces the Duke and Duchess of Sutherland's tour through the Scowrie or Western Division of Sutherland – for the first time visited by the Duchess:

Their Graces the Duke and Duchess of Sutherland, accompanied by the Marquis of Stafford, and their lovely eldest daughter, Lady Elizabeth, set out from Dunrobin Castle for the west, on Monday the 24th ultimo, together with James Loch Esq, M.P., when they passed the night at Lairg, and on the following day proceeded to Assynt. The illustrious party, on their arrival at Ledmore, were met by a large assemblage of the tenantry, with their respected clergyman, Mr. Gordon, at their head.

The Rev. gentleman was deputed by the people to address the Duke in their name, in order to convey their sentiments of affection for his Grace's person and family – to congratulate her Grace on her first appearance amongst them and to tender the parishioners' grateful acknowledgement for his Grace's unbounded bounty in having remitted the whole arrears of rents – an act of liberality, we may add, surpassing anything ever known in the north.

Upon Mr Gordon finishing this pleasing mission, his Grace replied with his wonted dignity, but yet kindly feeling, assuring the people that he and her Grace felt much pleased with the reception that they had met with, and of the deep interest they both took in the welfare of the Sutherland tenantry. The bond of union which has subsisted between the house of Dunrobin for generations, and the people of the ancient barony of Assynt, was thus renewed on the eventful occasion, with the warmest mutual attachment, alike honourable to the Duke of Sutherland and to his tenants.

After passing a couple of hours at Inchnadamph, and admiring the scenery, which is perhaps not equalled – to say the least of it, not surpassed by any in Scotland, and new to the Duchess, the party proceeded to Lochinver. Immediately on coming in sight of that splendid harbour and interesting village, the tenantry of that division of the barony, with the Rev. Mr. Davison and Donald Macdonald Esq., at the head of the procession, met the Noble Family in order to attest their esteem and gratitude. Their Graces acknowledged the reception in the best possible terms.

The harbour was studded with a variety of vessels, having their colours flying, which much enlivened the scene. The roar of cannon and the brilliant bonfires, in the evening, on the top of almost every hill, closed the day with a most delightful and imposing effect.

On Wednesday they proceeded to Store (*i.e. Stoer*). Here the people met them in crowds, and expressed their congratulations on seeing them while these sentiments of respect and attachment were kindly received and acknowledged by the noble party. After visiting all that was interesting, they returned to Lochinver in the evening, and the following morning set out for Scowrie.

The day was most propitious – a better opportunity for crossing the high hills of Unnapool and of viewing the surrounding scenery could not possibly be desired. On the carriages arriving at Glendhu Ferry, the party sailed up the Loch, gaining a view of the precipitous cliffs, high hills, water-falls, and cataracts, on both sides. Her Grace the Duchess was delighted beyond measure with the general appearance of the scenery – the grandeur of which a visit only can possibly convey any idea of. In the evening they joined the carriages on the north side of the ferry, and went to Scowrie, where they were met by a large assemblage of the Eddrachillis tenantry, with music, and banners bearing suitable devices, affording further proof of the people's attachment to his Grace, his amiable Duchess, and their family.

All nature seemed to smile on this occasion. The beautiful bay and islands of Badcall were seen to great advantage, and the vessels in the harbour being decorated with colours, had an exceedingly fine effect.

The discharge of the artillery, and blazing bonfires on almost every hill, in the evening, produced an effect truly worthy of the occasion – the remembrance of which cannot fail to be the subject of pleasing recollection to the illustrious couple, their interesting family, and the inhabitants of Sutherland, for many years to come.

Their Graces and party left Scowrie on Friday, and continued the journey to the parishes of Kenlochbervie and Durness. At Rhiconnich, they were met by a large section of the Lochinchard tenantry, and at Kenlochbervie by those of that district and Oldshores. The party sailed along Lochinchard, admiring the scenery, and her Grace was particularly gratified with the Alpine character of the great Reay forest – partly in sight of Lochinchard, the nearest harbour to Cape Wrath.

After this excursion, the party joined the carriages, and proceeded to Durness, where they arrived in the evening. At Gualin House, which has been erected by the Duke solely for the convenience of travellers passing along those high hills and morasses at inclement periods of the season, they were met by the gentlemen of the parish of Durness, who, after addressing his Grace and Duchess in congratulatory terms, on their visit to the district, followed in procession to near the inn of Durness, where the whole inhabitants of the parish had assempled to welcome their noble visitors. Here similar sentiments were interchanged with those already mentioned, and the day closed with bonfires and other demonstrative marks of the people's joy and attachment.

The following day (Saturday) the Duke and Duchess, Lord Stafford, and Lady Elizabeth, undertook the arduous task of visiting Cape Wrath and its Light House. Her Grace went to the top of the building, a task requiring much exertion, shewing a fortitude and activity seldom seen in a Lady of her exalted rank in society.

On Sunday they attended Divine service in the Church of Durness, when the Rev. Mr. Findlater delivered an admirable and appropriate discourse. There they remained over Sabbath, and on Monday visited the celebrated Cave of Smoo, from whence they took their departure, in high admiration of it, for Tongue.

The people were exceeding delighted with the Marquis of Stafford the 'roof-tree' of Dunrobin. He is all that his best friends can desire – amiable, affectionate and exceedingly intelligent for his years. The kind, urbane and amiable manners of the Duchess of Sutherland are well known. To exalted rank and great wealth, she joins qualities of a description calculated to render her an especial favourite with all classes. In the greatly admired Mistress of the Robes, we have the kind and condescending friend of the poor, the amiable mother, and the affectionate wife – qualities which justly adorn her high station, and which cannot fail to leave a favourable impression of her Grace in this, as in every quarter she may honour with her presence.

On Friday September 25 there appears an anonymous account by an intrepid traveller to the far north west of Sutherland. But, although the piece is very evocative of the time and of the country it describes, there is a sting in the tail.

The account is headed ORIGINAL COMMUNICATION by the paper's Editor and NOTES OF A JOURNEY TO CAPE WRATH by the author, and commences with a preamble which is almost as recognisable today as it was one hundred and sixty-eight years ago. It states:

Having lately made an excursion to the west of Sutherlandshire, it occasioned me considerable surprise, that a country capable of affording such ample gratification to the admirers of nature, should engage so little of their attention. This may, in some degree, be attributed to its remote position, limited intercourse with the neighbouring counties, and the want of regular conveyances. Formidable as those disadvantages are, I cannot allow myself to think that they are of such a nature as to restrain the curious. The comparative neglect of this beautiful county by travellers, may then be mainly attributed to the scarcity of information which exists regarding it, and the infrequency of it being brought under public notice. Thus, while every advertising sheet proclaims the merits of Guide Books to objects of historical interest (oftentimes by some unblessed ignorance never before heard of), and every *cairn* by the way-side is rescued with exemplary industry from an unhonoured oblivion, and embellished with innumerable traditions – scenes largely partaking of the sublime and beautiful, as in Sutherlandshire, remain unknown, and consequently unappreciated . . .

No tracts of country in Scotland have a greater dissimilarity of appearance than Sutherland and Caithness, the one being as mountainous, and the other as level as can be seen, a circumstance the more remarkable for their proximity.

The writer then proceeds on his journey via Reay – 'about twelve miles west of Thurso' – through Strathhalladale, Farr, Strathnaver and Tongue. He waxes lyrical in describing Ben Tongue and the Kyle and, to barely a lesser extent, Tongue House and its 'very superior gardens.'

He describes his journey westwards mentioning Kirkibol, the Rabbit Islands and Melness, and proceeds past Ben Loyal (or Lyall, as he names it) and Ben Hope to the village of Hope itself, and Loch Hope. Loch Erribol is 'about ten or eleven miles in length, variegated by numerous islands and bays.'

He describes Ardneakie's spectacular character thus:

The traveller is particularly attracted by the singular effect of a peninsular eminence, below the hill from whence Erribol is first disclosed, of a considerable length. It is joined to the mainland by a long low neck of land, over which the sea sometimes flows, leaving it, with the Inn of Heilam, perfectly insulated.

Durness is reached shortly after our traveller is overwhelmed by Smoo Cave. He regards its awe and wonder in much the same way as did Sir Walter Scott, who visited twenty five years earlier. After describing Durness and Faraid Head (or 'Far-out head,' as he calls it in the terminology of the day), and the old Kirk and graveyard and Rob Donn monument at Balnakeil, our early excursionist visits Loch Borralie ('Borley,' he calls it) and 'the Lake of Balnakeil.' Clearly the author here is relying on spoken place-names, which accounts for the spelling inaccuracies. The reference to the lake at Balnakeil is somewhat mystifying, as the wide open bay here is so obviously a coastal feature. The only possible explanation I can offer is that the author considered Balnakeil Bay to be a sea loch, and erroneously transcribed 'loch' as 'lake.'

> The Leviathan form of Cape Wrath bounds the prospect from Durness. This stupendous and dangerous headland is the extreme point of Scotland on the north-west

. . . is all that the writer has to say about the one feature named in the title to his travelogue. No description of the ferry crossing, or the exposed mountainous road, or the wilderness through which it passes, or the herds of red deer, or the spectacular views over the Kyle or from the cliffs of Cape Wrath, or of the lighthouse itself.

From this we must assume that the writer, who identifies himself simply as 'O,' never managed to achieve his objective; he did not, despite describing his journey to Cape Wrath, ever get there!!

On 20 August 1858 it published a brief account of the visit that month of the celebrated geologist Sir Roderick Murchison to the Parph and Cape Wrath. It is clear that the visit was undertaken in connection with the tour of the northern lighthouses by either the Engineer to the Northern Lighthouse Board (at the time David Stevenson) or the Clerk of Works (Alan Brebner), as the journey was made aboard the sloop *Pharos*; this vessel was, of course, owned and operated by the Board principally for lighthouse re-supply and inspection visits. The time of year suggests the summer inspection tour, as does the Zetland (Shetland) place of departure for Cape Wrath.

> DURNESS, Aug. 13 – VISIT OF SIR R. MURCHISON – On Friday, the 7th inst, Sir R. Murchison arrived, in the steam-ship 'Pharos' at Cape Wrath from Zetland, whither he had gone on a geological survey. On Saturday he walked, accompanied by that indefatigable and successful

discoverer and collector of fossils, Mr Peach, from Cape Wrath to the inn of Durine, a distance of 12 miles, without seeming in the least degree fatigued, notwithstanding that the day was very warm. The zeal of these scientific gentlemen may be guessed from the circumstances that they generally rise at 6 o'clock, and seldom retire to rest till between 10 or 12 o'clock and night. Mr. Peach was fortunate enough to discover in Unst, the most northerly island in Britain, two or three specimens of a plant called the *Armaria Norwegia* which does not occur in any other part of the kingdom. They proceeded, on Tuesday, to Stack Cottage, and thence they direct their course to Assynt and Ullapool.

(Sir Roderick Impey Murchison (1792–1871) was the foremost practical geologist of his day. After service in the Napoleonic Peninsula War he became an active member of the London Geological Society and by circa 1830 was its President. In 1855 he was appointed Director-General of the Geological Survey of Great Britain. At the time of his visit to Cape Wrath in 1858 Murchison was the pre-eminent and most celebrated Victorian geologist.

Charles William Peach (1800–1886) became a self-taught zoologist and botanist during his government Revenue Coast-guard service. He specialised in the identification of fossils in ancient rocks in Cornwall. In 1853 he was transferred to Wick and in the following year was the first to identify fossils in the Cambrian limestone of Durness.

Benjamin Neeve Peach (1842–1926), son of C.W. Peach, became a celebrated geologist in his own right after Sir Roderick Murchison supervised his education and early scientific career.)

Inverness Courier, 15 June 1876

In setting the scene, the unnamed visitor writes:

An interesting week's excursion might be made from Lairg to Scourie; thence northward to Durness, and along the whole North Coast from Cape Wrath to Strath-Halladale. The stages are Durness, Tongue,

Bettyhill (Strathnaver), and Melvich; and from Melvich there is a pleasant drive through Strath-Halladale to Forsinard Station on the Highland Railway. By this route the tourist will see all that is finest in Sutherland with the exception of Assynt; and that may well form an excursion by itself.

After spending a pleasant night at the Durine Hotel in Durness, a hostelry he describes as 'a comfortable, well-kept house, like all the hotels in the county,' our visitor braved the subterranean delights of Smoo cave and further explored Durness and its environs by visiting Balnakeil old church and the former summer residence of the Bishops of Caithness there, before turning his attention and exertions to Cape Wrath.

(At that time the Durine Hotel was the only commercial establishment offering accommodation to travellers in the far north-west. Fifty miles of poor quality roads separated Richonich and Tongue, the nearest other villages with public hostelries. Alas, the hotel no longer exists. It was destroyed by fire in 1908, the ruins remaining until 1959. Stone was recovered from the shell and used in the construction of an extension to Durness Primary school; the hotel site was utilised for the erection of the first Durness village hall and is now occupied by a car park for the remodelled village square, historical interpretation pillar and memorial garden. And how may modern day visitors repeat the itinerary of the mid-Victorian excursionist, but in significantly less than a week?)

The relevant part of the 1876 travelogue is, in full:

The distance from Durness to Cape Wrath is fourteen miles and a-half. From the hotel to the ferry is reckoned two miles and a-half; the ferry half a-mile; and from the west side of the Kyle a series of eleven milestones mark the journey. There is a good road all the way, and the visitor can have his choice of walking or driving.

There is, however, one inconvenience in driving, though it is more felt by the innkeeper than the traveller. The ferry-boats do not carry horses; and so the pony has to be sent away early in the morning round the head of the Kyle, and through the hills, where there is no road, and where the animal is very liable to receive injury. Another horse is sent with the conveyance to the ferry, and the conveyance itself is taken across in the boat, to be re-harnessed at the opposite side. Mr. Mackay is therefore not too anxious to risk his horses, although he is always ready to oblige visitors.

As the distance is moderate, many prefer to do it on foot, more especially as there is a chance, if one is very wearied, of getting accommodation at the lighthouse for a night. The walk is a solitary one; after crossing the ferry there are only three houses and a cart shed to be seen until the lighthouse is reached. The road lies through a brown, undulating valley, bounded by lofty cliffs to seaward, and inland by heathery hills which scarcely rise to the dignity of mountains.

Not a tree is visible – or at the most, one dwarf plant, struggling for life in a lonely garden; and the only sounds are the cry of the plover and the beating of the ocean, not seen but dimly heard at a distance.

The geological formation is a granite gneiss – scarcely distinguishable from granite to the inexperienced eye – varied by a spur of the old conglomerate. The soil is almost entirely gravel, on which lie scattered about large granite blocks and conglomerate, the latter consisting of sandstone and smooth rounded pebbles, resembling nothing so much as sweeties biscuits!

The pasture on one side, all the way from the ferry to Cape Wrath, belongs to the farm of Balnakiel; on the other, for most of the way, it is attached to the farm of Keoldale.

The last turn in the road brings us in sight of the Cape and the lighthouse. The summit of the cliffs here is covered with green grass, often watered by the ocean spray. Those marks of old dwellings on the slopes are probably the remains of huts, formerly used by the crofters who brought their sheep and cattle here for summer grazing.

The north west point consists of two cliffs, one about 500, the other about 400 feet high. The lighthouse is built on the lower one, surrounded by the keepers dwellings and a strong wall like a fortification. The nearest neighbour is five miles away; the postman comes but once a week in summer and once a fortnight in winter; but the inmates are perfectly happy and contented, attending to the lighthouse, the garden and the sheep which pasture on the slopes around them.

The loss of an occasional sheep by falling down the cliffs, or of a lamb killed by the hooded crow, is the sole cause of complaint. The sheep reared here are superior, just as the best cod are said to be caught off Cape Wrath. The principle of natural selection is fully recognised. 'None but the best fish can stem the currents' we are told; and sheep which can weather the storms find nourishing pasture on the Cape.

'At Sumburgh Head in Shetland' adds our informant, 'we could easily tell where fish were caught – those taken near the shore being weak and soft, and those taken further out among the currents being strong and firm'.

A good library helps to while away the winter nights. In summer an occasional visit breaks the monotony, and there are stated calls from the Commissioners of Northern Lights. There could be few more desirable spots in which to live a retired life, 'the world forgetting by the world forgot'.

There is occupation enough to prevent weariness, society enough among the two families (there are two keepers in the lighthouse) to check any feelings of loneliness, and variety enough to relieve and refresh the mind. The sea itself must be a source of interest; today calm as a lake, and tomorrow thundering against the cliffs, and throwing its showers of spray over the lighthouse.

Those precipitous granitic rocks present a rugged face to the waves. At one spot they rise straight up, 400 feet or more, flat almost like a wall; at another they are worn into deep furrows and sharp edges which strike their way like prows into the deep. Behind the lighthouse the gulleys thus worn by the sea penetrate far into the rock; and it is necessary to exercise a little caution to avoid stumbling into a trap.

A low rock, projecting into the sea, forms, we are told, the real cape.

It is certainly the furthest out point, and has been appropriated by the seabirds as a nesting place. Sunken reefs, marked by foam, seem to extend along the coast. On a clear day the view is extensive. To the south-west the Butt of Lewis is visible; to the east, Hoyhead of Orkney, and even the island of North Rona. But the weather on the occasion of our visit was slightly hazy.

During most part of the time nothing but sea could be seen; and only for a few minutes did the haze dissolve, and allow a glimpse of the Butt of Lewis and of an island in the distance which looks like a ship under sail.

But in every other respect the visit to Cape Wrath was most gratifying; and the pleasure was enhanced by the kindness with which a visitor, so entirely unexpected, was entertained.

One is struck by the timelessness of this account. Everything described is recognisable today, save the one notable exception of the lighthouse personnel. And the final paragraph is, we hope, as true and relevant today as it was in 1876.

CHAPTER II

VARIED VIEWS FROM 58 DEGREES NORTH

The following are previously unpublished recollections and random reminiscences by individuals formerly resident on Cape Wrath. Most are provided by former light keepers. Some accounts are printed exactly as written by the individual concerned and some I have written from brief notes and headings prepared by the interviewee. The remainder were prepared from notes taken by me in person or during telephone interviews. Where the account was not written directly by the person named, revisions were submitted to the interviewee until a finalised form was agreed.

With the obvious exception of the George MacKenzie account, all interviews were undertaken during 2006 at the very end of my researches. It is extremely important that these memories are preserved in a first-hand form. I feel particularly favoured that I have been able to meet each of the individuals concerned; some made return visits to Cape Wrath and I was able to make direct contact in that way, and others were introduced as 'a-friend-of-a-friend.' A short piece in the *Scotsman Magazine* of February 2006 produced yet more leads. Once initial reluctance was overcome, the memories flowed and these personal accounts could be preserved for posterity.

I really do hope that future editions of the book will include further submissions from former Cape Wrath residents. If you have personal experience of life on the very edge of the wild northwest, please consider putting it down on paper and/or contacting me via the publisher.

Marianus Cumming Davidson, Assistant Keeper 1957 to 1959

I entered service with the Northern Lighthouse Board in 1956. After three supernumerary posts I was appointed as Assistant Keeper at Cape Wrath in July 1957. My wife and I lived in the accommodation at the lighthouse.

We hold many happy memories of our spell at Cape Wrath, especially the clean fresh air and the kindness and friendship shown by the people of Durness, many who have now gone, unfortunately.

The Morrison family was our link to the mainland via Donald the Ferryman. If the tide was out Donald would hoist us on his back from or to his boat. On thanking him his favourite jocular expression was 'It's not your thanks or twopences – it's the two bobs that count.'

Billy Whyte our postman and messenger was our main link to Durness, making three trips (Tuesdays, Thursdays and Saturdays) each week by bike. When we had a night out in Durness we 'kipped up' with the Whyte family.

Tuesday was an eventful day for one family at the lighthouse – a trip to the ferry house to collect the station groceries from MacKays of Durness and meat from Lairg. Salmon we caught by illicit means at the Cape. Mrs Morrison's tea and pancakes was the highlight of our visit and we were always amused by her local expressions, e.g. 'I'm off tomorrow to buy a trouser for Donald.'

The station stores and fuel were off-loaded at 'The Clash' by the lighthouse boat *Pole Star* yearly in May and transported to the lighthouse by the station Land Rover.

We purchased a TV in early 1958, the first at the station, from Christie Campbell in Durness. One nightly weather forecast recorded Cape Wrath being the only place in Scotland with a high temperature (when in fact it was blowing a gale) the supernumerary having misread the temperature on his three-hourly weather report. He never lived that one down.

Summer months brought good weather, lovely sunsets and many visitors, bird watchers and a few famous faces. Our toilet was in constant use (no public toilets). Winter weather was wild and fearsome at the Cape – small fishing boats tossed about like matches in a howling gale. Certainly well-named.

My resignation in September 1959 followed a holiday, when we realised that our daughter, then fifteen months old, was amazed at seeing 'the outside world' with buses etc.

George MacKenzie, Principal Keeper 1962 to 1965

(George MacKenzie was interviewed for the BBC Radio Highland regional programme 'What a Life' by Bill Sinclair in the late 1970s. George retired to Durness and the interview was recorded there. His recollections ranged from the Scottish Highlands and Islands, to Australia. Many of his memories were relevant and personal to Cape Wrath; the following is a transcribed extract from that broadcast interview. George MacKenzie was posted to Cape Wrath light as Principal Keeper on 12 November 1962; he retired on 31 October 1965.)

I was born at Culkein Stoer, Assynt, in 1902. When I was twenty-one years of age I joined the lighthouse service. There was lighthouse keeping in our blood. My grandfather was a lighthouse keeper. He was relief light keeper at Stoer Head for more than forty years and I had an uncle who joined the lighthouse service and he served at many, many stations throughout Scotland.

I joined the lighthouse service (in 1923) and I was forty-one years ranging from the north of Orkney right down to the Isle of Man. I was appointed as an Assistant Keeper to North Ronaldsay in North Orkney. I arrived there on a Saturday evening and a Norwegian timber-laden ship went ashore in thick fog the following morning. He jettisoned all his deck cargo which was a godsend to the islanders, because they bought all of the wood from the Receiver of Wrecks.

Hundreds of tonnes came ashore on the beach. There was no fog signal at the station – it was just the light.

I went from Orkney right down to the Isle of Man, to Langness in the south of the Isle of Man. Later I was transferred to Dubh Artach light off Iona, one of the wildest rock lighthouses in the world. From Dubh Artach I was transferred to Skerryvore, another wild rock just twelve miles from Dubh Artach. I was promoted Principal Light Keeper there. Shortly after I left Skerryvore the place went on fire – probably an electrical fault.

Cape Wrath light was almost the same as being on an island. You have to cross the ferry – you *could* walk round to the main road, four miles through the hills from the end of the lighthouse road. The Lighthouse Board supplied a boatman there. When I arrived one stormy night - this was my native county, the first time I was stationed in a Sutherland lighthouse – it was blowing a gale when the lighthouse ship the *Pole Star* landed me. The following day a fishing boat went ashore and we managed to get the crew with rocket apparatus. Lightning struck the station that night. Gales up to eighty knots blew – that's over a hundred miles per hour. A repair crew came up to repair the boat, but the boat was smashed to pieces on the beach. The repair crew came up from Lossiemouth. I sent two of the crew in one of our Land Rovers and the other two in the second Land Rover. The two of them met on a blind corner in a head-on collision. That was my first weekend at Cape Wrath.

Cape Wrath was just as wild as Skerryvore. There are rails right round the whole station and you are hanging on to it when you go on watch at night or going to the engine rooms, because you just could not stand there. On one occasion there was a big Orkney chap – he was over six foot and weighed about seventeen stone – and a young Manxman on watch and he called him out at three o'clock in the morning to go on watch. This big fellow went out and the wind got him, in his back, and of course once you start running you can't stop, and he ran right into a wall and was lying down with a fractured skull. The other young fellow started ringing again when he didn't turn up – no sign of him turning up – so he came downstairs himself to see what happened. Just when he came out of the tower door the wind got him and flung him into a corner of the courtyard with a broken leg. So there was one fellow with a fractured skull and another fellow with a broken leg. Finally the big Orcadian came to and crawled up to the light and found the other fellow moaning with a broken leg, so we turned out the third man and they were rushed away to hospital the following day, and some reliefs came. That's the kind of wind they had up there – it's fantastic, the wind that's up there. We regularly registered eighty knots and more.

I was always interested in Natural History, particularly seabirds. When I was at Cape Wrath lighthouse I was recording (for the RSPB) on the famous Clo Mor cliffs, the highest sea cliffs in mainland Great Britain, almost a thousand feet high. There were huge colonies of seabirds nesting there – guillemots, razorbills, puffins, goodness knows what was there – all sorts of birds. I used to go and count them there for the RSPB. It is very difficult to stand on the edge of a thousand foot cliff and count, so what I used to do was tie myself with a rope and peg myself about ten yards back and lie over the edge and count them, with binoculars. If the edge gave way, you could never tell – you could never be quite sure about them.

George MacKenzie's son, now Lord MacKenzie of Culkein, recalls another occasion when the station suffered lightning damage. Early one morning when Principal Lighthouse Keeper MacKenzie had just come off watch and was making a cup of tea before going to bed, lightning struck the telephone line. The charge surge followed the line into the Principal's house, melting the telephone instrument and setting the hall on fire. Fortunately the fire was quickly contained with a hand-held extinguisher.

John Robinson, Minibus Driver, Cape Wrath 1973

In the early seventies I was living at Balnakeil Farm. Old Mr. Elliot let Jan Blankenstein and I have the use of the bothy at a very reasonable rent.

Mention of Mr. Elliot brings back memories of the one and only time I have ever driven a Bentley. Once we were in the old bar at the back of the Cape Wrath hotel enjoying what turned into a very long and convivial evening and, only to be expected, Mr. Elliot felt that he could not really drive home to Balnakeil. His car was a pre-war Bentley with controls firmly rooted in the days of what would nowadays be termed 'vintage' – outside handbrake about a yard long, clutch pedal requiring superhuman strength, etc etc.

Now Mr. Elliot had a wooden leg which, in his somewhat relaxed state, insisted on interfering with my operation of the clutch. But we eventually made it home.

Paul Brown was running the Far North Hotel at Balnakeil and the tourist minibus service to Cape Wrath lighthouse. I heard that he was looking for a driver and I got the job. The first problem to overcome was that of physically getting the bus over to the capeside from the Keoldale slipway. Paul and I fashioned a raft of sorts from salvaged aircraft drop tanks and a supply of six inch by two inch timber scrounged locally.

I drove the bus for that season, although the main driver was Hughie Morrison. The ferryman was John Muir. The ferry was a wooden boat fitted with a very small Seagull engine, as I recall, which often made little headway against the strong ebbing or rising tide. Oars were carried, and were often necessary. There were always problems with the shifting sandbanks, as now. Low water presented the most problems with the sandbanks.

The road to the light was similar in many ways and condition to what it is now, except that we had the ford at Daill instead of the military bridge. This was much more exciting for the tourists, splashing across the river. And it was not without its interests to the drivers – we had to dry out the brakes on the move by gentle application of the foot pedal without alerting the passengers that the brakes might not be operating at full efficiency after negotiating the ford.

Everything at the light was spick and span in those days, everything. The park walls were pristine, the lighthouse enclosure walls were painted white and all the buildings and workshops were maintained to the best standards. The grass was carefully kept. The air compressors which charged the fog horn were absolutely spotless, as was all of the machine room.

Lawrence (and Margaret) Tulloch, Assistant Keeper 1973 to 1975

It was December before the long-awaited phone call came from Mr. Dickson. I had been, for the previous five months, at Out Skerries in Shetland. This lighthouse was being made automatic but a light-keeping presence was required right up to the end. By this time I had been a Supernumerary for twenty months and I knew that my appointment was to be soon. When Mr. Dickson from the Northern Lighthouse Board's personnel department told me that I had been appointed to Cape Wrath I had mixed feelings.

Cape Wrath was not a popular station among light-keepers. It was one of the places that they did not want to go. On the other hand I was delighted that the time had finally come when Margaret and I could settle down and be together. We were newly married but already we had spent half of our married life apart. Most of our time as a courting couple and as an engaged couple we had been apart, me in the lighthouse service and she at college in Aberdeen.

Margaret knew nothing of Cape Wrath. She just wanted, as I wanted, for us to be together and have our own home. We had a great time at Christmas 1972 and New Year but immediately afterwards we had to pack up all our possessions and get them shipped to Cape Wrath. At this stage we owned little – four or five tea chests took care of the whole lot, except the three piece suite that was my parents' wedding present to us.

We flew to Wick via Orkney where we were met by a taxi driven by Richard MacKay. Richard became a good friend and the journey from Wick to Durness was a leisurely affair. We called, for refreshments, at every pub on the way. We stayed overnight in Dickie MacKay's hotel in Durness before going to the lighthouse the following day.

The weather, for early January, was lovely: not a breath of wind. We crossed the Kyle and were eager to see our new home. It came as no surprise, all lighthouse buildings had a sameness about them, and we soon settled in. In the early months life at Cape Wrath was a bit Spartan. We had no TV, no washing machine, no carpets and the fridge could not be used because the previous incumbent had washed it out with Jeyes's Fluid and the smell was there for evermore.

The station owned a Land Rover but that too, was out of action, broken down. We both came from a remote area of North Yell in Shetland, and we considered ourselves well suited to cope with things as they were. We looked forward to the New Year of 1973 with great anticipation. It was a time of great change nationally. Britain was the newest member of the European Common Market, as it was called then.

The Principal Light Keeper was Donald MacAulay from Lewis. He was married to Mima from Skye and they had one young son, Donald Angus, with another baby on the way. It turned out to be a girl, Shirley Anne, who was born later that year.

The couple next door was from Shetland. Brian, the First Assistant, was from Walls and his wife Babs came from Fladdabister. Bobby Morrison from Durness was First Occasional Keeper and Brian Kerr was the Second. I found my workmates good and friendly and the workings of the station easy enough to learn.

The two women were both friendly towards Margaret, and the novelty of the first few months made the time pass quickly. However, without transport there was no leaving the station and the only contact with the outside was the weekly phone call to the shop for messages which arrived thanks to an old banger that Brian had made into going order. Eventually the Land Rover got 'fixed' but it was so old and knackered that any fixing of it was temporary at best.

One of the most disagreeable aspects of Cape Wrath in those days was the lack of drinkable water. The water that came through the taps was the same colour as Newcastle Brown Ale and when a visitor to our house drank some of it he became ill. The water for cooking was what was catched off the roofs and it was not safe to drink unless it was boiled. Donald MacAulay in one of his many letters of complaint to HQ said that the water was 'no bloody good for babies or people!'

Donald and Mima had a lovely dog, a bearded collie, called Brandy. He seriously distorted the station's weather reports. We sent met. reports, by phone, to Wick every three hours. Brandy's sins came to our notice one day when the weather report I had sent was questioned. I had recorded four millimetres of rain on a day when no-one else had rain. Not only that, but my description of the clouds was inconsistent with precipitation of any kind. We kept a close watch on Brandy and saw him lift his leg against the rain gauge and pee with awesome accuracy into the funnel. From then on rain readings at Cape Wrath were somewhat haphazard.

Bobby Morrison was a really nice man and entirely dependable, but he had trouble with his legs. Whenever it was windy he could never make the trip between the bothy and the tower without hanging on, like grim death, to the handrails.

Some journeys were made even more difficult by the porridge. Bobby was very fond of porridge, but it usually upset his stomach and gave him bouts of rumble-root. He would therefore have to make all possible haste for the nearest toilet. One particularly bad day for Bobby came when we painted the stairs in the tower leading all the way up to the light room. The middle of each step was painted brown with the outsides painted cream. The stairs had to be usable at all times so we painted every second step. With his bad legs, taking two at a time was a big enough challenge but with his compelling need for relief it was a serious matter indeed!

Annual inspection day was a big day in the calendar. Women hated inspection days, because the Superintendent would come to the house to see that it was well kept. On the eve of the inspection, Margaret put on a pot to boil – it was bones of a chicken for soup. She went out and left it and forgot it. When she came back the pot had boiled dry and the soot was hanging in long threads from the ceiling. The light bulb was so caked that it showed hardly any light. There was a lot of hard work and cursing before the place was made presentable for the Super.

On inspection day, all the stores for the whole year arrived. Paraffin, diesel, petrol, coal, cotton waste (although never much), soap, uniforms, paint, furniture, brushes, mops, tools were just some of it. One year we had a large box landed. Nobody could even guess what was in it until Donald said 'It will be all my letters of complaint returned, it is about the right size!'

Brian Johnson left Cape Wrath. He made the switch from being a light keeper to being an Artificer, and until a new keeper arrived we had a succession of supernumeraries.

One morning when I went outside, I was aware of feverous activity in the engine room. When I looked in, it was the supernumerary with the entire year's supply of cotton waste on the floor. He was like a frantic farmer making hay on the one fine day of a wet summer. The floor was flooded with diesel fuel to about an inch deep in places. Normally, diesel had to be pumped from the big storage tanks outside to the header tank that fed the engines, but with the tanks being full to the brim it could flow with gravity and he had forgotten to close off the valve. It took most of the day to get it all mopped up. Goodness knows how many gallons of diesel were lost.

In the fullness of time, Alan Crowe became the first assistant.

After Stewart Pairman had been and gone, during which time I rose to the dizzy heights of first assistant. Alan was the ultimate paraffin-oiler. His family, in direct line of descent, had been light keepers since 1793. His wife Irene came from Sumburgh in Shetland.

In those days, anything that was unwanted was thrown over the cliff. Near the gate, the entrance to the lighthouse enclosure, there is a geo that served as the dump. Alan was aware that it was full of rats and he saw them as a potential hazard for the whole station.

One day he said to me that he wanted my help to give the rats a really bad day. There were several buckets of waste oil that we mixed with paraffin and poured down the geo among the rubbish. We then made four petrol bombs and threw them to the bottom of the geo. It was a windy day, a wind blowing on-shore. When all the rubbish took fire it roared up the geo like a giant flame-thrower, so much so that we were cut off from the station until it died down somewhat.

The spring of 1974 was very dry and the water supply, such as it was, ran out. We had to go with the tractor and trailer and take barrels of water from the river. Someone had set the heather on fire, and a big brae of peat burned for weeks on end.

At different times we thought it had gone out, but whenever it was dark, on a windy night, the deep glow was there to be seen. One day I did a very stupid thing. Margaret and I went to have closer look at the fire and I climbed up on top of the brae. The fire had made it hollow and it collapsed and I fell into the fire. It was a nasty moment, but I got out with no more than scorched trousers.

Eventually Donald MacAulay got what he wanted, a shift to Oban – he was to be the Principal at Hyskeir. His replacement was another MacAulay, Alex from Islay. Alex was a very different man from Donald and they were not related. Alex was very placid and easy going and all the station work was done at a gentle pace.

Alex and his wife Nancy had a grown-up family, so they were by themselves. In fact, I had met Alex before. We had been together on Rona when I was there as a supernumerary.

And so it was that after being at Cape Wrath a relatively short time, Margaret and I had been there longer than anyone other than the Occasionals. In the spring of 1975 we travelled home to North Yell to attend the wedding of close friends of ours, and it was at this time that we knew that Margaret was pregnant. While at home we went to Unst to visit the Muckle Flugga shore station.

Among others that we saw there was Tommy Georgeson. He told us that he was applying for a shift from Muckle Flugga, and he had good reason to believe that his request would be granted. This was my cue to apply, not only for a shift from Cape Wrath, but to ask for Muckle Flugga. Cape Wrath was not considered a suitable place for a woman having her first child. Doctors and hospitals were not handy, and my request was granted, albeit that it took time.

We left the Cape in August 1975 and said regretful goodbyes to the many friends that we made there. Some of those friends we keep in touch with to this day, thirty-one years later.

Nowadays Margaret and I look back on our time at Cape Wrath with nostalgia and fondness, and it is only now that we fully appreciate how happy we were roaming the hills and beaches without a care in the world.

Alex McAulay, Principal Keeper 1974 to 1978

We, (my wife Nancy and I) went to Cape Wrath in April 1974, and lived in the keepers' accommodation there for a couple of years before it was made a rock station and we had to move to Golspie, although I stayed as Principal until July 1978.

I served over twenty-nine years in the lighthouse service, starting at Kinnaird Head and later serving at Ailsa Craig – where I was once stranded for ten weeks without relief – and McArthur's Head, Islay, among many others. I transferred from Cape Wrath to Neist Point, Skye, from where I retired.

I was probably the only serving keeper at Cape Wrath ever to have walked in to my duty. We had been on holiday and on our return the weather was too bad for the ferryman. So we walked across the footbridge at Grudie overland to the ford at Daill. There was a rope bridge there, just two ropes, one above the other, and we clambered across because the ford was in spate. The station Land Rover collected us at the other side.

Our time at Cape Wrath was very happy as we had very good neighbours and never felt lonely. The Cape was a very wild place in winter. We had the Land Rover and went across to Durness to do our weekly shopping. The NLB supply boat came once a year with our stores. That was a big day, waiting to see what we were getting.

When we were at the lighthouse we had a paraffin fridge and a coal fire. Our fridge used to smoke a lot if it wasn't kept clean.

We had good New Year's at the Cape. Everyone joined in and Nancy baked a Clootie Dumpling.

Jan Blankenstein, Occasional Light Keeper 1974 to 1975

I always wanted to be a lighthouse keeper, ever since I could remember. I first visited Durness in 1964 with three friends while on a cycling holiday from Kirkaldy in Fife. As we passed the road end at Keoldale I saw the signpost pointing to Cape Wrath (a wondrous and magical place for me) and suggested a visit, but was outvoted. We cycled off southwards and the Cape receded into the distance, both geographically and emotionally. I returned to Durness on University field trips some six years later and the old magical pull returned.

After leaving University, I kept returning more and more often and for longer and longer periods and finally ended up staying. This was 1973. I had made friends with Dave Marshall, the wood-turner at Balnakeil Craft village and his wife Russ, who was the teacher in the village school in Durness, and I lodged with them. Despite the closeness of the Cape I didn't manage to visit, but the lure was still there.

One day Brian Kerr, another incomer who was the Occasional keeper at the light, told me he had been appointed as a full-time keeper and would I be interested in the Occasional's job? This was beyond my wildest dreams – perhaps I had stayed away from the light because it represented so many unfulfilled desires and ambitions. Anyway, I recall meeting the Principal, Alec McAulay, in the Cape Wrath Hotel, always the first stop on the way off the Capeside and probably the last stop on the way back on! We agreed to give it a try and I then had to arrange to spend two weeks training at the light. I was so ecstatic I went to Dickie MacKay's shop and bought TWO bars of chocolate.

My trip to the light started with the ferry crossing in the hands of John Muir, well-known consumer of large quantities of canned beer and teller of tall tales. John always had a few cans of beer concealed under various rocks around the ferry slip, in case he should feel a thirst come upon him. (Also, I suspect, to avoid the watchful and disapproving scrutiny of his wife Kath.) I bundled into the NLB Land Rover with the other keepers (how was it I always ended up in the back if there were more than three on board?) and we set off for the light. For me this was the first trip along that magical road with all its fascinating features: the ford at Daill, which varied in levels of excitement proportionally with the amount of rain there had been in the previous few days; the bridge at Inshore with the gate which always had to be opened; the road end at the lighthouse pier (Clash), and finally round that bend a few hundred yards from the destination to reveal the lighthouse close-up for the first time. I had seen it many times from Faraid Head, but that was away thirteen kilometres (eight miles) in the distance. The light was already lit and I recall the wonder as the red and white beams swept across the cliffs below the Lloyd's station to the south-east, a wonder that never left me.

I was settled into the bothy, set slightly apart from the other buildings, on the south side of the compound and thus started one of the, if not THE most pleasant periods of my life. I met the other keepers: Lawrie Tulloch who came from North Unst and who later returned to be keeper at Muckle Flugga, and Alan Crowe who was ex-Merchant Navy and was destined for great things. There was a peculiar line of succession in the NLB, determined not by merit but by time served, so 'dead men's shoes' was very much the way it was, but it meant keepers of Alan's quality had to wait for promotion. I recall Alan used to pace back and forward in the radio room while having a conversation, a throwback to his days at sea, but as the radio room at Cape Wrath was barely eight feet long, it made for a very short walk. I asked Lawrie one day what he felt about the job of light-keeper. He replied in all innocence that 'it had its ups and downs!'

Alec, the Principal, was from Islay. I knew little of his background, but he was capable of consuming vast quantities of whisky during his time ashore. But the following day he would be as right as rain, reporting that he had never had a hangover in his life – a statement I could well believe, having seen him recover from near unconsciousness to full function in about six hours! Brian Kerr was a fulltime keeper, but didn't live on the light. The keepers and their wives were all good decent human beings who were a pleasure to work with.

The duties of the Occasional or 'OLK' were the same as the other keepers, but I worked regular shifts or watches from Sunday to Tuesday while the full-time keepers worked a rolling roster. When folks enquired about life on the light, I used to say that it took four and a half keepers to man the light, and I was the half! The major duty was of course to attend the light and if necessary the foghorn. The light was like a huge Tilley lamp sitting on top of a huge grandfather clock mechanism, which drove the optic or lens system. When the light was functioning there was a constant loud hissing from the lamp and a constant clang from the striking mechanism which announced that the lens system was running. I think that the regulations required that the keeper on watch was present in the lamp room throughout his watch but everybody managed to arrange a line-of-sight view, sometimes with the aid of a mirror, of the light from the favourite armchair in the keepers' accommodation.

This (unofficial) system occasionally caused problems, especially on the 10pm to 2am watch, because a comfortable armchair, a blazing coal fire and television that finished well before midnight in those days could lead one to succumb to a rather lengthy snooze, resulting in a frantic hurtle up the tower stairs to rewind the weight and a prayer that no vessels of Her Majesty's Navy were on hand to report that the light was exhibiting an incorrect signal.

The daily routine, while constant in nature, did change with the time of year. Being so far north, the difference between summer nights and winter nights was huge. Around the summer solstice the lamp was lit for only around five hours, but in December it burned for about nineteen hours a day, it always being shown from sunset to sunrise. The mechanics of the lamp were such that the paraffin reservoir could be topped up only every second day in summer, but the fuel can had to be lugged up the tower daily in winter. There were two identical reservoirs, one for the paraffin and the other for the compressed air to pressurise the lamp. One had to shut the valve separating the air bottle from the paraffin bottle before opening the filler cap to add the paraffin or else the air bottle lost all its pressure to the atmosphere, resulting in mild cursing because the bottle was pressurised by a glorified bicycle pump and it took a lot of time, energy and sweat to pump up the bottle to working pressure from scratch. Obviously he who let it out had to put it back in again!

The foghorn was powered by compressed air produced by two massive Kelvin diesel engines which drove the compressors. These engines were started with petrol, which was the only use for petrol on the station, so it was actually poured into the carburettors from a whisky bottle, which surprised any visitors to the light. Of course we did nothing to disabuse them of the idea that only the best whisky was good enough for the Commissioners' engines (especially as Alec hailed from Islay). The foghorn was required rarely at the

Cape as fog was not a major problem but one was always aware of it starting during the night. One would be woken by its stentorian bellow then as one was dropping off again, ninety seconds later the process was repeated but usually by the third bellow one was again fast asleep leaving the world to bellowing monsters and watchful keepers.

Peter Hill in his book *Stargazing* suggests that being a lighthouse keeper was possibly the best job in the world, and I have to agree with him. For me the absolute zenith of the work was to be in charge of the light on the 2am to 6am watch in high summer. The light had been lit the previous evening at sunset by the keeper on watch at that time, but although it was sunset it was still bright daylight, indeed one could read a newspaper outdoors at midnight without the need of artificial light. When it came to putting the light out at sunrise, it was again already bright daylight. One stood in the lamp room, at about 3am, looking down onto a calm ocean four hundred feet below. The light had been clanging and hissing through the short night and then – silence, as the light faded away as the fuel was turned off and the lever thrown to disengage the optic. Whether one was a believer in a Divine Being or not, it certainly felt that I was God's deputy on earth giving the day permission to start, knowing that I was probably the only person awake, certainly on the Parbh, and probably for about five hundred square miles.

Another of the delights was doing the synoptic weather reports for the Met office, every three hours at 0300, 0600, 0900, 1200 *et seq*, *ad infinitum* and for some *ad nauseam*! I felt privileged to be part of a global team putting together a picture of the weather worldwide for the benefit of farmers, seamen, aviators, chocolate manufacturers and picnickers. One had to have a working knowledge of cloud types, cloud heights and a myriad of other little details – I was even allowed to attend a course at the Met Office College in Reading. They were surprised at the College that anyone would WANT to travel seven hundred miles for such a thing.

There were a number of events through the year that broke the steady routine – the arrival of the supply ship *M.V. Pharos* twice during the year – once to deliver coal for the keepers' houses and the other visit to deliver everything else – diesel for the generators and for the Land Rover, paraffin for the lamp and cleaning the paint brushes also delivered after the annual re-paint of EVERYTHING, mantles, Brasso, cleaning cloths, weed-killer. If it was needed, it was delivered by lighter from the ship to the jetty where it was manhandled up the slip, loaded onto the tractor and trailer and hauled the couple of miles to the light. Those were physically hard days when everybody pulled together.

After a year in the job I was given the opportunity to become a full-time keeper and to transfer to the light on the Isle of May in the Firth of Forth. I was delighted because it also meant I would be able to afford to buy the BMW motorcycle I had dreamed of for years. Then 84 (NLB headquarters at 84 George Street, Edinburgh, referred to by all as '84') said 'We'd better give you a medical . . .' Aahh, I thought. Disaster! I knew I was colour-blind but THEY didn't. Sure enough, I failed the medical because of my defective colour vision, the same thing that kept me out of the RAF. I WOULD HAVE TO LEAVE!

'Why?' I asked. The conversation went something like this:

'Because you can't tell ships' navigation lights.' (Correct.)

'Why does that matter?'

'You have to be able to tell which way the ship is steaming.'

'Why?'

'You have to warn them if they are steaming towards you, of course.'

'How do I do that?'

'You take the lighthouse torch and flash the Morse code for 'You are standing into danger.''

Now the lighthouse torch was a 19/6d (97.5 pence in new money) Woolworth's job, so I replied: 'If they can't see this 450,000 candle power above my head,' pointing upwards, 'how are they going to see this torch?'

'Aye, you're right enough!' they said, but I still had to leave. My BMW turned round and disappeared over the horizon. It would be nearly thirty years till it re-appeared!

So came to an end the best job I have ever had the privilege to do. One had to be a Jack-of-all-trades and Master of most – electrician, mechanical engineer, painter and decorator, stonemason, radio operator, meteorologist, metalworker, gardener. I was saddened when, as Bella Bathurst put it in *The Lighthouse Stevensons*, for the first time a complete profession had been consigned to history by advances in technology, and I thought that I had severed all connections with the lights. But no! They have discovered that they can't do without keepers after all and I am delighted to have my bosom buddy John Robinson following in my footsteps at Stour Head lighthouse. The job has changed, but the tradition hasn't.

Brian Kerr, Light Keeper and Achiemore Resident, 1973 to 1976

In the early 1970s I was resident in Eriboll, working on the Eriboll estate. A relief light keeper job became available at Cape Wrath and I did that for a year or so, which meant travelling around Loch Eriboll and through Durness to the Keoldale ferry (a one-way trip of around sixteen miles) and then an eleven-mile ride to the lighthouse. When an assistant keeper's post fell vacant I applied and got it.

I served as Local Assistant Keeper at Cape Wrath from 2 September 1974 to 31 October 1976, when I resigned. I was at Cape Wrath for about three years altogether.

About the time I started as assistant keeper I got the tenancy of Achiemore on Cape Wrath, which reduced the travelling considerably, and moved there with my wife and first daughter. There was always lots of planed timber being washed up on the beach at Daill, deck cargo lost in bad weather I suppose, with which I made the kitchen dresser, cupboards and other furniture. Much of it was still there on a recent visit.

At Achiemore we always kept hens. I recall collecting two 56lb sacks of hen meal from the ferry and taking them to the house in the station Land Rover. Lifting one from the back I snagged it on the rear door. The high wind blew almost the whole sackful around the house before I had chance to save it. Silly mistake, but the hens had a birthday and I did have another bag.

Another fowl-related incident was when my wife was surprised by a puzzled-looking road gang. Hens always laid eggs in the nettle beds around Achiemore. The best way to collect the eggs was to brush the nettles aside gently with a long yard brush. You could see the eggs on the ground under the leaves. Parting the nettles with a brush ensured that you didn't get stung. My wife one day became aware of a presence when she was involved in this exercise. The road gang were intently watching her, puzzled as to the purpose. 'Nice day for sweeping your nettles,' was the comment, before an explanation put things to rights.

At that time there was a rudimentary wooden hut at Achiemore used by soldiers posted to watch and guard during the shelling practice. On these occasions we were regularly approached by bored squaddies wanting to swap compo rations for fresh eggs. On a separate occasion, I recall a soldier disappearing off a cliff into the sea. His body was recovered months later, in Norway. It was identified by his dog-tag.

My second daughter was born whilst we were at Achiemore. My wife had to go to Dingwall for the birth. When she was due to return home I carried my first daughter all the way from Achiemore early in the morning to the head of the Kyle of Durness and waded across the water to meet the road and the service bus. It was blowing a gale and the ferry could not run. And I was spotted, of course.

I had a Triumph Herald to get from Achiemore to the lighthouse. Eventually the exhaust fell off (bad road and no bridge at Daill in those days) and it was glorious to be able to give it full throttle on the way to work. It sounded like a squadron of Spitfires, but it could be heard in Durness, apparently.

Mercedes-Benz wanted to film the launch of a new model in spectacular scenery, and chose the Highlands. The local constabulary would not permit them to film on a public road, but agreed that they could use the Cape Wrath road. So they arrived with camera crew and a helicopter and directors and stunt drivers, and spent a good deal of time with us. The section of road they used was the level stretch near Achiemore and round the corner to Daill. They spent hours splashing through the ford and hurtling along the road at anything up to seventy miles an hour. The car was covered in a white sheet with just a narrow slot for the driver's eyes. The sheet was gradually pulled away, to reveal the new model in all its glory. Somewhere in the M-B archives there is a can of film with frightening shots of a new Merc being driven erratically, under a sheet, on Cape Wrath.

The Principal Keeper in my time was Alec McCaulay – smashing guy – and the assistants were brothers-in-law Alan Crowe and Peter Caisley, both different in personality from each other. Cape Wrath became a rock station in 1975. That did not affect me as I was not living in the lighthouse accommodation.

We were expected to do all the external painting at the station. Painting the tower was uncomfortable rather than dangerous. The only scary part was getting into the cradle over the tower parapet. The brasswork had always to be kept polished and it was an unwritten rule that no-one ever touched it without gloves. The light was a paraffin burner in those days. It seemed to be that when the mantle broke and the light was shown one or two minutes late there was always a naval frigate off the Cape, ready to complain.

We had coastguard rescue equipment, which had to be tested occasionally. We used to fire the line by rocket across the gully next to the station and rig up the bosun's chair. The one who drew the short straw had the honour of being pulled across a two hundred-foot deep chasm.

Groceries for the lighthouse staff were ordered in Durness and delivered across the ferry for collection by the NLB Land Rover. On one occasion, ferryman John Muir left the box on the pier because he had to hurriedly return to the Keoldale side. The tide rose and the supplies sank at the edge of the pier. All the tins lost their labels, and mealtimes became a lottery. The mailbag was also submerged. In it was cash due to one of the keepers. The notes were pegged on the line at the station to dry them out.

One o'clock was always lunch time, so that wherever you were you knew the mealtime. It was always a cooked lunch. We watched the television news at lunchtime, followed by *Trumpton*. It just became a daily ritual. Even now I can remember the mantra of the characters' names.

Stores were landed from the NLB supply vessel at Clais Charnach and taken into the storehouse there. Paraffin barrels were hauled up to the lighthouse and stored in the base of the tower. We had separate stores for petrol, paint and diesel fuel for the generators.

There was an occasion when a man disappeared without trace from Kearvaig. He had gone up on the bus with camping equipment, and the driver realised a few days later that he had not returned. I went to Kearvaig and found his tent and possessions, but he was nowhere to be seen. The coastguards and mountain rescue teams did a search, but nothing was ever found. Months later the police returned his equipment to me, as I had reported the disappearance.

It was always accepted that there was an apparition in the Cape Wrath light tower. Alan Crowe experienced it, and I did too. A figure would manifest itself on the stairs between the tower entrance and the radio room. Everyone was aware of it and just accepted it, but it was never really discussed. I was walking back towards the station one night. It was pitch black and the sweep of the light would cross part of the hill below the Lloyd's building. A white figure glided silently through the light beam. I was momentarily convinced that it was another manifestation of the apparition, but I then realised that it was a short eared owl. Gulls make a noise, owls don't.

We had to eject a group of hippy types from the Lloyd's building. They arrived and seemed to take up residence and were often seen dancing on the roof at night in what might have been chemically-induced excitement. We made it clear that they would have to take themselves elsewhere.

Frequently we saw the *aurora borealis*. The wildlife on Cape Wrath always fascinated me. I spent a lot of time just walking the hills. Whales and dolphins were almost commonplace off the Cape. Otter kitts would play on the beach at Kearvaig within yards of me, sometimes climbing over my boots. And there were always rats about, ranging along the high-water mark and feeding in amongst the wrack. You see rats in a new light as part of nature in the wild, when the urban scare stories are discounted.

Cape Wrath is a magical place.

Donald MacLeod, Principal Keeper 1982 to 1989

I entered the lighthouse service with the Northern Lighthouse Board in 1954, and served as a probationer at Inchkeith, Fife. My first permanent posting was Barra Head, and I then served at Corsewall Point, Bass Rock (seven years), Barns Ness, Islay (north), Butt of Lewis, Sule Skerry and Neist Point throughout my career, before being appointed to Cape Wrath as Principal Keeper on 25 November 1982. The light was at that time classified as a rock station and, although there was accommodation for keepers' families at Cape Wrath, it was not used; the Northern Lighthouse Board provided homes for its personnel in Golspie, approximately eighty miles away on the east coast of Sutherland.

I served at Cape Wrath until 31 March 1989, when I retired from the service. I had over six very happy and contented years at the

Cape Wrath light. The following is a random selection of high- and not-so-high-lights from my time there.

My first four week tour of duty at Cape Wrath started on Christmas Eve with a near gale, and ended likewise. The wind blew the entire time. But we did enjoy some glorious weather there, and some of the sunsets were truly spectacular, the likes of which I have never see before or since. But I never succeeded in getting a good photograph of any one of the sunsets.

I had not been long at the Cape when one Sunday morning I was convinced that Old Nick himself had me marked for special treatment. I was leaving the radio communication room, at that time in the base of the light tower, and heading towards the engine room, when there was an almighty explosion and a flash of lightning. When the smoke cleared slightly I saw that the last telephone pole into the station was on fire. The underground cable from the pole was burnt out and all the instruments in the communications room were very badly damaged, even the drawers were welded together. That was a very near thing. And strangely it was a repeat of a similar incident which happened to me during my time at Sule Skerry. On that occasion, which happened in darkness in winter, some of the sleeping accommodation was set on fire.

Our station transport was a Land Rover and a tractor and trailer. The tractor and trailer were used mainly for transporting fuel and stores from the Clais Charnach landing to the lighthouse itself. At that time there were diesel storage tanks at the landing place. The concrete plinth where these tanks were placed still exists at Clais Charnach, with stainless steel bolts where the tank frames were. The tanks were protected from falling rocks by large steel wire nets, which are also still there. Some tanks were moved to the lighthouse before the station was automated.

When the weather was very wild at the lighthouse, especially during winter, it was necessary for the relief helicopter to land at the point where the main lighthouse road joined the road from Clais Charnach.

It was more sheltered there. On one occasion when I was going on duty on a very windy day (but not too windy for the helicopter to leave the supply boat), it was a different matter at the Cape. The pilot just could not get the chopper to descend, and we had to move further inland away from the cliffs. That was one scary arrival.

The station Land Rover was used to go to the ferry landing for supplies and mail. We ordered groceries and fresh food etc. from Durness and the ferryman brought it across for us. During military exercises we provided transport for the soldiers manning the guard posts at the boundaries of the bombardment range. If we needed to go to the ferry when the range was in use the military were very good. They suspended bombing runs until we could get back on station.

An off-duty man drove the military personnel to and from the guard posts. On one occasion after an exercise our man collected the guards to take them to the ferry. At one post one military man was missing – he was up on the hill protecting the range from walkers who might approach off-road. Our man went looking for him, but fell and broke his ankle. He waved to the passing minibus to attract attention but was lying injured in the heather for some time. When he was found we had to call in the helicopter to take him to hospital. His leg never properly recovered and he was unable to return to work. Sad, really. It shows how isolated and dangerous it could be at the Cape Wrath station.

The road could be very difficult in bad weather. Once when the Land Rover was being driven to the ferry in a long spell of wet weather, it sank without warning up to both its axles. The road foundations collapsed under it and the road just disappeared. It took a long time with the tractor and chains to recover the Land Rover, and then the road had to be made good.

At times we had some uncomfortable moments during bombing practices aimed at Garvie Island. Aircraft came in low over the sea and we could look down on the pilots from our station. We could trust our own RAF aircraft getting on the target, but the US F1-11s were a different matter. They seemed glad to let go anywhere. I heard later that on one occasion an American aircraft actually bombed Am Balg island, off Sandwood Bay, mistaking it for Garvie. Missed the real target by ten miles, but it is in the same county! It was all kept quiet for a few months until the newspapers got hold of it.

One of our boys out for a walk one day came across a bomb lying in a small burn running towards the sea. Luckily he didn't touch it. We contacted the police and coastguards, who informed Bomb Disposal. They arrived and confirmed that it was a live practise bomb with a 50lb charge in its nose. They exploded it and that was the last we heard of it.

I never cared much for the bombardment times. Planes were bad enough but shelling from ships was even worse. They were usually over the horizon and we seldom saw them. I remember one time when I was taking the soldiers from the ferry to the guard posts, when just as we arrived at the post nearest the lighthouse there was a huge thud in the ground beside the post. One of the guards went in and telephoned Faraid Head Range Control, and requested a repeat! Sure enough, another round came in and landed in roughly the same place. Scary indeed.

At one point during my time at Cape Wrath the MoD were practising with a new type of bomb which was supposed to explode three metres above the target, which most of them did, until on one occasion an aircraft dropped one which seemed to explode almost immediately. The plane was apparently travelling fast enough to get away safely. That was the end of that type of bombing and we never saw or heard that sort again.

During one NATO exercise one of the Sea King helicopters developed an engine problem and had to make an emergency landing at the lighthouse, just outside the boundary wall. The ground was quite soft there, and the chopper sank in over its wheels. A second Sea King arrived on site and lifted the first to firmer ground. The engine problem was sorted and the casualty eventually flew away.

During the summer months we seemed to have regular problems with tourist visitors. They always seemed to arrive just as we were disposing of old rags and used engine oil. We never just threw this over the edge (which would have been much quicker and easier) but always burned them near the cliff in a brazier made specially for the purpose. But there were many reports about this to HQ.

And many times we found people just wandering around our quarters. Some were under the impression that freedom to roam anywhere was acceptable, and others were just looking for toilets. We always said that we had none and that we used the nearest rabbit hole. It was really a shame that there were no public toilets when there were so many visitors to the area.

My colleague Jimmock MacKay used to tell the story that when he was questioned about the nets drying in the lighthouse courtyard he always replied, with a smile, that they were badminton nets, and that badminton was very popular at Cape Wrath! They were, of course, illicit salmon nets.

During my tour of duty at the Cape the most worrying time was after the Chernobyl explosion. We heard that the Lighthouse Board might want to close the Cape Wrath station temporarily because of the possibility of airborne radioactive dust drifting in our direction. The main reason for possible closure was that we used so much rainwater collected from the slate-roofed buildings just inside the boundary wall. The decision was taken to keep the station open when it was realised that the winds had taken any contamination more to the south. Water samples were collected every fortnight and sent for testing to Dounreay near Thurso. We were never told the results of the tests, just that the water was okay. It was worrying all the same. But keepers in the olden days used rainwater stored in underground lead cisterns, so we were not quite as at risk as they were.

CHAPTER 12

WHEELS TO THE NORTH WEST FRONTIER

THE CAPE WRATH MINIBUS SERVICE

The Service is Inaugurated

Intrepid excursionists could arrange to be taken to the very point of Cape Wrath within fifty years of the establishment of the lighthouse. And motor vehicles, although rarities, did penetrate the Parph during the 1920s, and probably before. These early attempts at organised tourist visits are described in the chapter entitled 'Magnificent Isolation.'

The road to the Cape Wrath lighthouse, built by the Northern Lighthouse Board (at a cost of £3520, according to a much later document), became a public road just a few years after its completion. For the convoluted story of the difficulties involved in maintaining this most isolated of roads see the chapter 'Scratching a Line in the Wilderness.'

Public roads require the pre-payment of the appropriate excise duty (formerly the road fund licence) for any motor vehicle proposing to use that highway. And public service vehicles operating on public roads are further subject to an additional array of driver and operator licences, not to mention public liability insurance and government-sanctioned maintenance, safety and inspection procedures. That is the situation which obtains to this day.

The first officially-regulated minibus service from the west Keoldale ferry landing stage to the lighthouse at Cape Wrath commenced in the mid-1960s. Paul and Yvette Brown and Hugh and Molly Powell jointly decided that a formalised minibus service would both fill a need for tourists visiting the far north-west of the Scottish mainland, encouraging them to stay a little longer, and might also generate increased numbers of visitors.

It must be remembered that at this time the impressive Kylescu Bridge did not exist; visitors travelling northwards up the west coast were obliged to use the small Kylescu-Kylestrome ferry service, which operated between the hours of 9 am and 7 pm. The ferry was privately-owned and operated until 1948, when Sutherland County Council bought it over. The two slipways were improved, the vessel enlarged to accommodate commercial vehicles and it became free of charge to the travelling public until 1975. The Kylescu Bridge was formally opened by H.M. the Queen in 1984.

The only two road routes leaving Durness were either eastwards along the north coast towards Tongue and Thurso, or south to Laxford Bridge continuing via the A.838 towards Lairg. These narrow roads were at the time single track with few passing places, making it virtually impossible to drive to and from Durness within a day. An additional visitor attraction in Durness could only be beneficial.

Paul Brown was granted a Traffic Commissioners Operators licence for the Cape Wrath minibus service on 18 July 1964. The first vehicle used on the service was an eleven-seat Ford Thames Martin Walter minibus registered 124 JUM. Then, as now, the major problem in starting a regular passenger service was physically getting the transport over the water to the Capeside peninsula.

The first raft to take the minibus across the Kyle of Durness was fashioned from ex-military aircraft fuel drop-tanks and a supply of wooden planks acquired locally. That it was a somewhat precarious exercise, not without its obvious dangers, is confirmed by the fact that willing council workmen were pressed into service to assist with the operation. These brave souls were deputed to drive the minibus onto the raft contraption at the Keoldale side, to accompany the whole edifice across the Kyle and to deposit the bus safely on the Capeside slipway. That the exercise was accomplished without mishap was perhaps in no small way due to an element of bribery. Paul Brown strapped a gallon bottle of whisky to the front passenger seat of the minibus and told the workmen that the bottle was theirs if they delivered it safely to the other side.

Ferryman Donald Morrison attempted to tow this first minibus across the Kyle with the open ferry boat employing a very rudimentary 'Seagull' outboard engine. He had to resort to the oars when it became obvious that the engine was making no headway against the incoming tide.

Later a more substantial raft was made from twenty-two oil drums and proper decking, following which two shallow-draft hulls were lashed together and the buses driven onto them for the passage across the Kyle. It has been only in more recent years that a purpose-made pontoon barge, complete with outboard motor, has been available. The barge combines stability with space, and the bus delivery and retrieval operation is now rather more stress-free than was the case in the early days. Even now the pontoon barge usually is assisted with a tow.

The Cape Wrath minibus service commenced with one vehicle. Runs to the lighthouse were initially scheduled to meet the ferry running at 9.45 am, 11.45 am, 1.45 pm, 3.30 pm, 5.15 pm and 7 pm every day, weather permitting. From this it is clear that six return runs each day were envisaged, a somewhat punishing schedule for both bus and driver. Fares were published as 10 shillings (50 pence) for the visit to the lighthouse and pier only, 12 shillings and sixpence (62.5 pence) for a half day return, or 15 shillings (75 pence) for a full day return. Children were charged at half-price in each case.

In 1965 brothers-in-law Derek C. Hulme and Allister Brebner expanded their 'Highland Safaris' tourist business across to Cape Wrath. Their trips into the Highlands of Scotland were restricted to the mainland until the operators licence was granted for minibus trips to Cape Wrath lighthouse. The inaugural Highland Safaris trip to Cape Wrath took place on 8 June 1965. Trips continued fortnightly, and weekly in spring and summer, for over thirty years. Highland Safaris organised official RSPB Bird Watching courses on Cape Wrath for ten successive years from 1966.

Hugh Powell (co-partner in setting up the service) holds a unique claim to fame, in that he must be the only PSV driver ever to have passed his competence test on Cape Wrath. He applied for a passenger-carrying vehicle driving licence when the Operators Licence was granted, and very soon after the inauguration of the Cape Wrath minibus service in 1965, a driving examiner arrived unannounced, intent on conducting the test there and then. All went well, and it is debatable who was the more surprised – the examiner at the state of the road, or the candidate at the special problems to be overcome during the test. The only place that could be found in which to carry out the three-point turn element of the test was at (and occasionally in) the river Daill. Thankfully the water level was low, and all was successfully accomplished without too much loss of face by either party.

By December 1969 a second minibus had been purchased. Both vehicles were used for a time as passenger numbers warranted. And during one quiet spell in the late 1960s the lower half of the original Ford Thames bus was painted yellow over on the Capeside. Passengers being collected at the lighthouse on that afternoon were convinced that they were boarding the wrong bus, until reassured by the driver. Paul Brown used a further two buses during his years of operation.

A Rival Service

Early in 1976 Hugh Morrison (son-in-law of the then ferryman John Muir) decided to apply for a Traffic Commissioners Public Service Operators licence for a Cape Wrath minibus service rivalling the established Brown/Powell operation. There must have been considerable doubt as to the viability of two separate services running along a single track road served by one tiny ferry boat.

A formal Traffic Commissioners' hearing, as required by law, was convened in Inverness to decide on the application. Witnesses were called both in support of and against the application. For the objectors it was pointed out that the single track road had few passing places and that the existing service ran efficiently, adequately accommodating all the potential customers. Doubts were further expressed at the limited Capeside pier turning space which had already to accommodate two vehicles, and that demand for the service was limited to the summer months only. It was also pointed out that a rival service closely associated with the ferryman would doubtless be favoured by the ferryman to the detriment of the existing operator. The applicant stated that he intended to operate an all-year service for fishermen and tourists, to a set timetable.

Hugh Morrison's application was successful; he was granted a Public Service Operators Licence on 17 February 1976 and proceeded to run a duplicate Cape Wrath minibus service in connection with his father-in-law John Muir's ferry operation across the Kyle of Durness. He used Ford Transit minibuses during his years of operation.

The ford across the Daill River was bridged in 1981, the full story of which is recounted in the chapter 'Scratching a Line in the Wilderness.'

The Service is Threatened, and Saved

During the late 1970s there were significant changes affecting the ferry and minibus service to Cape Wrath. The Northern Lighthouse Board decided that helicopter relief for isolated shore stations was the way forward. That in turn would mean there would in future be a very much reduced reliance on the ferry. The first helicopter relief of a mainland light was carried out at Cape Wrath on 17 January 1977. In the early years of the 1980s ferryman John Muir was compelled, by reason of ill health, to curtail and eventually withdraw from operating the ferry, although he had by that time provided his own boat and engine. And Hugh Morrison's surviving minibus now required major repairs, to the extent that it could not be used.

Iris Mackay of Durness had operated minibuses in northwest Sutherland for a number of years, but always on the 'mainland.' Indeed the Mathers, Iris's family, had traded as 'Licensed Motor Hirers' since the inter-war years. When it became generally known that the Cape Wrath lighthouse minibus service was threatened with closure (perhaps terminally) Iris agreed, at short notice, to run an emergency skeleton service for the 1982 season. This service was operated for a shortened six-week season using a hired blue and white Volkswagen Transporter minibus driven by Hugh Morrison on his own Operator's licence.

Iris MacKay was granted a Traffic Commissioners' Operators licence for the Cape Wrath service on 25 February 1983. The Mackays have operated the Cape Wrath minibus service every summer from that time. It remains the oldest continuous passenger bus service in Scotland run by the originating operator. During that same year the Northern Lighthouse Board disposed of the ferry rights to the Highland Council. Ferryman John Morrison has operated the smallest scheduled public passenger ferry in the British Isles, across the Kyle of Durness, from that time.

A second VW minibus was hired for the 1983 season, and Hugh Morrison again drove the service on Iris Mackay's behalf. Ferryman John Muir and his wife Kath obtained a house in Brora on the east coast of Sutherland towards the end of 1983. Because of bad weather and the problems presented by 'flitting' across the Kyle of Durness, they did not finally leave Ferry House until February of 1984.

For 1984 the service was placed on a rather firmer footing. This marked the era of Mackay owner-operated minibuses, which remains current to the present day. A pair of ex-GPO buses were obtained, the first a Commer, resplendent in Post Office red. This venerable vehicle did sterling service for some years in inhospitable country and arduous conditions before being sold, for use on the Capeside, to the owners of Balnakeil farm. It created an unfortunate precedent by being wholly consumed by fire a few years later.

A second ex-GPO Dodge superseded the Commer. Its front suspension was modified over on the Capeside to raise the ride height so that the green strip along the centre of the single-track road did not foul the vehicle whilst it was in motion.

The Dodge was replaced by a Talbot Express minibus, which in turn gave way to a Volkswagen Transporter. This vehicle, in 1989, continued the Cape Wrath propensity for self-immolation by destroying itself whilst in service near to the summit of the road just beyond Daill brae. A committal service was held at the spot, and the unfortunate event was recorded by commemorative photographs. The promised visit of the insurance assessor is still awaited.

The next minibus to penetrate Cape Wrath established the practice of utilising Mercedes Benz diesels on the service. So reliably did this vehicle perform that the decision was taken to rely on Mercedes minibuses as far as possible in future. A succession of Mercedes 307, 308 and 410 minibuses followed, to the present day.

The nature and surface of the road across the Cape Wrath wilderness exacts a very heavy toll in wear-and-tear on all the vehicles used there. This is especially so in the case of the minibuses, each of which covers approximately five thousand miles in a season. In the early days of the service it was usual for a bus to last no more than two years in the harsh terrain and environment. Advances in vehicle technology in more recent years now lead to an expected service life of approximately six years, although regular vehicle replacement and preventative maintenance place a heavy financial pressure on the operation. It is a measure of the MacKays' commitment to Cape Wrath that the service continues.

Even now the minibuses are fitted with an extra spring leaf all round, so that ground clearance is increased and passenger comfort maintained over the rougher sections of road. All servicing is carried out on the Capeside, as are minor repairs such as spring bush replacements. Punctures and disabling mechanical failures are mercifully rare occurrences. A set of bus tyres lasts a season. The drivers of necessity need rather more than basic mechanical knowledge. The majority of the route to the lighthouse is conducted out of range of mobile telephone or VHF radio. Self-reliance is an asset, and occasionally a necessity.

The Cape Wrath Minibus Service will continue for the foreseeable future, subject to the usual constraints of wind and water and weather. However: there is, it must be said, the ever-present threat of increased military disruption during the already short operating season. The minibus trip to the lighthouse at Scotland's far north westernmost corner is unique in an age of increasing uniformity.

Cape Wrath Minibus Data

	Reg. No.	Seats
Brown/Powell Operation:		
Ford Thames Martin Walter (new 6/1964)	124 JUM	11
Ford Transit Dormobile (acqd 12/1969)	TWY 50 F	12
Bedford CF2 Dormobile (new 7/1972)	TST 68 K	12
Ford Transit Dormobile (new 4/1974)	BST 479 M	12
Hugh Morrison Operation:		
Ford Transit Dormobile (ex Manson)	CNS 364 J	12
Ford Transit Tricentrol (new 8/1976)	JJS 816 P	12
MacKay Operation:		
Volkswagen Transporter (on hire 1982)	?	12

Volkswagen Transporter (on hire 1983)	?	12
Commer (ex GPO)	?	12
Dodge (ex GPO)	?	12
Talbot Express Dormobile (new 5/1983)	HKE 981 Y	12
Volkswagen Transporter Devon (new 4/1989)	F 482 RAS	12
Mercedes Benz 207D Whittaker (ex Monro)	RSO 977 X	12
Mercedes Benz 207D Devon (ex Morris)	E 227 LSX	12
Mercedes Benz 308D Steedrive	G 66 WBE	14
Mercedes Benz 308D Devon (acqd 2/2005)	M 281 FEG	15
Mercedes Benz 410D Autobus (acqd 2/2006)	N 235 WDO	16

CHAPTER 13

WILDERNESS WILDLIFE

Land and Marine Mammals, Birds and Plants
to be Found on and Around Cape Wrath

The area is internationally renowned for the numbers and diversity of its flora and fauna. Because the vast expanse of the Parph approaching Cape Wrath is uninhabited and unsuitable for anything but low-intensity sheep farming, the land remains almost entirely undisturbed – apart from the attentions of the military.

The coastline of Cape Wrath from Geodha Ruadh na Fola over four kilometres south of the cape itself, to Durness more than eighteen kilometres to the east, has been designated as a Site of Special Scientific Interest (SSSI) under the National Parks and Access to the Countryside Act, 1949, since December 1971. It is one of the most varied and exceptional sections of coastal landscape in Scotland; it includes cliffs of Lewisian Gneiss, Torridonian Sandstone, Durness Limestone, several mobile dune systems and the extensive sandy estuary of the Kyle of Durness.

Extensive climatological data was collected at the Cape Wrath weather station from 1940. The region has a high annual rainfall, with an average of over 1150 mm per annum. The predominant wind direction is south westerly, and gales and strong winds are common, especially in the autumn and winter months. The maritime influence on temperature ensures that during the summer Cape Wrath is regularly the coldest recorded site in Britain; prolonged severe frosts are, however, rare and winter temperatures are normally above those recorded in inland areas of Scotland.

A renowned spectacular feature is the 4.8 km long precipice of Clo Mor, which towers to over nine hundred feet, the highest coastal cliffs on the British mainland. (The highest sea cliffs in the British Isles are on St. Kilda, in the Atlantic Ocean to the west, and the highest unbroken vertical sea cliffs are on the island of Foula, north eastwards towards the Shetlands.) These cliffs are formed of Torridonian sandstone, and have been weathered and eroded by the incessant Atlantic storms to form tiers of horizontal ledges colonised by breeding and roosting seabirds.

Seabirds also nest and breed on the cliffs at the very point of Cape Wrath, and the Parph is one of the very few mainland locations in Scotland colonised by the Great Skua, or 'Bonxie' – these are more usually island-nesting birds. Puffins nest and breed around Cape Wrath and they can be observed bringing fish back to their young.

Buzzards are regularly encountered, and there is a thriving population on the Cape. Eagles may also be seen. Other raptors live and breed on the Cape, and there are numbers of Red Grouse to be seen towards Cape Wrath itself. And there is a large population of the ubiquitous Hooded Crow.

Land mammals will be encountered throughout the whole of the Cape. The large numbers of red deer are usually content to watch the passing of the minibus with an almost arrogant disdain. Only when a door or window is opened are they likely to be startled and lope away with their characteristically elegant gait.

Seals, Common and Grey, appear all around the Kyle of Durness and at Cape Wrath itself. Both species bear and rear their young in the area; a visit at any time during the period May to September will almost certainly reward the visitor with sightings of seals.

Porpoise and dolphin can sometimes be observed off Cape Wrath itself, or feeding in Kearvaig Bay, for instance. Orca (Killer) whales and Minke whales may also be seen occasionally, again off the Cape itself, in season.

The Kyle of Durness provides excellent angling. Salmon, sea trout and sea bass populate the waters and otters can often be observed near to the ferry landing stages. Angling permits and ghillie-accompanied trips can be arranged locally. The ferryman also conducts evening angling trips.

LAND MAMMALS

Red Deer

The Red Deer population is thought to number into the hundreds, roaming over the thousands of acres of Cape Wrath and the Parph. The deer herds are entirely comprised of the native Scottish Red Deer; Sika and Roe Deer do inhabit tracts of land to the south but they have not, evidently, colonised the Cape. The deer population is not managed for sporting or commercial purposes, as elsewhere in Scotland, although some low-intensity culling is carried out by the local deer management group in order to maintain the vitality of the stock and to keep the numbers of breeding males at sustainable levels.

Deer have been indigenous to the area for thousands of years. Grazing by deer and, to a lesser extent, sheep is the principal reason why there are no trees on the Cape. The deer nibble voraciously at all green shoots, and saplings just cannot survive into maturity. Gales and the salt-laden air further militate against trees growing and thriving near the wild western and northern coasts.

Deer can detect humans by scent more than two miles away, and can detect movement by sight over a similar distance. Your first sight of deer on the Cape will almost certainly be history to the deer.

Deer calves are born in June. There are many small sheltered valleys on the Cape providing plentiful supplies of fresh running water and grazing, where the hinds bear their young. Calves are light tawny or dappled in colour. They stay with the mother for approximately eighteen months; last year's calves, after the birth of this year's, are known as followers. The female followers are likely to stay with the group, the males being ejected. Young maturing bucks roam together in their own group, or collect their own coterie of breeding females, or fight with an ageing stag for dominance of an existing group.

The magnificent Royal Stag is a mature male of some seniority. He can be identified by the twelve tines or points on his antlers. The Red Deer is the largest of the all the native British mammals.

The stags shed their last season's antlers in early spring and new growth starts almost immediately. The stag remains separate from the hinds all through the summer and early autumn; his main concern and preoccupation is, besides grazing continuously to build strength and condition, clearing the velvet from the new growth antlers by rubbing them on any convenient shrub, rock, peat bank or wall. Discarded or lost fishing netting is sometimes to be seen entangled in a stag's antlers, even on Cape Wrath, which is an indication of how widely the herds range.

The new antlers should be fully formed and clear of velvet by 1 August. Stag stalking starts on 1 July and extends to 20 October.

In late summer the deer begin gradually to change the colour of their coat; it turns to a deep chestnut brown with a definite tinge towards red which, coincidentally with the colour change in the bracken and heather, is a natural camouflage. Late in the season the deer can be difficult to spot. It is often only their movement which reveals their presence.

The rutting season starts in late September, with the stag collecting his harem of hinds. This is the time when bellowing stags are most likely to be heard, defending territory and warning off usurpers. It is a very distinctive sound. The rut (mating season) normally extends only to September and October.

Hinds may be culled between 21 October and 15 February.

Smaller Land Mammals

As might well be imagined from its isolated, and therefore largely undisturbed, nature the Cape is rich in animal wildlife. There is a thriving fox population, a significant and constant danger to the sheep and lambs that are walked over the Kyle of Durness for summer grazing. Foxes may be seen over the whole extent of the Cape. At least one family has been established just south of the lighthouse boundary wall for some years – vixens and cubs are often seen there – and dog foxes appear particularly prevalent between Ferry House and Achiemore.

There are also badgers, which have been seen regularly to the east of Inshore. The best time to see these secretive animals is at dusk or during the hours of darkness, although I have seen a pair in mid-afternoon near to the three-mile marker.

Otters have been seen around the river Kearvaig and its tributary burns, and Scottish wildcat are known to be established in the same area and a little to the south of the lighthouse. Be on the lookout for otters also when waiting for the ferry at either landing stage; they have been seen here regularly.

There does not seem to be a large rabbit population on the Cape; the very many predators present would appear to keep rabbit numbers to a minimum. Only around the domestic settlements at Achiemore, Daill and Kearvaig is there any evidence of small sustainable rabbit populations.

Mountain hares have been encountered between Cape Wrath and Kearvaig. This is undoubtedly the most northerly habitat in Great Britain where they may be seen.

Many smaller mammals are also present on the Cape. Rats, mice, voles, shrews and moles provide a rich and diverse feedstock for the many predators. Stoats and weasels can be seen around the lighthouse at Cape Wrath; they are often to be seen scurrying around and in the dry stone walls, or at the top of the cliff faces feeding on stolen eggs.

Marine Mammals

Cetaceans

The coast of far north west Scotland is widely recognised as one of the prime locations in the British Isles to see whales, porpoises and dolphins, collectively known as cetaceans. Cetaceans are different from fish in that they need to return to the surface to breathe. It is at that time when they are most likely to be seen, although some species do ride the bow waves of boats, etc. The high sea cliffs of the Cape provide excellent viewpoints.

Several species pass along the coast and are regularly seen around the offshore islands. The main attraction is the rich feeding on giant shoals of pelagic herring and mackerel, the reproductive and migratory cycles of which drive them inshore so as to take advantage of the plankton that lies in the warm surface layers of the North Atlantic current. Small drifting shrimp-like creatures called Copepods are especially favoured. They occur super-abundantly in late summer in the waters around the north coast. Calanus is also a direct food source for the larger plankton-eating whales which pass southwards in August and September on migration to equatorial waters.

Gulls congregating offshore are likely to indicate a shoal of mackerel or herring near the surface. This in turn could indicate the presence of feeding cetaceans. Porpoises tend to be smaller than dolphins (i.e. less than 1.8 m in length), and dolphins are smaller than whales (i.e. between 2.5 m and 4 m in length). Whales generally are longer than 5 m, although Pilot whales do not as a rule exceed 4–5 m in length.

The dorsal fin on a porpoise tends to be triangular-shaped, whilst that on a dolphin is usually sickle-shaped. Orca whales have upright dorsal fins, though many species are without dorsal fins. The fin on a Minke whale is relatively quite small and two-thirds of the way towards the tail.

The Common or Harbour porpoise is the commonest cetacean in British waters, often seen in family groups close to headlands and in sheltered inshore bays.

There is a large concentration of Bottlenose dolphin in the Moray Firth; occasionally examples are seen off Cape Wrath or in the Kyle of Durness, or in Sango Bay, Durness.

White-beaked (up to 3 m) and common dolphins (1.7 m to 2.4 m) often appear in groups, as does the White-sided dolphin (2.7 m). All are acrobatic and will at times jump clear of the water. All have distinctive white or light brown markings on their flanks. The white-beaked dolphin is sometimes known as the 'squid hound,' as it feeds primarily on squid.

Risso's dolphin is the largest (3.5 m) likely to be seen in these waters. It has a large dorsal fin and a large bulbous head, and is often heavily scarred.

Pilot whales are almost always found in compact schools, grow to 5–6 m long, have large dorsal fins and flippers, bulbous heads and are almost all black in colour.

Minke whales are certainly the commonest of all the whales seen in the summer months around the British coasts. They have a tiny dorsal fin and grow to 9 m in length.

Orca or Killer whales swim in small groups or pods, usually around four or five in number, and are quite distinctive in their colouring. They have a long upright dorsal fin and a pointed head; the body colour is black with a white belly and white patch behind the eye. They grow up to 9 m long. They hunt close inshore feeding on seals.

Species	To Be Seen
Bottlenose dolphin	occasionally
Harbour (common) porpoise	common in summer, scarce in winter
Risso's dolphin	occasionally June–October, rare near shore at other times

White beaked dolphin	occasionally May–October, rare at other times
Minke whale	rare in spring, frequent June–August, occasionally autumn
Orca or Killer whales	occasionally May-October

Seals

Common and Atlantic Grey seals can be spotted at almost any time of the year. They breed and rear their pups all around the cliffs and coves of Cape Wrath, in the sheltered bays of the Kyle of Durness and Faraid Head. They can also be seen basking on the sandbars of the Kyle at low water and on the exposed rocks at Cape Wrath as the tide recedes. They will also commonly feed or float lazily by each of the two ferry landing stages, just watching their world go by.

Common seals, as the name suggests, are the most widespread of all the pinnipeds. They are sometimes also named Harbour seals. Half the world's population of Grey seals (also known as Atlantic or Atlantic Grey seals) are to be found around the British coasts and their numbers have doubled here since 1960.

Common seal adult males (bulls) grow to between 1.4 and 1.9 m in length with a weight of up to 170 kg; females (cows) grow to a maximum of 1.7 m and up to 105 kg in weight. Colours of both males and females vary between black, brown, grey and tan, with darker patches; the pups have a noticeably paler-coloured coat. There are estimated to be half a million individuals distributed between the north Atlantic and north Pacific oceans.

Common seals are opportunistic feeders, hunting fish, molluscs and crustaceans. They make regular short dives, usually to less than 100 m. They tend to travel no more than 20 km from the shoreline. They will be seen hauling out onto rocky foreshores, sand bars and beaches; they are gregarious and will usually be found in groups. Orca (Killer) whales are their only real predator here in the north west, though pups, born in the months of July and August, can fall victim to foxes and the larger birds of prey.

Common seals are not endangered, and their habit of remaining in one location for the majority of the year inevitably leads to conflict near to, say, fish farms. It is legal, under specific licence only, to shoot any seals that come near to commercial aquaculture sites. Commercial hunting is illegal.

Grey seals are generally larger and heavier in mature adults than the common seal. Adult males grow to 2.3 m and 230 kg, females to 1.8 m and up to 155 kg. Bulls tend to be larger than cows; colour ranges from dark brown through grey to almost black, with very pronounced blotches. Females tend to be paler then males. Grey seal numbers are confined to the north Atlantic.

Grey seals are voracious fish feeders, and fish represent their principal diet, although they will also take cephalopods (squid and octopus) and crustaceans. The pups are the most readily recognised of the two species due to their almost white coat. Pups are born in October/November and have a birth weight of approximately 15 kg. They gain weight at the rate of 2 kg per day during suckling. Three weeks after birth the mothers leave the group (rookery) to mate again, and the pup gradually loses the distinctive colour. Pups of both species are born in an advanced state of development, and can crawl and swim within a few hours of birth.

Seals are protected by the Conservation of Seals Act 1970, but individuals causing damage to fisheries can be shot. Seals of either species may not be shot during their breeding seasons (Grey seals September to December inclusive and Common seals June to August inclusive).

If you find a stranded cetacean please contact the Maritime and Coastguard Agency office in Aberdeen (telephone 01224 592334) as soon as possible. If you find dead cetaceans or seals, please contact the Scottish Agricultural College Veterinary Laboratory in Inverness on 01463 243030. The laboratory collates Scottish cetacean and seal mortality information.

Bird Life

Seabirds

The far north west of Scotland enjoys a widely-acknowledged reputation as one of the finest locations in the whole of the British Isles in which to see perhaps the largest diversity of seabirds, and Cape Wrath hosts one of the major seabird breeding stations in the whole of Britain.

The rich and substantial feeding grounds which lie in close proximity to the coast and the ideal nesting environment on the cliffs form the fundamental requirements for a thriving seafowl community. Many species have been recorded breeding here. Small fish such as Sand Eels and Norway Pout, crustaceans, seaweeds and algae provide some of the vital food sources that support the predominant avian species inhabiting the far north west coastal ranges.

The sea cliff faces support a number of micro-habitats each containing its characteristic avifauna. The lowest part of the structure with its fissures, talus and caves provides the main breeding areas for Shags and Cormorants. Black Guillemots, our scarcest and least sociable indigenous Auk, are scattered in small loose colonies in suitable secluded crannies and boulder fields around this level. Sheltered ledges beneath overhangs and narrow crevices are favoured by Razorbills, which breed in large numbers.

The middle and upper zones are dominated by Kittiwakes, the most maritime of our gulls which breed abundantly on the narrowest of ledges, cementing their nests to the rock with a mixture of algae and guano. The largest Kittiwake colony on the British mainland is situated at Clo Mor. Vast numbers of the gregarious Guillemot breed on the wider ledges of this storey, laying a single pear-shaped egg that has evolved so that when nudged it does not roll off the ledge.

Clo Mor was the first site in mainland Britain to be recorded (in the 1890s) as colonised by the Fulmar. They breed on well vegetated ledges and shallow embrasures around the higher level of the cliffs.

Perhaps the most iconic bird to be found at Cape Wrath is the Puffin. There are breeding colonies all around the headland, stretching from Clo Mor in the east to the twin sea stacks of A' Chailleach (the Old Woman) and Am Bodach (the Old Man) a little to the south of Cape Wrath. Most people are familiar with the colour and markings of the Puffin, but many visitors are surprised by the small size of the birds when they first see them in the wild, a result, perhaps, of photographs not usually giving an idea of scale. Puffins normally grow to a maximum length of 32cm with a wingspan of 55cm; they nest on all the precipitous headlands and cliffs. Please be aware of the dangers in these locations if you are watching or photographing the beguiling Puffin.

Puffins nest underground in burrows. Often the best chance of seeing them in close detail is when they return to the nest with small fish for their chicks. They may also often be seen clambering over the rock or cliff face near to their burrow; a good pair of binoculars or a camera with a close focus lens will be a definite asset. Their multi-coloured triangular beak, black and white body markings and orange/red legs and feet are sure identifying characteristics; not for nothing are they sometimes called 'the clown of the sea.' Their rapid, shallow wing beat may also help with identification.

Puffins hatch and rear their young during the summer months; they tend to leave Cape Wrath in the last week in July to fly north and west into the mid-Atlantic. They spend the majority of the year at sea, and return to nest and breed at the end of April or May.

Between April and July the dense colonies of seabirds with their eggs and young are concentrated in a relatively small area, and consequently they are vulnerable to many predators. The opportunistic and powerful Black-backed Gull is an omnivorous scavenger, taking a wide variety of food including adult Puffin and the young and eggs of other seabirds. It is the largest of our gulls and breeds in the vicinity of the Puffin colonies and on the less-disturbed offshore islands.

The Lesser Black-backed Gull is less prevalent on the Clo Mor area, preferring generally more level breeding sites with short vegetation. The bird is smaller and more agile than its larger cousin and much less a scavenger, relying on food piracy and feeding at sea.

The Herring Gull is the most abundant and opportunistic of the predators on Cape Wrath and is also most catholic in its choice of both breeding sites and food.

The Cape is one of very few mainland nesting and breeding sites for the Great Skua, or 'Bonxie.' Several pairs now nest on open moorland; they harass and steal food from other avian thieves and have been known to attack sheep and humans straying too close to their nests! The smaller Arctic Skua is also seen in fewer numbers around the Cape.

A few pairs of Ravens, the largest of the corvids, breed on the coast. Smaller and more distinctively-marked Hooded Crows are quite widespread throughout the Cape, usually appearing in pairs along the Kyle of Durness and near to the road to the lighthouse.

Most species of terns (Common, Arctic, Little, Sandwich) may be seen around Durness, the Cape and the Parph, though you are most likely to see them whilst awaiting the arrival of the ferry. And there are many Oystercatchers to be seen in these same locations. The very many discarded shells on the beaches and around the ferry landings are clear evidence of their presence.

Raptors

The magnificent Golden Eagle is widespread throughout the more remote parts of north west Scotland and there are many breeding pairs in the immediate vicinity of Durness. These majestic birds are also established on the Cape; they are to be seen occasionally between the ferry landing stage and Diall and around the Kearvaig

River. Carrion, rodents and other small animals form their principal diet and they may also take small lambs and seal pups. Nest sites are usually on craggy ledges. The Golden Eagle is one of a very few birds present throughout the year.

White-tailed Sea Eagles may also be seen occasionally. A bird often mistaken for the eagle is the Buzzard, of which there are many breeding pairs widespread over the Cape.

The Peregrine Falcon, our fastest aerial predator, also breeds on the Cape. The Falcon is strictly a bird hunter and its functional design for pursuit and capture of flying quarry reaches a degree of perfection unmatched by any other raptor. From late spring Merlin, the smallest of our falcons, may also be observed in pursuit of other avian summer visitors.

Other Large Birds

Heron can be seen in some numbers in the Kyle of Durness from the ferry landing stages and at the Daill and Kearvaig rivers.

Red Grouse will often be seen in late spring or early summer. They are more commonly encountered in June and July when their chicks have hatched but not yet gained sufficient confidence to fly freely. Clutches of small chicks are sometimes encountered on the road towards Clais Charnach; drivers have to be vigilant in the early summer to avoid these small birds, which tend to prefer the road surface rather than the heather for their journeys before they have mastered the art of flight. They usually allow themselves to be carefully lifted clear of the road. There are also a few pairs of breeding pheasants.

You may also be fortunate in spotting one of the secretive Divers during the bus journey to or from the Cape. Great Northern, Red-throated and Black-throated Divers have been recorded on the small lochans visible from the road, at Inshore (Lochan nam Breac Buidhe) and nearer the Cape towards Clais Charnach.

Ptarmigan have been recorded on Fashven and Sgribhis-bheinn, the hill to the right after passing Inshore in the very centre of the Ministry of Defence Bombardment Area, overlooking the main target of Garvey Island. This is the most northerly point and the lowest altitude that this bird has been recorded in mainland Britain.

FLORA

The combination of extreme exposure, isolation and northern latitude make the Cape Wrath peninsula one of the best examples in Scotland of montane and maritime heathlands at unusually low elevations. Over one hundred and fifty plants of various species have been recorded thriving well in the rich diversity of habitat available.

In the coastal areas tall heather predominates alongside tall ferns in the more sheltered peat fissures, with heather and juniper heath occurring on the more exposed parts. Erosion surfaces up to two hundred and fifty metres back from the cliff edges support waves of dwarf heathers leading to fellfield vegetation and crowberry heath. On some of the eroded areas there are thriving stands of moss campion and purple saxifrage.

To the east of Cape Wrath, least willow occurs at one hundred and thirty-five metres, one of the lowest elevations in Great Britain for this species. At Cape Wrath itself lime-rich sand blown over the headland has created an unusually high-level small dune system with remarkably conical marram hummocks. On cliffs sheltered from the north and north west gales there is strong development of woodrush and tall fern, leading down to rose root and wild angelica ledges.

In the upland habitats around Sgribhis-bheinn there is fine development of a mixed heather/juniper/bearberry/alpine bearberry/dwarf shrub heathland. As altitude and exposure increases heather and juniper heath give way to alpine clubmoss and least willow.

Early in the season, during April and May, there is always a spectacular show of close-packed striking yellow gorse in flower alongside the road climbing Daill brae from the wooden bridge crossing the Daill River. And later in the season, in August and September, the Highland heather is in full colour over much of the moorland all the way to the lighthouse. There is usually a memorable display in the valley of the Kearvaig River.

The local colonies of sedge, orchid, thistle, gentian, rush, forget-me-not, buttercup, and campion (moss, red and sea) will all be of interest to amateur botanists. But please do be aware of the dangers of the Cape Wrath cliffs and of the special care needed if venturing into the former Ministry of Defence gunnery ranges and the current bombardment and shelling areas around the Clo Mor cliffs. Do not enter when the red flags are displayed and do not approach or touch anything which might be unexploded ordnance or parts of discarded military hardware. Observe and adhere to the military warning signs.

CHAPTER 14

CHALLENGING CAPE WRATH

The Strenuous Way West Towards Tír Na Nóg ('Land of Youth')

The very fact that Cape Wrath exists is sufficient reason to draw people there. These are three examples of the ways in which people can get to Cape Wrath under their own steam.

The Cape Wrath Fellowship

A certain breed of cyclist has long been attracted to the more inaccessible places on the British mainland, and there are fewer more inaccessible places than the Cape Wrath lighthouse if the intention is to complete the journey there on a bike. Crossing the Kyle of Durness presents similar problems to the cyclist as it does to the conventional bus passenger. Weather, wind and water level can present insuperable problems on any day and forward planning can be thrown awry by any or any combination of these. And use of the military bombardment and firing range is another limiting factor, although the public notification and advance warning procedures claimed now to be in place should make frustrations of this nature a thing of the past.

In July 1949 cycling journalist Rex Coley formed what became known shortly thereafter as the Cape Wrath Fellowship. To qualify for membership, cyclists were expected to ride from the capeside landing place all the way to the Cape Wrath lighthouse. At the time of the inauguration of the Cape Wrath Fellowship it was, of course, possible for verification of the visit to be provided by the resident light-keepers, and the visitor's book could be signed. Successful cyclists could in those early days submit an account of their expedition to Rex Coley together with any documentation and photographs supporting their claim for validation. By September 1949 certificates had been issued to seventy-five successful cyclists; certificate 1681 was issued in 1981.

Later research shows that Mr J.S. Wallis and Mr. H. Dibble cycled to Cape Wrath on August 15 1927, twenty-two years before the formal implementation of the Cape Wrath Fellowship.

The Cape Wrath Fellowship rather declined after Rex Coley retired. Record-keeping was taken up and maintained *by Cycling Weekly* magazine journalist Peter Knottley, who in turn retired in 1992, and the Cape Wrath Fellowship again approached terminal decline.

But eventually the Cyclists' Touring Club came to the rescue and took on the scheme's record-keeping and administration. The name was changed under the CTC's aegis to the 'Cape Wrath Challenge.' A certificate and badge are available to all successful participants. Verification data relies nowadays principally on photographs taken of grinning cyclists with the lighthouse tower in the background, the permanent light-keepers having departed in 1998. With a change of administrator within the Cyclists' Touring Club, the name has now reverted to 'The Cape Wrath Fellowship.' This not only avoids any possible confusion arising from the similarly-named annual running event but also emphasises the exclusivity of the original concept developed by Rex Coley.

In 1980 Holdsworthy Ltd, manufacturers of Claud Butler cycles, launched a revolutionary new machine under the name 'Cape Wrath.' It was claimed to be the best touring bicycle ever built. And where better to launch the new concept than Cape Wrath itself? This was not to be a simple photo opportunity and back into the Winnebago. Holdsworthy arranged a three-day tour of north west Sutherland for seven cycling journalists and four company representatives, covering two days and one night on the Cape. Bicycles and riders were ferried across the Kyle. The party then headed for the lighthouse and returned to Kearvaig Bay by a most unconventional route. The party camped at Kearvaig and returned to the ferry the following day. Altogether an unusual product launch, which attracted considerable coverage in the cycling press.

Planning by the cyclist visitor is essential, and probably more necessary in view of the longer period of time the cycle-borne visitor is likely to spend 'capeside.' It is essential that a food supply is carried. Flowing groundwater on the whole of the Cape Wrath peninsula is potable if slightly peaty. There are numerous streams and burns from which it is safe to drink. Do not drink from standing water; it will be brackish and could be injurious to health. There is no fresh water supply at the lighthouse. There is some shelter provided by lighthouse buildings. There is the possibility of the proposed café and interpretation point within the former compressor buildings being in operation. Cycle maintenance tools should, of course, be carried, for this is an extremely isolated wilderness. There is no mobile telephone reception with seven miles of the lighthouse.

Should a real problem develop it may be possible to beg a lift back on the minibus, and on occasions bicycles have been carried back to the ferry by this means. On the one emergency occasion in recent years when it was necessary to transport a tandem back to the ferry, the machine had to be largely dismantled.

The Cape Wrath Challenges

What is now a well-known and well-supported highlight in the annual running calendar came about by happy accident. In 2000 the Island Race, a round-Britain relay event covering 4,200 miles spread over 100 days came to Durness for stage 93. An ultra-marathon of 27 miles from Durness to the Cape Wrath lighthouse and return, involving a ferry crossing on the outwards and return legs, was organised.

It was immediately recognised that this really ought to be developed into a week of running events amongst spectacular mountains, clear air, deserted beaches and little road traffic. The idea of the Cape Wrath Challenges was born.

The inaugural Cape Wrath Challenges week took place in May 2002; it set the scene for an event which has now become a keenly-anticipated annual event in the running calendar. There are organised runs around Loch Eriboll, beach runs at Balnakeil, mountain events on the lower slopes of Beinn Ceannabeinne, and a run along the spectacular valley from Gualin between the peaks of Farrmheall and Cranstackie by the side of the Kyle of Durness back to base. There is also a wide range of daytime and evening social events.

The culmination of the week's running events is the Cape Wrath Challenge proper, held on the Saturday prior to the evening feasting, music and dancing and awards ceremony. The Challenge Marathon or Ultra Marathon is open to single runners, and two or five member relay teams. Every successful competitor receives a certificate recording their time.

The event increases in popularity every year. Up to two hundred runners of varying levels of expertise enter from Britain, Europe and internationally. The third week in May is the week of the Cape Wrath Challenges, when the days are long, the weather kind to the runners, and the midges yet to be a serious inconvenience!

The Cape Wrath Trail

What is arguably the most arduous long distance trek in the United Kingdom starts in an unprepossessing manner in Fort William, by skirting a supermarket and a large housing scheme before following the line of the Great Glen via the towpath of the Caledonian Canal. The published route then crosses some of Scotland's wildest wilderness areas before emerging, 194 miles/323 kilometres later, at Cape Wrath lighthouse.

At Blairmore, north of Kinlochbervie on the B.801, there is a small car park with public toilet well patronised by less serious walkers intent on a stroll to Sandwood Bay and back. This makes an exceedingly pleasant day in the wilds along a well defined track and footpath, the goal being a visit to one of Scotland's most stunning beaches. The fact that it is well publicised, and consequently busy in the summer months, can often detract from its singular beauty.

The final stretch of the entire Trail, from Sandwood Bay northwards is very exposed, encompassing river crossings which can be impassable when in spate, no habitation or shelter and certainly no track or footpath. Sheep and deer tracks can tend to lead the unwary astray. A large scale Ordnance Survey map is essential, as is a compass and the ability to use it properly when visibility is not clear. Foul weather clothing and adequate food supplies are also vital.

There is no official or optimum route. Choose your own having regard to the time of year, the weather forecast (sometimes little more than a recorded message in these parts) and your own abilities. A route closely following the coast will reward with spectacular scenery – cliffs, sea stacks and the possibility of dolphin and whale sightings – but the downsides are unavoidable descents and scrambles in gorges becoming steeper as they reach the coast. A route further inland to the east will ascend to over 200 metres, with views to Lewis and the Western Isles, Orkney and the headlands along the north coast towards Dunnet Head.

A wise precaution before embarking on the last stage of the Cape Wrath Trail would be to advise both the minibus operator (Iris MacKay 01971 511343) and the ferryman (John Morrison 01971 511376) of your estimated arrival time. Although adverse weather, tides and use of the military range can affect the minibus and ferry service, every effort will be made to accommodate your arrival with transport back to the 'mainland.' The bus and ferry service operate between May and September inclusive.

The published guidebook to the whole of the Cape Wrath Trail is by Denis Brook and Phil Hinchliffe under the title *North to the Cape* (ISBN 1 85284 285 1) and published by Cicerone, Cumbria.

For those preferring to make the final stage of the trek southwards from Cape Wrath (and thus eliminating transport uncertainties in accessing the lighthouse) the recommended publication is another Cicerone Guide: *Backpacker's Britain: Volume 3 Northern Scotland* (ISBN 1 85284 458 2) by Graham Uney.

ACKNOWLEDGEMENTS

The text of this effort is mine; I accept responsibility for any errors, misinterpretations or textual inaccuracies. The reader might consider that I tend towards verbosity, sesquipedalian expansionism or an excess of zeal over proficiency (or, indeed, all three). I can only apologise for the occasionally obvious excess of enthusiasm – Cape Wrath does that to some people.

Whilst the effort is mine and I take responsibility for it, it would not have been possible without the support and encouragement of a host of individuals possessing greater knowledge than I; all were free with their advice, expertise and suggestions. Without them the work would not have emerged in the comprehensive format that it has.

The kernel of the idea for the book germinated from happy chance, or Sutherland serendipity. I had the great good fortune, purely by chance and without planning or prior intention, to fall into a Bank Holiday driving job on the Cape Wrath road when there was a dearth of available drivers in the height of the tourist season. I did it for ten days or so, and became addicted to the uniqueness of the place and the vast diversity of the visitors; all human life is there, for an hour or two. Not quite the expected career move for a contentedly retired constitutional lawyer. And seven years later I still drive to the lighthouse at Cape Wrath around three hundred times a season. Excitements on the Lighthouse road, indeed.

Not a great deal has been written about Cape Wrath as an individual subject. There are varied descriptions of its unique geology, and wildlife, and geographical location, and its military and defence connections, and of course of the lighthouse at the very north-western-most tip of the British mainland. But all these diverse references seemed to me to be brief and somewhat superficial in nature, out of context and missing to a large extent the real attraction and stark epic grandeur of 'The Capeside Experience.'

I intended initially to set out a brief booklet answering all the usual questions from visitors generated by the open ferry-boat voyage across the Kyle of Durness and the twenty-two-mile round trip along an unmade single track – er, track – built in the 1820s for horse-drawn transport, the chief advantage of which nowadays would appear to be its unerring ability to sort out the digestive problems of any enfeebled passenger. Rapidly it became apparent that there was a real wealth of data available, which needed recording and codifying within the covers of one single publication. And the more I looked, the more I found.

Documentation concerning the Stevenson family of Lighthouse Engineers, their long and close association with the Northern Lighthouse Board, the Board's planning for and completion of the Cape Wrath Lighthouse and its history over past centuries is dispersed to record archives around Scotland. My initial approaches to these various bodies produced immediate and genuine offers of help in the project.

My first (and perhaps most obvious) avenue of approach was to the Northern Lighthouse Board. My initial letter of enquiry produced a courteous reply and a wealth of data, including suggestions for further avenues of research. The Board's Information Officer, Lorna Hunter, proved an efficient and ever-helpful contact; she willingly cast her experienced eye over my draft typescripts of those chapters having some relevance to the early years of the NLB and its dealings with the lighthouse at Cape Wrath. Indeed Lorna offered to read through the drafts even before I summoned up the courage to make that very suggestion. There must be ESP at the NLB.

Other NLB personnel to whom I owe debts of gratitude in varying degrees are Ali Rae, Jim Hunter, Colin Dingwall, Charles Laidlaw,

Fraser Byers and Jim Henderson. Special mention must also be made of Thomas M.P. (Tam) Cairns B.Sc., I.Eng., M.I.I.E., Area Maintenance Engineer (North), who is directly responsible for the lighthouse and whom I have been privileged to meet and talk with at length on his regular visits to the far north west. Charles Laidlaw and Tam Cairns each provided a great fund of technical data and historical detail on the work of the Northern Lighthouse Board in general and the Cape Wrath light in particular. In another context another commentator saluted 'you, and your indefatigability.' I can offer no greater nor more genuinely-held praise.

Former keepers and other residents of Cape Wrath provided many fascinating insights and reminiscences of their experiences. Their enthusiasm to place on record their memories so many years after leaving the far north west outpost attests to the uniqueness of life on the Cape, now sadly disappeared and consigned to history. Lord MacKenzie of Culkein generously agreed to cast an eye over the almost completed typescript and suggested many valid correction and improvements obvious to a career lighthouse keeper, in addition to providing elucidation on some of the more technical aspects.

Northern Lighthouse Board archives recording its formative and early years have been transferred to the National Archives of Scotland for proper safe-keeping. Staff there from whom I received a sympathetic hearing were Tessa Spencer, Patrick Watt, Amanda Noble, Leanne Swallow, Ruth Jones and Neil Miller. All were ready with advice or assistance and all produced at one time or another copies of various original documents vital to the story of the Cape Wrath lighthouse and the keepers stationed there between 1842 and 1921. The staff of the British National Archives at Kew similarly provided valued support.

Stevenson correspondence and reports relative to Robert Stevenson's close association with the lobbying for and the design, specification and erection of the Cape Wrath lighthouse are lodged in the Manuscripts Division of the National Library of Scotland.

Senior Curator Sheila MacKenzie readily extracted relevant Cape Wrath documents and arranged for copies to be supplied to me.

The original Stevenson plans, drawings and sections for the Cape Wrath lighthouse, and documents detailing later developments of equipment at the light, are held by the Royal Commission on the Ancient and Historical Monuments of Scotland. Veronica Fraser and Iain Fraser each provided ready assistance in reply to my enquiries.

Stephen Freeth, Keeper of Manuscripts at the Guildhall Library of the Corporation of the City of London identified the very early records of the Lloyd's of London Signal Stations and proved of great assistance in my teasing out the history of the once imposing hilltop structure overlooking the Cape Wrath headland.

The records of the Museum of Scottish Lighthouses at Kinnaird Head, Fraserburgh (the Museum is housed in the very first lighthouse built by the Commissioners for Northern Lights in December 1787) produced the Station Register recording the details of keepers at the Cape Wrath lighthouse from 1919 to its automation in March 1998. I am grateful for the help provided by Jimmy Oliver (Assistant Keeper at Cape Wrath 1996 to 1998) in this regard.

Mike Budd of the National Motor Museum, Beaulieu assisted with the identification of several motor vehicles shown in illustrations used within the narrative, and Mark Waters of the Cyclists' Touring Club contributed significantly to the chapter describing the Cape Wrath Challenges. Andy Chisholm, Caithness born and now retired to the south coast, is a retired telephone engineer (he worked in Durness from 1957 to 1960) who contributed the technical data concerning wartime telecommunications technology.

I count myself as fortunate indeed in being supported in my quest for the esoteric facts of a bygone age by Alex du Toit, Assistant Archivist at the Highland Council Archives in Inverness. Alex extracted from the Council and committee records of a local authority consigned to history over thirty years ago more data than I could have hoped to manage on a first visit, and all this without the aid of epitomised or indexed minutes. Praise be to the unsung but dedicated local expert. I also record my gratitude for the assistance rendered by Edwina Burridge, Fiona MacLeod and Alison Brown at the Inverness Archives. Nicki Blackburn and Shirley MacLean of Brora Library and Gail Inglis of the North Highland Archive in Wick, Caithness also assisted with valuable data and documents.

At the very start of my researches I was very fortunate to meet Yvette Brown, who was instrumental in setting up the first licensed minibus service to the Cape Wrath lighthouse in the 1960s. Yvette loaned some early photographs and provided some vital early contacts. As a direct result of my discussions with Yvette I was put in touch with Derek Hulme; Derek organised walking tours in northern Scotland under the Highland Safaris banner and was probably the first regular customer of the newly-instigated Cape Wrath minibus service. His meticulous record-keeping and undeniable photographic skills made the task of sorting out the early days of the service so much more pleasurable.

I was also fortunate in meeting Kath Muir, who lived at Ferry House with her husband John when he was ferryman in the 1970s and 1980s. Kath loaned some photographs, and further contributed reminiscences which helped to colour the detail of the early years of the joint ferry and minibus service from her personal knowledge and memories.

Malcolm Bangor-Jones is a published researcher and author well-versed in Highland matters in general, and those of the Reay and Sutherland estates in particular. He generously guided me in the direction of contemporary newspaper and other texts containing relevant Cape Wrath references, and I am grateful to him for his enthusiasm and interest in my project and for his capacity to respond with such immediacy.

One of the joys of operating the Cape Wrath minibus service is that every day is different and every day brings the guarantee of different people with different stories. Two such occurred in the summer of 2005, firstly when one of the minibus passengers appeared more interested than usual in the buses and in the practicalities of the service. Geoff Lumb eventually provided copies of the photographs reproduced within this book showing the Northern Lighthouse Commissioners' Commer and Morris-Commercial vehicles in use on the Cape during the middle years of the twentieth century. To him I owe a debt of gratitude; without his visit and his interest these illustrations just would not have been available for inclusion here.

The second occasion was the appearance of Mr. and Mrs. H.C. Davidson. Mr Davidson served as assistant keeper at Cape Wrath between 1957 and 1959, and throughout that time lived there with his family in the domestic accommodation provided by the Northern Lighthouse Board. The Davidsons provided splendid period photographs of ordinary life at Cape Wrath, including some capturing the more mundane tasks required to be carried out by resident light keepers. Painting operations, involving swinging in a not too secure-looking cradle around the light tower or straddling the fog horn directly over a two hundred and seventy-foot drop into the north Atlantic, were exertions then expected of resident lighthouse staff in the course of their everyday duties, but which nowadays would provoke cardiac arrest in any half-competent Health and Safety Officer.

During the 2006 season, Richard Mellor travelled as a passenger to the lighthouse. Whilst awaiting the arrival of the ferry for the return crossing, Richard mentioned his interest in small independent bus operations. The result of our subsequent correspondence was a very much clearer picture of the early Capeside bus operators and the vehicles they employed in this most remote of locations. I am indebted to him for much corroborative data included in the chapter describing the history of the Cape Wrath minibus service.

All of the many Durness residents I have met have invariably been welcoming, and willing to answer what sometimes might have appeared to be strange, esoteric questions. Donald Mitchell, the Highland Regional Council's local Countryside Ranger, allowed himself to be inveigled into acting as overseer and fact-checker for the chapter detailing the Cape's wilderness wildlife. I am privileged to be a member of that select band of happy individuals able to acknowledge having been assisted by the Lone Ranger.

Hugh Powell readily provided a fund of detail concerning the early days of the Cape Wrath Minibus service and of life on Cape Wrath in earlier days. And no publication in any way relevant to Durness and its parish can hope to consider itself complete without recourse to Ronnie Lansley; his encyclopaedic local knowledge allied to an impressive, almost demonic, skill with camera and computer, made my efforts so much more rewarding.

The contribution of John Carbreck the ferryman has already been touched upon in the main body of the narrative. His occasional gruff exterior masks a lifetime's local knowledge with a sardonic sense of humour. There can be no more stimulating start to the day during the tourist season. It really is beyond enjoyable knowing that the day will begin with a laugh, and that the laugh will doubtless continue, by VHF radio, throughout the day, within the hearing of a bus full of passengers. Carbreck combines a certain celebrity on the local panto circuit with piano-accordion virtuosity. But what is an accordion? Just a concertina with attitude and braces.

Kevin Crowe of Balnakeil Press was the first publisher I approached with a view to publication. That he was at the time considering starting his own small publishing house with an emphasis on local subjects was a happy accident indeed. Kevin provided sustained encouragement, valuable advice and suggestions for improvements to my raw initial manuscript at the very time they were most needed. Aspiring authors really have no right to expect such good fortune.

Tony Dean introduced me to the Capeside experience and the uniquely challenging road; Donnie MacDougall kept me on it during those first two exciting weeks. John Ure was always on hand to help with the occasional brief calamity – he is indeed Cape Wrath's own Fourth Emergency Service.

It really is a very great and continuing pleasure for me to meet and be greeted by all of the friends I have made in Durness.

But my sincerest gratitude must be extended to Iris, Donnie and Yvonne Mackay. I am privileged to count them all as close friends. No longer do I feel a stranger in a strange land. That is the measure of the welcoming nature of this gentle, genuine, generous community in the far north west, Duracell clones excepted.

Finally, I do not expect that this effort will be either definitive or exhaustive. But I do hope that some readers might be prompted to contact me should I have made incorrect assumptions or misleading interpretations; please do correct me if my explanation of research material is demonstrably inaccurate. And I am always interested in old photographs, documents or reminiscences bearing any relevance to Cape Wrath.

I am continually uplifted by my successive visits to the spectacular north-western-most tip of the British mainland, and the fascination is ever-present. I am privileged that my life has brought me here. It would be a tragedy of immense proportions if the majority of the Parph became a military playground with access limited at the whim of the drab serge heroes. Polite they may be, but with that closed blankness that soldiers often assume when talking to suspicious civilians they are not allowed to kill. Cape Wrath deserves better, and every visitor with an interest in Britain's wilderness places deserves to be able to participate in the 'Capeside experience' without let, or hindrance, or restriction. The close involvement now of the Durness Development Group will surely protect the area for the enjoyment of everyone. The Group deserves your support and I commend it to you.

Cape Wrath is a special place; long may it remain especially so.

APPENDICES

I – 31 March 1802
Observations by Robert Stevenson concerning the establishment of a Light-House upon Cape Wrath addressed to John Tait, Esq, Writer to the Signet (W.S.)

II – 1802
Memorial by John Tait, W.S., relative to the erection of a Light-House at Cape Wrath

III – 16 July 1802
Letter from Robert Stevenson to John Tait, W.S.

IV – 1802
Direction by Subscribers to the Light House Petition to John Tait, W.S.

V – 21 November 1805
Letter from Lord Reay to the Honourable the Commissioners for Northern Lights

VI – 12 May 1826
Specification of a Light House to be Erected upon Cape Wrath

VII – July 1826
Memorandum by Robert Stevenson for Mr. Slight on Cape Wrath Survey

VIII – 11 July 1828
Specification of the Stone and Lime walls to Inclose a Piece of Ground for a Small Park at Cape Wrath Lighthouse

IX – 1828
Specification of the Boundary Wall of the Lighthouse Ground at Cape Wrath as proposed to be built in Rubble stone or Feal or Turf

X – 26 February 1828
Specification by Robert Stevenson for a Road to be made from the Lighthouse Store on the Kyle of Durness

XI – March 1828
Sketches, Estimate of Costs and Specification of Bridges on the Cape Wrath Road

XII – 20 March 1828
Letter from Alexander Gibb to Robert Stevenson concerning the Bridges on the Cape Wrath Road

XIII – March 1828
Contract for the Erection of the Cape Wrath Lighthouse

XIV – 10 November 1828
Notice to Mariners – Inauguration of the Light-house at Cape Wrath

XV – 1791 – 1799
First Statistical Account of Scotland: Cape Wrath references

XVI – September 1834
New Statistical Account of Scotland: Cape Wrath references

XVII – 13 August 1906
Letter from Northern Lighthouse Board to Board of Trade, London; Special repairs to Cape Wrath Lighthouse

XVIII – 24 November 1919
Arrangements for Maintenance of the Ferry to Cape Wrath Lighthouse and War Signal Station

XIX – 5 December 1947
Analysis of Claim for Grant to Repair Cape Wrath Road; Wartime Damage.

XX – 1 September 2005
Width and Weight restrictions applied to the U.70 Cape Wrath Lighthouse Road

APPENDIX I

Observation concerning the establishment of a Light-house upon Cape Wrath addressed to John Tait, Esqr, Writer to the Signet.

Cape Wrath situated upon the north coast of Scotland in West Long. 5 degrees 30 minutes and North Lat. 59 degrees is one of the most noted Headlands in Great Britain – whether it is considered in regard to the boisterous seas which wash its shores – the rapid currents which set round it – or the Rocks which lie scattered about it – or viewed as a great Turning-point in the course of a large proportion of the vessels which navigate the North-seas – it will be found strongly characterised as a proper situation for a Light-house.

The coast between Cape Wrath and the Orkney Islands, a distance about eighteen leagues, lies perfectly exposed to the swell of the Atlantic Ocean, causing at all times a very heavy sea upon it, and rendering the passage round the Cape with <u>contrary winds</u> extremely tedious and <u>practicable only in very moderate weather</u> – nor is there upon this tract of coast a single place of safety for a vessel except Loch Eribol suitable for ships easterly bound, which makes this passage be the more keenly contested as in the event of bearing-away Orkney is the nearest place of shelter, in such cases the Mariner would feel much convenience and protection from a Light-house upon Cape Wrath – and likewise in making the land from the sea in long voyages – he would also be at all times to judge of his situation in regards to those Rocks near the Cape, and that <u>Sunk Rock lately discovered about four leagues North-by-West from it</u> and with such a Light in view a vessel could be laid-to in safety during the longest Winter night – nor would there be any danger of vessels being put ashore by the Flood tide, setting upon their broadside when upon their Larboard-tack, beating round the Cape, under night to Westward, the cause of many of the wrecks which happen about Cape Wrath.

The experience of a few years have served to show that accurate Charts with an increase of Land-marks are to the coasts of a country what the opening of Roads, and similar improvements are to Inland parts – accordingly we find that previous to the Marine survey of Orkney and the Highlands by the late Murdoch McKinnie undertaken by Order of the Lords Commissioners of Admiralty and until Commissioners were appointed by Act of Parliament to erect Light-houses upon the Northern Parts of Great Britain – Mariners were left to grope their way round these shores without any assistance and instead of a more direct course they generally kept north of the Orkney, and even the Shetland Islands, then steering west they stood without the Lewis Isles into the Atlantic, exposed to many dangers and unable to avail themselves of the advantages of the Sounds and Harbours in the Highlands – hence the difficulties of the navigation of this part of the coast and a great bar in the way of that flourishing trade carried on through these Sounds from Liverpool etc to the Northern Continent of Europe – it was also a great drawback to the improvement of the Highlands, and to the extension of the British-fisheries.

In addition to the work about to be executed on the Start-Point of Sanda in Orkney, by Order of the Commissioners for Northern Lights, two things seem chiefly to be wanting to complete the navigation of the Highlands and Islands, Viz, a Light-house upon Cape Wrath, and one upon, or near the Island of Tiree, which together with a few Buoys and Beacons for Sunk Rocks and the entrance of some of the principal Lochs and Harbours, seem to be all that is wanting to render the Navigation as secure upon this as any tract of coast about the Kingdom. And perhaps to obtain any, or all of these, it may only be necessary for the Mercantile Interest to apply to the Commissioners, under whose auspices six Light-houses have already been erected, and are maintained much to the safety and accommodation of seafaring people.

Robert Stevenson
Edinburgh
31 March 1802

APPENDIX II

Memorial relative to the Erection of a Light House at Cape Wrath

Cape Wrath, situated upon the North west point of Sutherland, is one of the most noted Headlands in Great Britain – And whether it is considered in regard to the boisterous seas which wash its shores-the rapid currents which set round it – or the Rocks which lye scattered about it - or whether it is viewed as a great turning point in the course of a large proportion of the vessels which navigate the North Seas – It will be found strongly characterised as a proper situation for a Light House.

The Coast between Cape Wrath and the Orkney Island (a distance of about Eighteen Leagues) lies perfectly exposed to the swell of the Atlantic Ocean, causing at all times a very heavy sea upon it, and rendering the passage round the Cape, with contrary winds, extremely tedious – Nor is there upon this tract of coast a single place of safety for a vessel, except Loch Erriboll, which is suitable for ships easterly bound – And if they miss Loch Erribol (sic) they are obliged to bear away for Orkney as the nearest place of safety – It is evident that the delay in turning the Cape is greatly increased by the want of a Light house – for with the assistance of a Light house , the Mariner would be enabled to judge of his situation with respect to Land and Rocks, and he might lye-to, during the longest winter night, in perfect safety. – Nor would there be any danger of vessels being put ashore by the flood tide setting upon their broadside when beating round the Cape under night to the westward, the evident cause of many shipwrecks – From such a Light house too the Master of a vessel missing Loch Erriboll would find much assistance in steering his course to Orkney – and Mariners making the land from long voyages would find evident advantage and protection from such a Light house.

The delay and danger in passing Cape Wrath has of late greatly increased by the discovery of a sunk rock, which lies off the Cape about 4 leagues, in a North and by west direction from it – Upon which it is believed many vessels have been totally wrecked, and mariners are now so apprehensive of danger from this rock, that in place of keeping at agreed distance from the Cape in the Night time, as formerly, they now steer as near to it as possible, so as to avoid what they consider to be a still greater danger – In this way they have to encounter much stronger tides, close upon shore, and being thereby drove from their expected course, without a light to guide them, they are dashed upon the Rocks and undone!

To mention every instance of delay and loss which has occurred would swell this paper to a great length indeed! – the delays are obvious and many of the losses are well known, But there is reason to believe that the losses are to a greater extent than is generally known, Because vessels have frequently been seen labouring off the Cape in the Evening, but which before morning have totally disappeared; Hence it must be concluded that many vessels, supposed to have foundered at sea, have been lost in the neighbourhood of Cape Wrath.

As a specimen of the Losses, the history of a single night only shall be given – Upon eighteenth October 1797 the DAEDALUS of London, with a valuable cargo of Tallow, Flax and Iron, from the Baltic to Chester, was totally lost and only two men saved – the SHEPPERDESS of Liverpool, with a similar cargo, from the Baltic to Bristol, was, at the same time, dashed to pieces and all hands drowned - And the NEPTUNE of Banff with a cargo of meal for Fort William was lost also and all perished! – The two men who survived from the wreck of the Daedalus were examined by the Admiral Substitute, and declared that on the day prior to the loss, when on their passage betwixt Orkney and the Cape, they heard the Mate of the Daedalus observe to the Master that he feared they were steering a course too low or westerly to clear the Cape with ease, and that the Master replied that his reason for shaping so westerly a course was in order to avoid some sunk rocks said to lie off at sea from the Cape, and he supposed the vessels astern, meaning the Shepperdess and Neptune, were steering equally low for the same reason – Hence it is evident that these three shipwrecks were occasioned by the apprehension of danger from the rock lately discovered, and by the want of a Lighthouse at Cape Wrath – And many, many, other wrecks might be mentioned – all which a Light house at Cape Wrath would most certainly have prevented.

It is hoped that the Preservation of Lives and Property, and the general Interests of Trade and Commerce, will induce the Honourable Commissioners for Northern Lights, to direct that a light house be immediately erected at this most necessary point of Cape Wrath.

Jo. Tait, W.S.
1802

APPENDIX III

Sir,

I inclose your Memorial regarding Cape Wrath.

I am greatly obliged by your affording me a reading of it - it appears to me to be perfectly correct.

I am

Sir,

Your most hale servant,

Robert Stevenson
No. 1 Blair Street
16 July 1880

John Tait Esqr.

APPENDIX IV

Direction by Subscribers to the Lighthouse Petition, 1802

We the Subscribers, being materially interested in the Navigation of the North seas, and in promoting such measures as may render that navigation safe and expeditious, and having considered a Memorial relative to the erection of a Light house at Cape Wrath

We, cordially Approve that measure, as tending most essentially to the benefit of the Navigation and Commerce of the Country,

And We Direct an application, by petition, or otherwise, to be made in our names, to the Honourable the Commissioners for the Northern lights, to attain this important object –

And We Authorise Mr. John Tait WS, Edinburgh to prepare, sign and present that Petition, and to take such other steps as may be necessary, he from time to time acquainting the Committee named by us of the Procedure had.

We the within Subscribers appoint the following persons as a Committee with whom Mr Tait is to correspond, viz

For London .. ..

For Bristol .. ..

For Liverpool .. ..

APPENDIX V

Letter from Lord Reay to the Honourable the Commissioners for Northern Lights.

Edinburgh, 21 November 1805

Gentlemen,

I have been for some time in the County of Sutherland and have paid a good deal of attention to several matters connected with that part of the County where my property lies.

According to my information many shipwrecks have happened, and trade has been considerably impeded by the want of a Light house at Cape Wrath, situated near the entrance of the Pentland Firth from the Atlantic, where the strength of the Currents upon a bold coast, and the dread arising from a sunk rock lately discovered, render an establishment of that kind peculiarly desirable.

I therefore beg leave to submit the matter to your consideration and have no doubt that if you shall be pleased to direct the necessary inquiries to be made you will be satisfied of the extent of the dangers to which I refer, and of the advantages trade would derive from the establishment proposed.

I have the honour to be,
Gentlemen
Your most obedient (indistinct, illegible)

(signed)   Reay

APPENDIX VI

Specification of a Lighthouse to be Erected upon Cape Wrath

The site of the Lighthouse and Buildings to be herein after specified is on the promontory forming the north-western point of Sutherlandshire, known to Mariners by the name of Cape Wrath; but the precise spot will be marked out upon the ground by the Engineer, or the Clerk of Works, for the Direction of the Contractor, previously to the commencement of the building operations.

Preliminary Works

Harbour and Road

From the present want of Harbours and Road at or near Cape Wrath, for building, and conveying building materials to the site of the proposed Lighthouse, the following Preliminary operations are to be immediately executed and undertaken by the Contractor, viz: The small creek, known by the name of Clais Cairnach is to be deepened and improved by the removal of the boulder stones, and blasting, or otherwise excavating the rock in a manner, and to an extent, calculated to afford shelter and passage for boats drawing not less than 2 feet water to float landward to low-water mark of Spring-tides. These, together with works of dry stone Masonry, are to be employed to an extent sufficient to form a permanent Landing-slip, from low-water to high-water of Spring-tides; the length of which, between these points, shall not be less than 15 yards, nor the slope more than at the rate of one perpendicular to four horizontal: the surface of the Slip being two feet above the level of Spring-tides, measured at the line of high-water as ascertained on the present beach; and upon the whole executed in a manner calculated to give the greatest possible facility to the landing of materials for the immediate works and ultimate use of the Lighthouse.

From the Landing-slip above described, to the site of the Lighthouse, a cart Road is to be formed and made in a line of direction, which, in the manner alluded to shall be pointed out upon the ground extending in length to two statute miles, or thereby. This Road is to be formed 14 feet in width, metalled, or laid, with broken stones from rock or gravel of approved quality, to the width of 10 feet and of 6 inches in depth, provided with proper side and cross drains at all points where such may be found requisite for keeping the Road in a dry and workable state. The line of draught is to be made as easy as the natural difficulties of the ground will admit; but, nevertheless, so as nowhere to be of greater acclivity than at the rate of one perpendicular to 10 horizontal. When this Boat-harbour and Road, herein before described, shall have been executed and completed to the satisfaction of the Engineer the Contractor will be entitled to receive the sum of £952.12s.0d as the full price and remuneration of said work. It is further provided, that the said Boat-harbour and Road shall be kept in good order and repair by the Contractor for his own use, and be delivered by him in good order and condition at the conclusion of his contract-works, agreeably to a certificate in writing under the hand of the Engineer; and that under a penalty in case of failure of One Hundred pounds Sterling to be deducted from the contract-price of the Lighthouse-works hereinafter described.

Storehouses

Further, as preliminary operations, two Storehouses are to be erected and completed; the one at Clais Cairnach, and the other at the Kyle of Durness, agreeably to the accompanying Plans and Sections. The sites of these Storehouses are respectively to be pointed out by the Engineer, or Clerk of Works; their dimensions over walls being each 26 feet in length by 18 feet in width, and 9 feet in height, from the sole of the door to the top levelling of the walls which are to be not less than 2 feet in thickness, founded on rock and built entirely of the best rubble masonry, laid flush in good Lime-mortar, prepared agreeably to the Schedule of directions for the other works. In each Storehouse a door is to be formed, measuring 7 feet in height by 3 feet 9 inches in width, with two windows, each 4 feet in height, and 2 feet 6 inches in width.

There is also to be a chimney or fire-place of 3 feet in width by 3 feet in height, placed agreeably to the Plan, with a circular or oval flue carried from the chimney to the height of 7 feet above the levelling of the walls.

The fire-place and chimney-top, together with the door, windows, and outward angles of the House, are to be formed with pick-dressed scantions and corners. The roofing is to consist of the best memel timber, rising in the pitch to the height of 6 feet above the level of the walls. Rafters to be 7 inches in breadth by 2 and a half inches in thickness , placed at not more than 14 inches apart, to be properly knit at the top, and connected at the foot with a collar joist of 7 inches by 2 and a half inches, dovetailed into the rafter, at 12 inches above the toe. The Sarking to be of 7/8th inch boards, and the roof covered with the best Easdale Slates, laid with sufficient cover, and well shouldered with good Lime mortar. The four corner panes, the ridge and gutter, and flanks of the chimney-stalks to be finished with Sheet lead, weighing 8lbs per square foot, and of sufficient breadth to form a cover over the slating of not less than 5 inches; the panes and ridge being previously formed with a hatter of 2 inches in thickness, and standing not less than 3 inches above the slating.

The doors are to be in every respect similar to the outside doors hereafter described for the Lighthouse, and the windows are to be filled with a 7/8th inch deal shutter, fitted into a frame built into the opening for the windows, and closing from the inside with a cross-bar and staples: the whole to form a good and secure fastening.

The foundations of the walls are to be carried to the depth of two feet under the level of the door-step, but if more or less building than this be requisite, any difference in the quantity of masonry will form a deduction, or addition, as the case may be, to or from the Estimated price. These two Storehouses are to be completed in the course of the summer of 1827; and when so completed, in a proper and workmanlike manner, and agreeably to this Specification, a Certificate under the hand of the Engineer shall be given to the Contractor, who is to receive the sum of £333.12s.6d, as the full and complete price of the Storehouse works.

Lighthouse Works

From the exposed situation of the coast of Sutherland and of Cape Wrath in particular, the whole of the works of their several kinds, herein now Specified and herein-after to be described, are required to be executed of the very best materials, and of the most substantial style of workmanship, described and set forth in this Specification, and agreeably to the accompanying Plans.

General Dimensions

The general dimensions of the Lighthouse Buildings may be stated as follows: the Lighthouse tower is to be 43 feet 7 inches in height from the level of the bottom of the basement course to the upper surface of the balcony course; and from the said basement course downward to the level of the oil cellar floor, 9 feet 4 inches. The tower is to be 18 feet in diameter, overall, immediately above the basement course, diminishing to 16 feet 6 inches in diameter immediately under the corbel course under the Balcony. The inside diameter of the rubble wall is to be throughout 11 feet 6 inches, and the Brick-lining to be 10 feet of internal diameter. The Tower Storehouse, which is to be semi-circular and concentric with the Tower, is to be formed to a radius of 19 feet 6 inches over walls; and its height, from the bottom of the basement course to the top of the coping of the walls, 11 feet 9 inches. The main body of the Dwelling-house is to measure 70 feet 6 inches in length by 31 feet 6 inches in width, over walls, immediately above the basement course; and to measure in height, from the bottom of this course to the top of the coping of the walls, 13 feet 9 inches. The wings, which form the offices, are to measure each 15 feet in length of front by 24 feet 9 inches in width, immediately above the basement course, and the height, measured as in the Main-house, is to be 12 feet, except the Ash-pits, which measure as above only 5 feet. The open court, forming the space between the Dwelling-house and the Lighthouse tower, is to measure 59 feet 6 inches by 32 feet 3 inches, within walls.

The dimensions of all the doors and windows are to be made agreeably to those marked on the Plans and Drawings of the respective compartments of the works: it being understood that the dimensions so noted refer to the finished parts of the timber-work, for doors, and to the daylight size of the Stone-work for the windows; the height of all the doors, not otherwise marked or described, being 6 feet 6 inches in the clear, when finished.

Works of Masonry

Polished Work
The inside pavement of the Tower and its stair, the pavement of the Dwelling-house, stone skirting, chimney jambs, inside soles of the Tower windows, pavement of the Dry-store room, and inside pavement of the Privies to be all executed in Pavement of finely polished work.

Axe-Dressed Work
The upper surface and head of the Balcony-course, are to be done in axe-dressed work.

Pick-Dressed Work
The Basement course and coping courses of all these buildings, together with the Corbels of the Tower-cornice, scantions of doors and windows, and corners, to be all done in that species of workmanship technically termed Pick Dressed Work.

Droved Work
The pavement of the Oil-cellar, the entrance to Privies, and breasts of Ash-pits, with all the outside paved footpaths, and water cisterns, are to be in Droved-work; or, in the event of using Caithness pavement, it is to be laid with the natural face properly selected.

Linings and Other Brick Walls
The whole of the outward walls of the Dwelling-house, from the level

of the middle of the basement-course, to the lower side of the Roof joisting, is to be lined with the best description of Brick of the common size, laid on bed, and having a space, or vacancy, of 3 inches in width, between the said Brick wall and the internal surface of the rubble walls of the house. The tower-walls are, in like manner, to be lined as above described, from the level of the Oil-cellar floor, up to the lower bed of the upper course of the corbels of the Balcony; but for the interior of the Tower, the Bricks are to measure 12 inches in length, 6 inches in breadth of bed, and 3 inches in thickness, prepared for the purpose of this work.

All the division walls of the Dwelling-house and the Privies are to be of the best description of common brick laid or built on bed founded on the rubble walls and carried up to the lower side of the roof-joisting: all those not falling under beams being furnished with wall plates of 4 and a half inches in breadth by 1 inch in thickness, on which the joisting is to rest. The newel of the stair of the Tower is to be built of Brick, similar in their dimensions to the lining of the Tower, but to be moulded to the circle of the newel, and the whole of the Brick walls are to have bond timber built in as hereinafter specified for doors, standards, skirting and foot-base, &c. The arching of the Oil-cellar is to be done in Brick-work of 9 inches; or to consist of 2 Bricks in thickness.

Causewaying

There are to be two species of causewaying in these works, viz: the one termed Aisler, and the other rubble causewaying. In either case the face of each stone is not to exceed a superficial area of 32 square inches, and to be 6 inches in depth: the whole laid in a stratum of clean sharp sand of the depth of 6 inches and bonded at all the exterior edges, and the junction of Aisler and Rubble causeway, with a line of Kerb-stone of 10 inches in depth, and 5 inches in thickness.

Rubble Building

All the works of masonry in these buildings as delineated on the accompanying Plans and Drawings, with the exception of the parts already specified, are to be executed of the best hammer-dressed rubble work, having a sufficient number of Bond-stones. In the tower at the progressive height of every 10 feet, or thereby, a course of header-stones is to be laid of not less than 10 inches in thickness: their length to be equal to the full thickness of the walls at the respective places where these courses are introduced. All the spaces between the joisting and beams of the roofs at their bearings are to be filled flush to the level of their upper surfaces with rubble masonry. The whole of the masonry to be laid flush in good Lime mortar, prepared agreeably to a schedule of direction furnished by the Engineer.

Excavation and Upfilling

When the precise site of the Lighthouse buildings has been pointed out and fixed upon by the Engineer, or the Clerk of Works to the Lighthouse Board, the lower bed of the basement course of the Buildings shall be laid at the level of the surface of the natural ground, taken at the point so determined upon for the centre of the Tower, and to this point all other parts or dimensions of the buildings shall be referred.

Upon this site an excavation is to be made of all the earthy matters contained within the area of the buildings, and at such other points beyond this area where earthy matters occur. Above the level of the basement course, there are to be excavated to the level of that point all round the buildings, and to the distance of 15 feet from the basement course, beyond which, if required, the excavation is to run out in the form of a ha! ha! or slope, rising at the rate of one perpendicular to three horizontal. In excavating for the foundation of the Tower and Oil cellar, should rock occur within that area before reaching a sufficient depth it is to be excavated to the depth of 11 feet under the level of the basement-course.

Where the natural surface of the ground falls under the point of comparison above alluded to, upfilling is required to be made to the level of the basement-course, extending 20 feet in breadth from the face of the walls. From the extremity of this level border, the upfilling is to slope downward at the rate of one in 3 till it run into the natural surface of the ground at the bottom of said slope.

After the foundation walls, as hereinafter described shall have been carried to the level of the basement-course, all the spaces between these walls shall be filled, from the rock to the level of the bottom of the basement-course, with dry stone shivers, hand laid. Round the exterior walls of the Oil Store-room, and the Tower, a backing of dry-stone, 2 feet in thickness, carefully hand laid, is also to be carried up to within 12 inches of the bottom of the basement-course.

Foundations

The area of the Buildings being prepared as above described, the surface of the rock is to be dressed, where necessary, to receive the masonry on level beds. The walls of the Building, including the foundations of brick division-walls, as well as all the main walls and court-walls, are also to be founded upon the rock. The walls to be of the dimensions or thickness marked on the respective parts in the Plans and Sections: - that is to say : the Tower and Cellar walls to be of the thickness marked on the ground-plan, together with a footing of 4 inches by 12 inches in height on the side where the pavement is to be laid. The walls of the House and Offices are in like manner to be made agreeably to the dimensions marked on the ground-plan, together with the thickness for a footing of 4 inches on the side where pavement is to be laid, and of 3 inches where basement-course is to be laid. These footings respectively to be carried up to within 3 inches of the level of the pavement, and of the bottom of the basement-course. The court-walls are to be founded of the thickness of 2 feet 3 inches, with a footing of 3 inches in each side, formed at 3 inches under the level of the basement-course of the Buildings. All the foundations at and under 2 feet 3 inches in thickness (in thickness) if carried lower than 5 feet under the level of the basement-course are to be increased in thickness, by footings of 2 inches on each side for every 2 feet of additional depth; and it is hereby declared and understood that the Contractor is to excavate to an average depth of

5 feet under the lower bed of the basement-course. But should it so happen that works fall short of, or should they exceed this depth, the difference shall form an addition or deduction upon the Contract-price, as the case may be.

Dwarf Walls

The pavement floors of all the apartments of the Dwelling-house, the Tower and the Oil Cellar, and Dry Store-rooms are to be laid on Dwarf-walls of 12 inches in thickness, raised on the surface of the dry-stone upfilling, already described, or upon the surface of rock, or the back of the arches of the Store-room, where such occurs. These Dwarf-walls and Pavement-stones are to be so disposed of and arranged that the central line of each wall may fall under the corresponding joints of two of the pavement-stones; but where the slabs of Pavement are of such dimensions that the distance between their bearings would exceed 15 inches, additional walls must be raised so as to reduce the points of bearing within these limits.

Brick and other Arching

The Brick Arching over the Oil Cellar is to be constructed agreeably to the span and spring of the Arch marked on the Sections. All interior voids of doors and windows are to be arched with stone or brick above safe lintels not less than 9 inches in depth, 15 inches in breadth, and rising 1 and a half inch for every foot of span in the void or opening.

Basement Course

The Basement course is to extend round all the external parts of the Dwelling-house and Offices. The Tower and Store-rooms and the front of the Court-wall, laid at the height already specified, to be 14 inches in height, projecting 2 inches beyond the face of the wall with a washing or chamfer on the upper bed of 1 inch on the projection, prepared in pieces of not less than 3 feet in length and 12 inches in breadth of bed. In the basement of the Dwelling-house and Dry Store-room, and round the foot of the Tower walls, perforations of 2 inches in diameter are to be made communicating through the walls with the leaden gutters of the void between the rubble masonry and the brick lining, so constructed and laid out as to admit air, and draw off the moisture that might percolate through the walls and collect in the leaden gutters of the voids hereinafter described.

Corners

The cornerstones of these buildings are to be not less than 2 feet 6 inches in length and 10 inches in bed, and from 12 to 15 inches in height.

Rybats

The Rybats or Scantions of doors and windows outhand stones are to be not under 2 feet 6 inches in length, 10 inches of bed, and 12 to 15 inches of height, and the inhands to pass to the inside of the Brick-linings, if stone of that length can be procured; failing which pick-dressed Scantions are to be laid, chace-hand fashion, with the outhand stones.

Soles & Lintels

The soles of windows, and lintels of doors and windows are to average 12 inches in breadth of bed, 8 inches in depth for soles, and 12 inches in depth for lintels; the length to be not less than 15 inches above the extreme day-light width of the respective openings.

Torus or Band

Along the front and back of the Dwelling-house a Band or Torus course is to be laid of 5 inches in thickness, and projecting 2 inches with a washing of 1 inch:- to be in pieces not under 2 feet 6 inches in length, nor under 12 inches in breadth of bed.

Coping

The outward walls of the Dwelling-house and Offices, the outward wall of the Tower basement and the Court-wall, are all to be finished with a coping of Pick-dressed stone. The walls of the house, offices and store- rooms being all reduced above the level of the roof to 18 inches in thickness, and the court-walls to the same thickness at the top, the coping for the whole is to be 20 inches in breadth, projecting 1 inch on each side of the wall and 10 inches in depth, , pick-dressed to the semi-circular form, and in the heads and joints, and the latter carefully pointed with Roman cement, after the coping has been all laid. The copings of the pediment on the front & back of the house, are to be of the same breadth, 8 inches in thickness, and all dressed square on the upper bed. The plinth, forming the bottom of the pediments, is to be 6 inches in thickness, and projecting 2 inches; the whole of these copings are to be formed of stones of any convenient length above 18 inches.

Tower Cornice

The Cornice of the Tower is to be formed with corbel and space alternately to consist of 24 blocks, or corbels with the alternate spaces, and these surmounted by a Plinth or Balcony-course. The blocks are to be 1 foot in breadth, built in two courses each one foot in depth. The tails of the lower course to reach to the inward face of the Brick-lining, and the heads to project 7 and a half inches over the outward face of the wall; the upper course of the corbels to have a bearing on the solid of the walls of not less than 1 foot 9 inches, the heads to project 7 and a half inches beyond the lower course, and to be completed to the inward face of the former course with a ring of Pick-dressed stones not under 15 inches in breadth of bed for the support of the iron beams of the Light room floor. The spaces between the corbels are to be filled with rubble masonry, the same as the other parts of the work. The Balcony-course is to consist of 24 stones, whose joints must fall upon the central line of the corbels. The extreme diameter of this course will be 19 feet 4 inches; the length of each stone 3 feet 11 inches, and to be of the thickness of 10 inches. The tails formed full, and to be Pick-dressed to the circle of 11 feet 6 inches in diameter. On the upper bed of this course there is to be a washing outwards of one and a half inch, from the boundary line of the Light room parapet wall to the extremity of the course. The joints to be all carefully dressed to the square; and in laying they are to be grouted flush, from the depth of 5 inches, with a mixture of white lead, sand, and linseed oil well beaten together.

Light Room or Parapet Wall

The stones for the Light room or Parapet wall, as delineated in dotted-lines on the Drawings, to be furnished by the Lighthouse Board, and laid down at the Lighthouse in a worked state, ready for laying, the Contractor is only to provide lime and (mortar) labour for building the same.

Chimneys

The Kitchen chimneys are to be 3 feet 6 inches in height, the jambs to have 8 inches of breadth of face and 20 inches of depth, projecting 3 and a half inches beyond the finished walls of the apartments. The room chimneys to be 3 feet in height, the jambs 6 inches of breadth of face and 1 foot 6 inches in depth, projecting 3 inches beyond the face of the walls, the width of the whole being respectively as marked on the Plans. These chimneys to be formed first with plain Pick-dressed scantions, and the jambs and lintels to be formed of pavement slabs, the fronts and lintels not under 3 inches in thickness and the covering slabs 2 inches in thickness, the whole securely fixed to the rubble scantions with copper bats at the rate of 3 lbs of copper to each chimney.

Chimney Flues

The chimney Flues are to be formed upon an elliptical mould whose diameters are to be 14 inches and 10 inches, which is to be progressively drawn up as the building rises. In the Lighthouse-tower-wall a Flue or void of 12 inches in diameter is to be formed on a cylindrical mould, and carried exactly perpendicularly from the level of the floor to the tower bed of the Balcony-course. At the bottom of the Flue an opening or door is to be formed communicating with it measuring 3 feet in height by 18 inches in width, and at the top another opening of 12 inches square or thereby. The surface of all the flues is to be carefully plastered over with good lime mortar.

Chimney Stalks

Three chimney stalks on the Dwelling-house and one on the Store-rooms as shewn on the Plans are to be carried up of sufficient dimensions to contain the flues which terminate in them: that is to say, the exterior walls of the stalks shall not be less than 9 and a half inches in thickness, nor the divisions between the flues less than 7 inches; those of the Dwelling-house carried to the height of 8 feet above the level of the top of the coping of the walls; and that of the Dry-Store-room 6 feet above its coping. The Cope-stones of the chimney-stalks are to be 10 inches in thickness and batted together with copper bats, run up with lead at the rate of 2lbs of copper for every joint that may be formed in the cope-stones.

Stair

The Tower-stair is to be formed in steps of 7 inches in height, or rise; and the tread to be such that twenty-four of them may form a complete wheel, or circle, of the Stair. These steps are to be built of pavement-slabs; the tread and breasts being in separate pieces. The length of the slabs of which the steps are formed is to be 4 feet 4 inches apportioning this length to 3 feet 4 inches for the clear of the step between the brick lining and the newal, 6 inches at each end for a resting on the said lining and newal; they are not to be under 2 inches in thickness the breast to be 5 inches in height, neatly jointed and the tread or sole of such breadth as to project one inch over the front of the breast on which it rests, and 2 inches under that of the succeeding step which it supports; the front projecting being neatly rounded as a bottle. This stair is to ascend from the level of the Oil-cellar floor to within 8 feet 6 inches or thereby of the upper bed of the Balcony-course. In that space three landings are to be formed: the first, and lowest, at the door leading to the Dry-store-room, which is to have a horizontal extent equal to three steps; the next at the entrance door of the Tower and to have a horizontal extent of nine steps and the third landing forming the stair head is to have an extent equal to eleven steps. These landings like the stair steps are to be constructed of slabs of Pavement, averaging not less than 1 foot 6 inches in breadth, not less than 3 inches in thickness, their joints forming radii of a circle, and to be half lapped to the breadth of one inch. The bearings of these landings or plates on the lining and newal walls of the Stair are to be the same as specified for the steps.

Door Steps

The floor of the Dwelling-house being placed 14 inches above the bottom of the basement course, the ascent to each house will be made by two solid sandstone or limestone steps, rising from the outside causeway, the same number and description of stone steps are required at each of the Ash-pit doors; but the three steps required from the Tower-stair to the Dry-store-room will be of the same description as those for the Tower-stair. The above described steps will be formed with a rise of 7 inches and the breadth of the tread 12 inches. The three doors of the Court, and both of the Byre-doors are respectively to be furnished with a neatly pick-dressed stone sole, equal in breadth to the thickness of the respective walls, and not under 6 inches in thickness, which may be laid in two breadths if necessary.

Pavement

The whole of the Dwelling-house, including Kitchen, Rooms, Closets, Passages, Store-rooms and Presses, as also the Tower, Dry-store-room, Tower-window-inside-soles, and the Privies and similar parts of the building are to be floored or laid with Polished pavement not under one and a quarter inches in thickness, neatly jointed and laid flush on Lime-mortar. The Oil storeroom and the passages of Privies are in like manner to be floored with droved or unpolished pavement not under 2 inches in thickness neatly jointed and laid as above:- the whole of these pavements are to be laid on dwarf-walls, as already described.

Stone Skirtings

The Tower with its stair and the Oil Cellar, Dwelling-house, Passages, and Privies are to be finished with Stone Skirtings; that for the Stairs to stand 3 inches above the rake of the steps and on floors and landings 6 inches above the Pavement on which it rests; in all cases the Skirtings are to project three-quarters of an inch beyond the face of the finished Plaster-work.

Apron Courses

In all the walls where leaden aprons are to be laid a course of Pavement not under 2 inches in thickness is to be laid on which the Aprons are to rest; this course is to be 18 inches in breadth, or equal to the thickness of the respective walls which they pass through, and to be not under 9 inches in breadth, where Aprons are only single. The stones may be of any convenient length, neatly jointed and laid flush; the edge over which they hang being worked off to a greater round. For the single aprons a raglet is to be formed in the wall, immediately above the apron course, by building in steps of timber 3 inches in breadth by 1 inch in thickness, which are afterwards to be withdrawn.

Ash-pit Breasts

In the passage to the Ash-pits, a breast stone is to be set up equal in length to the width of the passage, 3 feet 4 inches in height, and 3 inches in thickness, if formed of Pavement, and 6 inches if common stone be used. These Breast-stones are to be droved or pick-dressed, according to the quality of the stone used.

Causewaying

A border of 3 feet in width is to be formed all round the court, and from the Tower-door across the court to the front of the Dwelling-house; also along the front wall of the court and Store-room is to be laid with Aisler causeway – the stones not exceeding 4 x 8 inches of face; but the remaining parts of the court, together with the space included between the Ash-pits and Screen-walls, as also a border of 3 feet in breadth all round the remaining parts of the Dwelling-house, Offices, Byres, and Ash-pits are to be laid with Rubble-causeway. The surface of all the causewayed borders next to walls or Basement-course is to be laid on a level with the bottom parts of it, and to slope or fall outward 1 inch on every 3 feet. In the Court the causewayed spaces on each side of the central border are to fall on all sides to the a-b, marked on the plans.

Drains

A covered drain of rubble-masonry, measuring 18 inches by 12 inches, formed with a hammer-dressed stone sill is to be carried round the Dwelling-house and offices at the distance of not less than 1 foot from the outward walls. From this drain a branch of the same description and dimensions is to be led off at the nearest point towards letters a and b , marked on the plans of the court; from thence they are to run in a curved direction to another point marked c on the Plan, where they unite and form a junction with a Drain of similar dimensions, which is to be carried round the Tower and Oil Cellar walls. From this junction of these Drains, one measuring 2 feet 6 inches by 2 feet is to be carried forward to the distance of 120 feet from the front of the Tower. These Drains are to be laid with a declivity of not less than 2 inches in every 3 yards of their length: to be built upon, or cut into rock, according to circumstances, so as to form a fair and clear run for the soil and drainage water; and at each of the points marked a and b a perpendicular eye or opening is to be formed, measuring 18 inches square, built of rubble-masonry with mortar, communicating with the Drains below. These eyes are to be covered with flat stones of at least 2 feet 6 inches square, and 8 inches in thickness, or with two stones making up these dimensions – having a perforation of one foot in diameter, formed in the middle prepared for a cast iron grating or perforated basin. From each of the Water-cisterns and the Ash-pits a small waste Drain is also to be made, leading to the nearest principal drain, for carrying off the superfluous water.

Water Cisterns

Two cisterns for collecting the rain water from the roofs of the houses are to be formed each measuring 5 feet in length, 3 feet 6 inches in width, and 2 feet 6 inches in depth: to be made of good sound Arbroath Pavement, not less than 3 inches in thickness; the top, bottom, sides and ends being each respectively in one stone to be reyleted or groaned in all their joinings, and put together with a mixture of white lead paint, linseed oil, and sand, well compounded. The cisterns are to be set in a position near the foot of the Rain- pipes, and covers to be placed one foot under the surface of the causewayed border in front of the house. Each cistern is to be furnished with a waster and washer of sufficient size for cleaning and passing off superfluous water into the drains.

Skreen-walls

Two pieces of Skreen-walls, as represented on the plan are to be erected in front of the Offices, which are to be of similar dimensions with the court-walls, except in their height, which, including the coping, is only to be 7 feet above the surface of the ground.

Materials of Masonry

The materials for the Tower-stair, and all the Chimney-jambs, Stone-skirting, apron-courses, inside soles of windows, and all hearths are to be taken from the Turin or Carmylie Quarries in Forfarshire: all other pavement stone is to be taken from the best quarries of Mr. Trail of Castlehill, in Caithness-shire, excepting the outer door-steps, which shall be of good sound sandstone, or Limestone; and for all other purposes, either in dressed or rubble work, the materials are to be taken from such Quarries, within one mile of the Lighthouse, as shall be approved of and pointed out by the Engineer, or the Clerk of Works: the same not being nearer than 200 yards from the Lighthouse Tower. The lime for the use of the Lighthouse works is to be taken from the Limestone Quarries in the Parish of Durness, or any other of approved quality, equally suitable for the work to be duly prepared with clean sharp sand, and pure fresh water, well compounded, as agreeably to a Schedule furnished by the Engineer, and beaten to the satisfaction of the Inspector of the Works.

Provision for Altering the Specification

Should it be found on trial that the quarries in the neighbourhood of the Lighthouse will turn out an abundance of materials fit for axe-dressed work, it is hereby provided, that the Specification shall be altered insofar as it refers to Rybats, Soles and Lintels of doors and windows, and to substitute the following article, viz: window rybats to be worked with a breast of 6 inches, and a check for the sash-frame of 3 and a half inches in depth, door rybats for the entrance-doors of houses and tower to be worked as in-gates to the depth of 1 foot 9 inches or thereby, and then a check of 2 and a half inches in depth for the door frame; Rybats for the Court-doors to be double headed and worked with a check of 2 and a half inches, in depth in the middle of the thickness of the walls to receive the door-frame; for other outside doors the Rybats to have a breast of 8 inches in depth, and a check of 2 and a half inches; soles of windows to be worked with a washing of ¾ of an inch, and lintels of doors and windows to have a check of 2 and a half inches in depth agreeing with the Rybats as respectively described. All the parts non-specified under this head, including also a margin of the breadth of 6 inches round all doors and windows are to be neatly axe-dressed. Contractors are therefore required to estimate and make offer of the difference of expense at which they would engage to execute these parts of the work as now described under this article; Provided that materials may be found applicable to that purpose, and on order for the same being given under the hands of the Engineer.

CARPENTER AND JOINER-WORK

Roofing
The Roofing of all these buildings, except the Tower, is to be constructed as platforms with main beams and joisting framed into the beams. The beams for the dwelling-house and offices are to measure 13 inches by 8 inches; the former being laid in two lengths meeting on the middle wall. The beams for the Store-rooms are to measure 13 inches by 6 and a half inches. The joisting is to be 8 inches by 2 and a half inches, and placed at 13 inches apart so as to alternate on the opposite side of the same beam & to be dovetailed into the beams to the length of 2 inches and to the depth of 5 inches, the remaining 3 inches on the depth of the joisting passing half across the top of the beam, and resting lightly upon it: the whole being laid out agreeably to the plans of these parts of the buildings. The declivity drips and gutters are also to be made

agreeably to the Plans and Sections in the following manner, viz:- the surface of the platforms at the highest point is to be placed 4 inches under the level of the coping of the walls, from which point they are to fall at the rate of 2 and a half inches in 3 yards toward the lower side of the roof. In the Dwelling-house Roof the inclination is to be from the back towards the front, having a drip of 4 inches in depth formed along the centre of the middle stone wall or thereby, and a gutter of 12 inches wide at the top and 8 inches at the bottom, where deepest, formed along the inside of the front wall, which shall be 3 inches in depth at the shallowest points, falling from the two extremities, and from the centre point at the rate of 2 inches in 3 yards towards the points d.e. marked on the plans, where the discharge will be made. In the roofs of the office, the inclinations are to be in the same direction with a gutter and drip at the wall separating the Byre from the Ash-pits, and another gutter at the front wall of the Privies. In the Store-house roof, the inclination is to be from the outward wall toward the Tower, round which, and along the Court-wall, a gutter is to be formed, falling to each side from the point f, marked on the plan. These drips and gutters in the roofs of the Offices and Store-house are to have the same fall and dimensions as those specified for the Dwelling-house.

The boarding of the Platforms, Roofs, and gutters, is to be of battens cut from Meniel timber not exceeding 4 inches in breadth, and to be 1 and a quarter inch in thickness, grooved and feathered in the joints and brought to uniform thickness so as to be all flush on the upper surface: to be properly nailed down to the joisting with blind nails, punched over head into the boarding and covered with putty. The ends of all the beams, and the ends of joistings which rest upon the walls, are to have a hold of at least 12 inches of the stone wall laid on wall plates of 8 inches in breadth, and 2 inches in thickness.

Safe Lintels

The safe lintels of timber over all voids are to be in the proportion of 1 inch in thickness for every foot of length; the length to be 1 foot 6 inches more than the width of the opening, the breadth always being equal to that of the space to be lintelled over.

Ceiling Joists

The ceilings of all the apartments, passages and other parts of the Dwelling-house, Dry Store-room, Privies and the back of the Tower-stair are to be levelled by means of ceiling-joists measuring 4 inches in breadth by 1 and a half inch in thickness placed at 12 inches from centre to centre, and properly secured to the beams and joisting.

Lathing

All the ceilings, doors and window Scantions throughout the whole of the buildings, and the back of the Tower-stair are to be lathed with Split-laths not exceeding 1 and a quarter inch in breadth and properly nailed.

Windows

The windows of the Dwelling-house are to be 5 feet in height by 2 feet 4 inches in width, the Tower windows, of which there are to be six in number, three of them are to be 5 feet, and three of them to be 4 feet in height, and to be each one foot in width. The Oil-store-room window is to be 3 feet in height by 2 feet in width. The materials of these windows to be of the following finished dimensions, viz; Soles 4 inches in depth; sashes 2 and one eighth inches in thickness; pulley stiles 5 and one quarter inches in breadth and 1 and one eighth inch in thickness; inside facings 1 and one eighth inch in thickness and 4 inches in breadth; astragals or window bars three-quarters on an inch in thickness, and having a glass check of 1 inch in depth.

Door standards in brick-on-bed-walls are to be 2 and a half inches in thickness, and of such breadth as to sink the plaster on both sides to reach the full height of the apartment; and besides the top and bottom fixtures, they are to be nailed to three bond timbers on each side of the door of 14 inches in length, and 4 and a half inches by 2 and a half inches, built into the brick wall. The lintels to be of the same dimensions as the standards, and properly saved from the load of the incumbent wall. The standards for inside doors in stone walls to be not less than 4 inches in breadth, and 2 and a half inches in thickness, properly nailed to at least four bond timbers, previously built into the walls. These timbers are not to be under the dimensions of those already specified. For all outside doors the standards are to be of the same dimensions as those last specified; but in place of bond timbers, they are to be fixed with a like number of copper split-bats, each weighing not less than half a pound.

Doors

All the doors of these buildings are to be made 6 feet 6 inches in height, except when otherwise marked, and the width in all cases to agree with the dimensions marked on the Drawings. All the outside doors, including those of the court, the dwelling-house and the offices, with the oil cellar door, and those of the Privies, are to be made of plain deal 1 inch in thickness, the boards not exceeding 4 inches in breadth, feathered and grooved, and beaded on the joints and properly fastened with copper nails to a frame of 1 and a half inch in thickness. The stiles of the frames to be 4 inches in breadth, morticed upon three rails, each 10 inches in breadth, and joined with a bead moulding. The joints of all the framing and boarding of these doors are to be put together with white lead paint.

Two slip doors are to be made for the Ash-pits, each 3 feet in width by 2 feet in height, formed in a similar manner to those above described.

The inner door of the Tower, as shewn in the Plan, is to be made 2 and a quarter inches in thickness, in two leaves, half checked in the meeting joint; the lower half being framed bead and flush on the face on one side and moulded and plain panelled on the other side; the upper half being fitted each to receive a plate of glass to be furnished by the Lighthouse Board. The entrance doors of the dwelling-house, and of the Tower and the court, are respectively to be formed in two leaves, half checked in the meeting joints: all the other Doors of the House and the Tower are to be four panelled bound doors, the bottom and middle rails being 10 inches in breadth, and the other parts of the frame being 4 inches in breadth. The principal doors of the Kitchens and Rooms, and the Dry-Store rooms and the Tower-landing-doors, are to be 2 inches in thickness; those of the closets, store-rooms and presses 1 and a half inch in thickness, and the whole moulded on both sides with a substantial planted moulding, and filled with plain panels of one half of an inch in thickness. At the bottom of the drop-hole or void in the Tower-wall, and both at the top and bottom of the newel, there is to be a small door 3 feet in height by 1 foot 6 inches in width, and 1 and a half inch in thickness, framed bead and flush panelled and fitted with proper frames.

Window Shutters

All the windows of these buildings, except those of the Tower-stair and oil-cellar, are to be finished with bound shutters of two panels in height, framed of 1 and a half inch deal, and half inch panels, and moulded to correspond with the doors. The shutters of each window are to be fitted with a closer not less than 3 inches in breadth of 7/8th inch deal, clamped on the ends, and where the shutters are not of sufficient breadth when opened to fill up the scantion, reeded pilasters are to be put up to fill the space.

Door Furnishings

The Doors in brick-walls are to have capes 5/8th inch in thickness, and of such breadth as to cover the remainder of the door-posts after the door has been hung: all other doors to have capes not under 4 and a half inches in breadth, and 5/8th inch in thickness, moulded on the edge. The doors in Kitchen, closets, Store-rooms, Oil Cellar, Court and Privies are to be finished with plain facings of 4 and a half inches in breadth, and 5/8ths inch in thickness, beaded and moulded, where necessary: all other doors not named or described as above, being those of the Rooms and Passages of the Dwelling-house, and those of the Tower-stair, are to be finished with single architraves of 4 and a half inches of breadth of plate, and 5/8ths inch in thickness, with a substantial moulding.

Window Finishings

The Window Finishings of the different apartments are all to be as follows: viz – the Kitchen and Storeroom Windows are to be fitted with plastered soffits and breast and elbow linings of ¾ inch plain deal with plain facings of 5 inches in breadth, and 5/8th inch in thickness, beaded and moulded on the edges and fixed upon proper grounds, which are to be put up previously to plastering the walls. The windows of the Tower, Oil Cellar and Privies are to be finished with polished pavement soles, plastered scantions and soffits and a ¾ inch corner bead round all. The windows of all the other apartments are to be finished with bound soffits, breast and elbow linings, framed of 1 and a half inch deal moulded on one side agreeing with the shutter, plain panelled, and with architraves similar to those of the doors, but to be 5 inches in breadth and fixed on grounds as described for the facings. All the window linings are to have copings and skirtings after the usual manner.

Skirtings and Foot Base

All the apartments as Kitchens, Store-Rooms, Closets and Presses specified to be finished with plain facings, are to have a plain skirting all round of 5 inches in depth, 5/8th inch in thickness and all the apartments already specified to be finished with architraves, the Dwelling-house passages excepted, are to have a solid foot-base of 6 and a half inches in depth and 1 and one quarter inch in thickness, moulded on the upper edge. The whole of these to be fixed upon grounds of 3 inches in breadth, by 5/8th inch in thickness, properly secured to bond timbers previously built into the walls for that purpose, the bond timbers being so applied as to serve also for fixing the lower edges of all such skirtings and foot-base, and further : the spaces below all such grounds are to be filled flush with plaster lime and allowed to perfectly dry before the finishings are applied.

Jamb Mouldings

Each of the Room chimneys is to have a substantial Jamb-moulding and Coping put round it, projecting 1 and a half inch beyond the face of the jambs, and fixed upon proper grounds.

Shelving

Each of the Wall Presses is to have four tiers of shelving of the full depth of such presses, and one inch in thickness, cleaned on both sides, and fitted in before plastering. Besides these shelves for the presses, 250 superficial feet of the same description of shelving are to be fitted up, and properly supported upon brackets, or otherwise, in the Storerooms and closets, as shall be afterwards pointed out by the Clerk of Works.

Privies

The Privies are to be fitted up with one seat each, having a polished pavement front, and a double top, the upper one having a bead and flush hinged flap. Above the seat a lining of plain 5/8th inch deal is also to be put round the back and ends: the whole rendered complete without the apparatus of a Water closet.

Tower Stair-Head

On the upper landing of the Tower-stair a door is to be formed, as shewn in the Plan, and finished as already specified. From this landing the ascent to the Lightroom is to be by a neatly finished (trap) wooden trap-ladder of 20 inches in width, formed of 1 and one quarter inch deal, the sides and steps of which are to be 8 inches in breadth. The steps are to rise each 9 inches, or thereby, to be morticed into the sides, and the whole ladder twisted to the circle or sweep of the walls between which it stands, agreeably to the Plans. The sides and steps are to finish on the front edge with a Torus, and the back lined up with 5/8ths inch deal: the whole to be neatly finished and fitted to its place.

Materials of Carpentry

All the roofing, including the boarding of the Platform, windows, all plain deal doors, safe lintels, bond timbers, and all door standards, and frames, are to be of the best Memel crown timber, or of American pitch-pine : all inside doors, shutters and other finishings are to be of the best

American yellow pine : the whole of the timber used in these buildings is to be perfectly free of sap wood and other blemishes.

Plaster Work

The plaster work of the walls and ceilings of all the apartments of the Dwelling-house, kitchens, rooms, storerooms, closets, passages, and presses, the Tower-walls and back of stair, and walls and ceilings of the Dry store-room and Privies, are to be finished in three coat plaster, the Oil store-room and the passages of the Ash-pits in two coat plaster, and the walls of the Byres and fuel stores to be done in one coat plaster. The Kitchens, Rooms and Passages of the Dwelling-house are to be finished with a plaster cornice, proportioned to the size of the apartments.

Glaziers Work

All the windows of these buildings are to be glazed with first crown glass, well bedded and filled with putty, compounded of Linseed Oil and Dry-pounded chalk, with a due proportion of white or red lead, carefully prepared and beaten up. Previously to glazing the outside parts of the windows are to be laid over with two coats of white lead paint.

Plumbers Work

The Plumbers works of the roof are to be executed with the best cast sheet lead of the weight of not less than 8 lbs to the superficial foot, with gutters and aprons of the same quality and weight, ascertained to the satisfaction of the Clerk of Works; the whole of the Platforms and gutters being laid out as delineated on the Plans, and described under the head of Carpentry. The Platforms are to be properly seamed, the upsetting for each seam being 3 inches on the one sheet, and 4 and a half inches on the other, neatly folded and rolled over. The breadth of the sheets from seam to seam, when finished is to be 2 feet 4 inches, or thereby, for the square roofs and 2 feet 6 inches at the broad end of the sheets in the circular Roofs. At all the drips and gutters, bands, or doubling pieces of lead, 5 inches in breadth and the same strength as the Platform lead, are to be laid flush with the surface of the Platform boarding to the breadth of 2 inches and fixed down to the boarding with composition nails. Over these bands one inch of the Platform sheets is to be doubled, and then both parts folded down on the face of the gutter, to the depth of 3 inches over the upsetting of the Platform, or gutter, as the case may be. The lead of the gutter is to be set up on the side next to the Platform as high as the surface of the Platform, and on the outside, or that next to the walls, it is to rise as high as the top of the leaden apron. In all external walls, the aprons are to be built in of the full breadth of the wall on which they rest; this in all cases is not to be less than 18 inches, to hang over or over-lap the upsetting or gutter or Platform lead as the case may be, not less than 4 inches; and to hang over the lip of the wall, on the outside, not less than 1 inch, nor more than 2 inches. These aprons, which are laid into prepared regles, are to have a hold of not less than 3 inches, and to hang or overlap 4 inches as above specified. Two rain water pipes for the Dwelling-house, two for the Offices, and two for the Tower-basement of 3 inches diameter are to be brought from the discharging gutters of the respective roofs down to the ground, and the four pipes first mentioned are to be continued directly to the water cisterns. The water from the latter two being first received in to a small cistern of 12 inches square and 12 inches deep, formed of lead weighing 12lbs to the square foot, set in masonry lined with pavement stone and covered on the top with pavement of 2 inches in thickness, placed under the surface of the ground. From these small cisterns a pipe of 1 and a half inch diameter is to be laid to convey the water to the large cisterns. At the foundations of all the brick-linings and 4 inches under the level of the pavement a leaden gutter is to be laid, extending over the whole length of these voids; one edge of this gutter is to be laid into a reglet prepared for it on the stone wall on a level with the bottom of the gutter; and, with the perforations already specified, to be formed in the outward walls, and having a hold of the wall of not less than 3 inches. The other edge of the gutters, or that next to the brick linings, is to be upset to the height of 4 inches against the brick-wall; and an apron 7 inches in breadth laid on the course of brick at, or immediately below, the level of the floor pavement, is to hang or lap over the upset edge of the gutter 2 inches. The lead for these gutters is to be of the same quality and weight as specified for the roofs.

SMITH WORK

The entrance doors of the Dwelling-house and the Tower-door are to have each an iron rim lock. The doors of the Inspectors rooms, the Dry-store-room, and the door on the Stair-landing to have each an 8 inch mortice lock. The Light Keepers store-room doors to have each a 7 inch iron rim lock. The doors of the kitchens, bedrooms and bedclosets of the Dwelling-house to have each a 7 inch iron mortice latch with snib-bolt. Presses and small closets, to have each a press-lock. The Oil-store room, the Byres, and the Fuel store-houses are to have each a Stock and Plate lock. The Court doors, and doors of the Ash-pits and Privies are to have a Brass Thumb-latch. The Tower inside door to have a brass mortice Thumb latch with two handles, and all the doors that are in two leaves are to be furnished each with a pair of 9 inch brass case bolts, with proper fixtures for the first leaf of the door.

Hinges
Hinges for all deal doors to be brass cross-tailed, those of 2 inch bound doors to be brass 7 inch edge hinges; for 1 and a half inch bound doors, to be also brass 7 inch edge hinges; and those for window shutters, small doors in the Tower, and flaps of Privies, to be and a half inches; and those for window-closers to be 2 and a half inches.

Sash-Pulleys and Fasteners
In each window of the Dwelling-house, and Tower, one sash is to be hung with 2 inch brass axle-pullies, best white sash-line, and cast-iron weight; and each window in the Dwelling-house is to be furnished with sash and shutter fasteners of the value of twelve shillings for each window.

Sundry Conditions

The Commissioners of the Northern Lighthouses are to furnish all Locks and Hinges as above described, the Contractor being only bound to furnish the workmanship for fitting and applying these article to their respective places and purposes in a workmanlike manner.

In case of any alteration being found necessary in the course of executing the Plans to which this specification refers, it shall be in the power of the Commissioners to extend or lessen these operations, or the extent of the buildings; it being understood that for such extension the Contractor is to be paid agreeably to his Schedule of Estimated Prices of the respective articles or species of work: but, on the contrary, should such alteration lessen the extent of such operations, or Plans, the same shall form a deduction from the estimated sum, and in either case, the addition or deduction is to be regulated by the annexed Schedule or list of prices furnished by the Contractor in reference to his offer. In case of anything relative to the finishing, or completing of these Works, as intended to be executed, agreeably to the foregoing Specification, and accompanying Plans, therein set forth and described, shall appear to have been omitted; or in case of any difference as to the true meaning and spirit of the Plans, and Specification, the part or parts involving such difference shall be referred to the explanation of the Engineer for the Works, whose opinion and decision, it is hereby declared shall be binding on the Contracting Parties.

The Contractor is bound in the course of the current year 1827 to make all the necessary excavations, to quarry and lay down all the necessary materials of all kinds for the building operations, and also to prepare Carpenters and Joiners work, and to build the whole walls of the Lighthouse buildings to the height of the level of the Basement course, or to such other height as to the Engineer may seem advisable; it being understood that the building operations are to be suspended from and after the first day of December 1827, till the month of April 1828. It is further provided, that all the Works of Masonry, including the Light Room Parapet shall be completed by the first day of August

1828; and the whole of the works completely finished, and ready for being inhabited by the term of Martinmas 1828.

Certain proportions of the Contract-price shall be advanced during the progress of the works, on the production of Certificates under the hands of the Engineer, or his Inspector, in the following manner, viz: the sum of £952.12s.od when the Boat harbour and the Lighthouse road are certified to have been completed; and the sum of £333.12s.6d when the Store-houses at Claiscairnach and Kyle of Durness are certified to have been completed agreeably to the foregoing conditions for Preliminary Works: further, in liquidation of the special Contract-price, for the Lighthouse Tower and Dwelling-house, One Tenth part shall be paid when the contract is signed by the parties; One Tenth part when the quarries have been opened for the Lighthouse Works and building materials laid down to the extent of 100 tons; One Tenth part when the whole of the walls in the Dwelling-house, Offices, and Tower have been founded; One Tenth part when the whole of the buildings have been brought up to the level of the basement-course; One Tenth part when the Tower is carried to the full height and the Balcony-course is laid; One Tenth part when all the sea-borne materials have been landed within two miles of the Lighthouse; One Tenth part when the Dwelling-house and Offices are roofed in; One Tenth part when the Plumber Work, and all the Works of Masonry, including pavement and brick-work, have been completed; and the Balance of the Contract-price shall be paid when the whole works are certified to have been completely finished, and approved of by the Engineer, for which three months are to be allowed from their date of completion as certified by the Resident Inspector.

Schedule of Prices Referred to in the Foregoing Specification of Cape Wrath Lighthouse:

Excavation and Removal of Rock to a distance of

100 yards	per cubic yard	3s 6d
Ditto Earth or Gravel,	per ditto	1s 6d
Rubble Building,	per cubic yard	15s 0d
Common brick-on-bed,	per superficial yard	5s 9d
Axe—dressed Aisler,	per superficial foot	3s 6d
Pick-dressed ditto,	per ditto	2s 6d
Polished Pavement,	per ditto	1s 6d
Droved ditto,	per ditto	1s 4d

Joisting 8 by 2 1/4 inches, 15 inches from centre to centre,

including 1 1/8 inch Platform boarding,	per superficial yard	13s 6d
Beams and cubic timber,	per cubic foot	4s 0d
Bound-doors and Shutters,	per superficial yard	11s 0d

Plain deal doors, 1 1/8 inch boarding on 1 ½ inch frames

	per ditto	9s 6d
Windows Glazed,	per superficial foot	4s 6d
Lineal Single Architraves,	per lineal foot	6d
Ditto Base and sub-base,	per ditto	6d
Ditto Door-posts 6 inches by 2 ½ inches,	per ditto	1s 2d
1 inch deal Shelving,	per superficial foot	9d
3 Coat Plaster,	per superficial yard	1s 3d
2 ditto	per ditto	9d
1 ditto	per ditto	6d
Plain Plaster Cornice,	per lineal foot	1s 2d
8lb lead,	per superficial foot	2s 6d
Lineal Drains, 30 x 24 inches	per lineal yard	10s 6d
Ditto, 18 x 12 inches	per ditto	7s 6d

Roofing 7 x 2 ½ inches and 14 inches apart, with

¾ inch Sarking and boards for slates,	per superficial yard	10s 6d
Causewaying 6 inches in depth,	per ditto	3s 6d

APPENDIX VII

Memorandum by Mr. Stevenson for Mr. Slight

Memorandum for Mr. Slight on Cape Wrath Survey July 1826

First

To Proceed for Rispond with the 'Regent' where, circumstances permitting, Captain Souter will accompany him (on?) an ambulatory survey of the coast, from thence to Cape Wrath and Laxford.

Second

To notice that the object of this general view of the coast, in company with Mr. Souter, is not only to give Mr. Souter an idea of this tract of country, but also that he may assist Mr. Souter in examining such creeks and sundry places as it may be thought advisable to bring more particularly into view, in the course of the Survey which is understood to be bounded by the sea on the one hand and the line of the road as nearly as may be on the other.

Thirdly

To make a particular survey of the site of the proposed Lighthouse making sections in reference to its height above the Tide mark.

Fourth

To have further in view the necessary quantity of Land for a Garden or grass for four or five cows for the use of the light-keepers.

Fifth

To have in view the best line or lines of road which the country will conveniently and at a moderate expense afford between the anchorage and Anchorages, suitable for the Lighthouse ships and the lighthouse station and also from such creek or flood harbours on the coast as may occur between Rispond and Laxford.

Sixth

To take memoranda regarding building materials, and the situation of quarries capable of producing them: to mark thereupon the Hew if within its space, to collect hand-specimens of all such building materials.

Seventh

To communicate generally with Mr. Anderson at Rispond, & Mr. Dunlop of Cape Wrath, on the object of these memoranda.

Eighth

To correspond with Mr. Stevenson as usual, & to return to Edinburgh by such conveyances as may be conveniently had when the survey is completed, bringing the surveying instruments and if conveniently practicable his whole apparatus with him.

APPENDIX VIII

Specification of the Stone & Lime Walls to Inclose a piece of Ground for a small Park at Cape Wrath Lighthouse.

The extent and position of the wall to be pointed out on the ground.

The foundations of which are to be dug through the moss to the hard ground and the wall to be founded at the thickness of 2 feet 3 inches if the depth does not exceed 2 feet 6 inches, but in any place where it shall exceed this depth to increase in thickness at the rate of 2 inches for every 2 feet in depth, on each side, at the surface of the ground, the wall is to be 2 feet thick, and built up to the height of 5 feet 8 inches from the surface of the ground to the under bed of the coping where it is to measure 1 foot 3 inches, the coping to be 10 inches thick, hammer dressed round on the top and projecting one and a half inches over the wall on each side; In this wall a gateway is to be placed in the middle of the side wall next to the Lighthouse, and two gate pillars of pick dressed stone properly bonded is to be built of the size of 2 feet 6 inches on the square and so placed as to hang a 7 feet gate, the height of which pillars is to exceed the height of the adjoining walls the height of their copings and plinths.

The whole of these walls to be built of rubble masonry with good lime mortar having regularly distributed a sufficient number of bond-stones, and the whole done to the satisfaction of the Engineer for the Northern Lighthouses or his Inspector.

11 July 1828
John Reid

APPENDIX IX

Specification of the Boundary Walls of the Lighthouse ground at Cape Wrath as proposed to be built in Rubble stone or Feal or Turf

Stone Wall

The position, direction and extent of the walls of Stone and Turf respectively are to be pointed out on the ground by the Inspector of Works at Cape Wrath.

A trench is to be dug out of the Moss to reach the Rock or hard ground on which the walls are to be founded. This trench is to be of sufficient width to receive the thickness of the wall agreeably to the dimensions after specified.

The height of the walls above the natural surface of the ground is to be 5 feet including the coping course. The thickness at the surface taken as above to be 2 feet 3 inches and to diminish in thickness to 1 foot 3 inches immediately under the coping. The underground position of the walls being of irregular height varying with the depth of the Moss is to be founded of such thickness as to admit a diminution of one inch on each side for every foot in height that may be required under the natural surface of the ground and the wall brought to the uniform thickness of 2 feet 3 inches at the surface as above specified.

The Walls are to be built in dry stone rubble Masonry properly bonded and pin(n)ed and having a sufficient number of through bond stones placed at regular distances through the Work

The coping course is to average 9 inches in depth to project at least two inches over the face of the wall on each side and blocked with the hammer to a roundish form on the top. The coping course is to be bedded and pointed with lime Mortar.

The stone for building the above described Walls are to be taken from any part of the ground that the contractor may find most suitable and convenient and the Earth or Moss which may be left over after filling in the foundations is to be removed from the line of the walls and spread into the nearest broken or hollow ground or to fill up such excavations as may be made by quarrying within the Lighthouse & ground.

Turf Dyke

A ditch is to be formed of 4 feet in width, 1 and a half feet in width at the bottom and 2 feet in depth. At the distance of one foot from the edge of the ditch the Turf wall is to be founded of 4 and a half feet in thickness at bottom to be 5 feet in height and 2 feet in thickness at the top. The face of the wall toward the ditch is to be batter one foot on its whole height and the opposite or inwards face is to be batter one and a half foot. The sods or Turf taken from the ditch are to be applied to the erection of the Wall so far as they will go and the remainder is to be taken from the Lighthouse ground along the margins next to the wall. The Turfs are to be laid with the sward downwards except the coping course and none of them are to exceed 6 inches in thickness. The whole of the works herein described are to be executed to the intire satisfaction of Robert Stevenson, Engineer for the Northern Lighthouses.

The Contractor will receive payment to account at the rate of four fifths of his Contract price for every 30 roods of 36 square yards each of Stone wall that is completed and a like portion of his contract price for every 20 roods of 6 lineal yards each of Turf dike that is completed under certification from the Inspector of Works and an order thereupon to draw being granted by the Engineer.

The Balance of the Contract price is to be paid when the whole work is completed measured by or inspected by or under the direction of the Engineer which inspection it is hereby declared shall be made within three months from the date of the completion of the works.

APPENDIX X

Specification for a Road to be made from the Lighthouse Store at the Kyle of Durness to join the road leading from the Store at Claiscairnach to Cape Wrath Lighthouse, by Robert Stevenson, Civil Engineer. 26th February 1828

General Description

The road to be made between the Kyle of Durness and Cape Wrath extends to 8 and a half miles or thereby in length. It is to be formed in a line of direction marked by pits agreeably to a Plan by Robert Stevenson, Engineer to the Commissioners of the Northern Lighthouse, to whose satisfaction the works herein after specified and described are to be executed in a substantial and workmanlike manner at the site of an Inspector acting under his directions.

Formed Roadway

This Road or Bridle-track is to be formed of the width of 9 feet within the said drains when the ground is flat and marshy; but where the ground is firm or where side cutting becomes necessary the Breadth of the formed Road is to be only 6 feet in width between the drains. In all places where the line of road passes through moss or marshy ground requiring to be cut it shall be covered with strong swarded turf to its full breadth, the greenside lain undermost over which hard stuff is to be laid cleared of all stones of the size of a hen's egg or upwards. The surface of the Road thus formed by cutting the soil as the case may be in all cases to the depth of not less than 4 inches and embanking the hollows with turf in a substantial manner so as o form throughout a regular and uniform surface having a line of Draught nowhere worse than at the rate of one perpendicular than ten horizontal – two rows of turf verges are then to be laid at the distance of 4 feet 3 inches apart in a neat and compact manner for the boundary of the metal or gravel bed. The turf for this purpose is to measure 12 inches in breadth and 4 inches in thickness.

Gravel Bed

The metal of the Road shall be composed of the best quality Gravel which the country will produce within distances of Five Hundred Yards of the line of the direction of the Road. The Gravel laid upon the Road is to be free from Moss or any other Earthly particles. It is to measure 4 feet 3 inches in width. Where the ground is soft the gravel bed is to be 8 inches in depth in the centre and dressed off at 7 inches at the verges or sides; but where the ground is firm or hard the gravel bed is only to be 6 inches in depth at the middle and 5 inches at the sides dressed off on either side to allow the water to run off. Care must also be taken to lay the rounder gravel at the bottom and the smallest particles at the surface.

Drainage

Side Drains are to be made along the whole line of the Road where necessary, of such form and such direction as shall at all times prevent surface or spring waters from lodging in the Road. Where the ground is soft and marshy the side drains are to be kept at the distance of 3 feet without or beyond the turf borders. In such situations these drains are to measure 2 feet 6 inches in width at the top 1 foot three inches at the bottom and to be not less than 15 inches in depth where the ground is firm and hard they are to be 18 inches in width at the top 9 inches at the bottom and 9 inches in depth.

Cross drains of rubble stone are to be built, where necessary, on the line of the Road. The bottoms of these drains are to be paved to such an extent that their side walls shall rest on the paving at least 4 inches on each side. These side walls are to measure not less than 14 inches in thickness and to be finished with covering stones not less than 3 inches in thickness and to such lengths as to have a rest of not less than 4 inches upon each of the side walls. These drains according to the situation of the ground are to measure in the clear or void respectively

9, 12, 15 & 18 inches square they are to be laid sufficiently low in the line of draught to admit of covering turf of 2 inches in thickness between the upper surface of the stone covers and the bottom of the gravel bed of the Road. The intake or mouth of the drains is to be properly sloped, paved and directed for the receiving of the water and their outfalls or tails are to be formed and cut with a sufficient declivity and paved to a sufficient extent for conveying off the water.

Back drains are also to be cut and paved where necessary in a proper form and manner for preventing the surface and spring waters from injuring the road.

Rubbish

The Rubbish of the works of excavation are to be spread out upon the ground and the spoil banks dressed on the surface. Large stones are to be removed and pointed Rocks are to be cut down that the whole extent of the road may have a complete and finished-like appearance.

General Conditions

The Commissioners of the Northern Lighthouse are to relieve the Contractors of claims of surface damage. They are also to be at the expense of building the necessary Bridges on the line but the cross-drains will be estimated by the lineal yard according to their respective sizes. The Contract price is to be paid by the Lighthouse board upon the certificates of the Engineer in manner following: viz one third part when three miles of the Road shall be declared by the Inspector to be made; one third part more when six miles of the Road have been made and the remaining third part of the Contract price (excepting the sum of fifty pounds) together with the price of the cross drains shall be paid when the work is declared to be in a finished state. The balance of fifty pounds above alluded to shall also be paid when the works are found by the Engineer to be in a complete state and are taken finally of(f) the hands of the Contractors; it being expressly understood that the Inspection for this purpose shall take place within three months after the Contract period of finishing the Road which is hereby declared to

be the first day of September 1829 providing the work shall then have
been finished

5th February 1829

Appendix

First

On all parts throughout the line of the road when Embanking is required
either on one or both sides of the road it is to be formed of the breadth of
one and a half feet beyond the Turf borders and such embankments are
afterwards to be increased in breadth at the base so as to afford a slope
from the foot of the embankment to the edge of the formed roadway at
the rate of one and a half horizontal to one perpendicular. Such cross-
drains as may be found to be necessary in these embankments are to
extend to the full breadth of the embankment at its base.

Second

In all places where cutting occurs either on one or both sides if exceeding
2 feet in depth from the bottom of the side drains a Retaining face wall
of dry stone Masonry is to be carried up to within two feet on an
average of the height of the natural depth of the bank the remaining
two feet of height is to be sloped or dressed back at the rate of one and
a half horizontal to one perpendicular.

For the dimensions of the cross drains as specified at page third (i.e.
above) the following are to be substituted viz : 12, 15, 20 and 24 inches
square instead of 9, 12, 15 & 18 inches.

Third

The Back or Catch water drains are to be made 2 feet 6 inches in width
at the top, 1 foot at the bottom and 1 foot in the depth laid out with a
uniform fall and direction to the mouths of the nearest cross drains.

APPENDIX XI

Estimate of Costs and Specification of Bridges on the Cape Wrath Road

Estimate of Bridges on the Proposed Line of Road from Durness Storehouse to Claiscairnach

For Kerwick Water 30 feet Span
- 2 Foundations of Abutments
- 2 Abutments up to Springing
- 1 Arch stones
- 4 Spandrill Walls
- 2 Backing behind Arch
- 4 Wing Walls
- 2 Parapet

Centre of Three Ribs
- 15 Uprights
- 6 ditto
- 6 pieces
- 18 Diagonals
- 3 Stringers
- 3 Sole pieces
- 3 King Posts
- 6 Queen Posts
- 6 Jack Posts
- 6 Spurs
- 3 Segments
- Cleading
- Slack Blocks

Total amount for 30 feet span = £125.4s.2d.

For a Bridge 10 feet Span
  Cubic in Masonry
  Cubic in Centering
Total amount for 10 feet span = £30.16s.4d.

———————

Amount for both Bridges = £156.0s.6d.

Specification of the Bridges on the Proposed Line of Road from Durness Storehouse to Claiscairnach

The Bridge of 30 feet Span is to be 9 feet across the Soffit, thickness of abutments 5 feet, length of wing walls 10 feet and thickness 2 feet, depth of Arch stones 15 to 18 inches, thickness of Spandrill walls 2 feet 6 inches, the length of Parapets 40 feet, thickness 18 inches and height 4 feet above the Arch stones, Rise of Arch 10 feet.

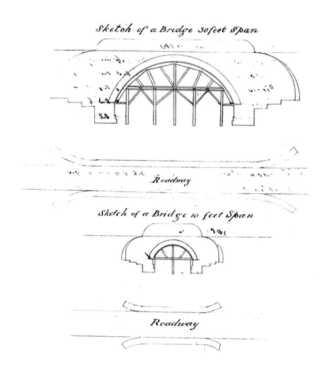

Sketch of a Bridge 30 feet Span

Roadway

Sketch of a Bridge 10 feet Span

Roadway

The Bridge of 10 feet Span is to be 9 feet across soffit, rise of Arch 3 feet 6 inches, thickness of Abutments 2 feet 6 inches, length of Wing Walls 5 feet, thickness 2 feet, depth of Arch stones 12 to 15 inches, thickness of Spandrill walls 2 feet 6 inches, length of Parapets 20 feet 6 inches, thickness 18 inches, height above the Arch stones 4 feet.

Both Bridges to be built of rubble stone and Lime mortar, the haunches to be backed up, the Parapet Coped with hammer dressed stones set on edge not less than 9 inches deep.

The whole work is to be executed in a workman like manner in terms of this Specification and to the satisfaction of Robert Stevenson Esquire, Civil Engineer or the Superintendent of the Works.

March 1828

APPENDIX XII

Letter from Alexander Gibb to Robert Stevenson concerning the Bridges on the CapeWrath Road

Aberdeen
Twentieth March 1828

Sir,

Agreeable to your desire contained in my Father's letter to me of the eighteenth Curto Annexed I beg to send you a Sketch, Estimates and Specification of the Bridges for the Proposed line of Road near Cape Wrath. Not having a Section of the site of the Bridges I could not include the excavation for the foundation which will have to be added to the estimate.

The rise of the arches I have supposed one third of the Span. The prices are those stated in our Schedule for Cape Wrath Lighthouse it being understood the Bridges and Centering when finished are to be measured and paid for according to said schedule.

Owing to the narrowness of the Road a cart cannot go along it, consequently the lime and timber will have to be conveyed on horse backs from Claiscairnach to the site of the Bridges the smallest of which is about six miles from Claiscairnach.

I shall not be away from this place for three days so that if you wish any alteration I shall be glad to hear from you.

I am,
Sir
Very respectfully
your obt. Servant
(signed) Alex. Gibb

Robert Stevenson Esqr
Civil Engineer
Edinburgh

APPENDIX XIII

Contract for the Erection of the Cape Wrath Lighthouse

It is contracted agreed and ended between the parties following Viz. Charles Cunningham Writer to the Signet Clerk and Cashier to and having the authority of the Honourable the Commissioners of Northern Lighthouses on the one part and John Gibb Architect in Aberdeen as principal and Alexander Low Manufacturer in Aberdeen and Donaldson Rose Timber Merchant there as cautioners and sureties for the said John Gibb to the effect herein after mentioned on the other part, in manner following,

That is to say, whereas the said Commissioners have resolved to erect a Light-house on Cape Wrath in Sutherlandshire conforming to plans, elevations, sections and Specifications made out and subscribed by Robert Stevenson Engineer of the said Commissioners and all subscribed by the parties as relative hereto;

And whereas the said Commissioners have preferred and accepted of an offer made to them by the said John Gibb for executing the works in the said specifications, plans and elevations at the price and under the conditions after expressed –

Therefore and in consideration of the said Contract price herein-after specified the said John Gibb binds and obliges himself and his heirs executors and successors whomsoever to execute in the most substantial and workman-like manner the whole works contained in the said specification and in the plans, sections and elevations before mentioned and in every respect agreeably to the Conditions and directions therein and herein-after expressed and of which specification and description the tenor follows (here take in the specification referred to in Appendix VI) and the said John Gibb binds and obliges himself and his foresaids to execute and complete the whole of the work contained in the specification above engrossed and in the plans, sections, elevations and drawing above referred to of the very best materials and in the most substantial style of workmanship to the entire satisfaction of a fit person or persons as an Inspector or Inspectors of the works under the direction of the said Robert Stevenson or of any other Engineer or Inspector the said Commissioners may appoint who shall have power to judge of the sufficiency of the quality of the materials and execution of the works as the same proceeds according to the true meaning of the above specifications and the foresaid plans, sections, elevations and drawing signed by the parties relative hereto, and in case it shall be found that anything has been omitted in the before-written specification necessary to complete the buildings in every respect according to the intent and meaning aforesaid the said John Gibb binds and obliged himself and his foresaids to furnish and perform the same as if such article omitted had been fully specified described and represented, and that without his being entitled to any allowance over and above the Contract price after specified;

But it is hereby stipulated that if in the course of the execution of the work it shall be found necessary to make any alteration by adding to or enlarging the building or any part thereof such additional work shall be executed by the said Contractor agreeably to the specification above engrossed and in case any such alteration shall occasion any additional expense or labour to the said Contractor it shall be paid for at the rates specified in the schedule of prices hereunto annexed and subscribed by the parties as relative hereto and that over and above the Contract price after specified and in like manner if it shall be found necessary to make any alterations on the said specified works or any part thereof by lessening the same or leaving any part thereof unexecuted a deduction according to the schedule shall be made from the said Contract price proportional to the saving of labour or expense which shall be thereby occasioned and it is hereby expressly declared that any alteration so to be made shall not be considered as any deviation from this Contract and that no claim for any extra expense or additional charge shall be allowed unless the said Contractor shall have received express orders in writing to that effect from the said Robert Stevenson or the Engineer for the time and the said John Gibb binds and obliges himself and his foresaids to furnish and provide at his own risk and expense all stones, lime, lead, iron and wood of the descriptions above specified and all other materials and tools requisite for the above works all of the very best quality (excepting in the case afterwards provided for of the Commissioners exercising their power to furnish all the articles for which prices are fixed by the said specification) and to furnish, set up and take down the whole machinery, scaffolding, gangways &c which may be necessary for the same and also in like manner to furnish and provide vessels, boats and carriages for procuring and conveying the said materials and implements and every other requisite according to the above specification declaring that nothing stated in the specification above engrossed or represented on the plans, sections, elevations and drawings subscribed as relative hereto shall be made use of or construed by the said Contractor into any cause or pretence for furnishing or employing materials of inferior quality or for altering the work herein described he being understood to have completely satisfied himself previous to entering into this Contract regarding all particulars connected therewith more especially regarding the situation of the Light House to be erected and of the roads and other accommodations for landing and carting the materials and implements

And it is hereby further declared that the said John Gibb or his son Alexander shall personally superintend the works hereby contracted for and shall not be at liberty to underlet or enter into sub-contracts for any part of the said works to any person or persons whomsoever excepting the Plumber work or such other parts of the said works as may be approven of by the said Engineer for the Commissioners and it is further declared that if in the course of conducting the operations it appears that the said John Gibb is not furnishing proper materials or is not carrying on the works agreeably to the specification, plans, sections, elevations and drawing above mentioned and according to the directions of the Engineer or that the works are not proceeding with proper expedition the said Engineer or Inspector for the time shall in any of these events give notice thereof in writing to the said John Gibb and if notwithstanding of such notification the defect complained of shall not be rectified the said Engineer for the time shall have power to suspend or stop the work until the said Contractor shall satisfactorily show that he is to remedy the defect complained of and should he still fail in the performance of his obligations the said Commissioners shall have full power on notice given in writing to take the works out of the hands of the said John Gibb and to declare this Contract at an end and the said John Gibb to be not only liable in the penalty incurred through failure but also in the whole loss damage and expense the Commissioners may sustain in consequence thereof and in getting the work completed by others and the said Commissioners shall have full power to enter into new Contracts with other persons for the said works or to employ workmen under the superintendence and direction of the said Engineer or Inspector for the time to finish the remainder of the works hereby contracted for at the sole risk and expense of the said John Gibb in which case the said Commissioners shall be entitled and they are hereby authorised to retain from the Contract price herein after agreed to be paid for the execution of the said works the amount of the sums so laid out in the employment of other workmen as the same shall be ascertained by the receipts of the workmen themselves or if the sums thus laid out shall exceed the said Contract price or balance of the same in the hands of the said Commissioners at the time the said John Gibb shall be bound and obliged as he hereby binds and obliges himself and his foresaids to repay and make good to the said Commissioners whatever balance may stand over unpaid of the said expense after getting credit for the said Contract price or balance thereof and it is also hereby declared that the said Engineer or Inspector for the time shall have full power and authority to cause to be pulled down such part or parts of the work as shall appear to be improperly executed and the said John Gibb binds himself at his own expense to alter the same to the satisfaction of the said Engineer or Inspector for the time;

Moreover the said John Gibb hereby binds and obliges himself and his foresaids during the Current year Eighteen-hundred and twenty-seven to make all the necessary excavations for the building to quarry and lay down the material of all kinds requisite for the building operation and also to prepare Carpenters and Joiners work and to build the walls of the whole Lighthouse buildings to the height of the level of the basement course or to such other height as to the Engineer may seem advisable.

It being understood that the Building operations are to be suspended from and after the first day of December 1827 till the month of March 1828 unless he shall receive special orders from the Engineer to the contrary and the said John Gibb binds and obliges himself and his foresaids to have all the works of Masonry including the Light-room parapet completed by the first day of August Eighteen-hundred and twenty-eight provided the said Commissioners have the prepared stones for the said parapet which they are bound to furnish at the site of the Light House in time or so as not to retard the completion thereof and the whole of the works completely finished and ready for being inhabited by the term of Martinmas Eighteen-hundred and twenty-eight;

For which causes and on the other part the said Charles Cunningham binds and obliges the said Commissioners and their successors in office that they shall pay or cause to be paid to the said John Gibb the sum of £5756.1s.10d being the sum for which by his offer made and accepted of as before mentioned he has engaged to execute the whole of the said works and that in manner and by the statements following viz:

The sum of £952.12s.0d sterling when the Boat harbour and the Lighthouse road are certified to have been completed and the sum of £333.12s.6d sterling when the Storehouses and Clais-cairnach and Kyle of Durness are certified to have been completed agreeably to the foregoing conditions

– one tenth part when quarries have been opened for the lighthouse works and building materials laid down to the extent of one hundred tons

- one tenth part when the whole of the walls in the dwelling house offices and tower have been founded
- one tenth part when the whole of the buildings are brought up to the level of the basement-course
- one tenth part when the Tower is carried to the full height and the balcony course laid
- one tenth part when all the sea borne materials have been landed within two miles of the Lighthouse
- one tenth part when the dwelling house and offices are roofed in one tenth part when the Plumber work and the whole of the Masonry including the pavement and brick works have been completed
- one tenth part when the plaster work is completed
- and the balance of the Contract price shall be paid when the whole works are certified to have been completely finished and approved of by the Engineer for which three months are to be allowed from their completion as certified by the resident Inspector

It being hereby agreed that each of the above instalments shall be payable on Certificates under the hand of the Inspector for the time when they shall become due respectively declaring always as it is hereby expressly provided and declared that the said sum of £5756.1s.10d shall be held to be complete satisfaction and payment to the said John Gibb for the execution of the whole works above specified and that no claim whatever for any extra work shall be admitted unless such extra work shall have been specially condescended on and agreed to by the said Commissioners previous to the execution thereof and authorised by a writing under the hand of the said Robert Stevenson or other Engineer for the time all as above provided for declaring that in the event of the said John Gibb being required to make the alterations on the rybats soles and lintels of said building as mentioned in his said offer and on his making the same to the satisfaction of the said Engineer or Inspector for the time then a further sum of £200 shall be added to the said Contract price and further declaring that it shall be in the power of the said Commissioners that if they think proper themselves to furnish all or part of the locks hinges and other articles necessary for the said works whereon prices are fixed in the said specification above engrossed and to deduct from each of the Instalments of the foresaid Contract price as include the period of work in which such articles shall be used the specified price for each and every article so furnished by themselves and that without any allowance whatever being demandable by the said John Gibb in lieu of such furnishings provided always that due notice shall be given to the Contractor of the intention of the Commissioners to avail themselves of this reserved power and provided the articles shall be furnished in due time to allow for the work proceeding and being executed in terms of this contract and to admit of the Instalments being paid as above specified and the said John Gibb hereby agrees that in case any difference shall arise between him and the Inspector or Inspectors of the works for the time regarding the execution of the plans or the sufficiency of the workmanship reference shall be made to the said Robert Stevenson or the Engineer for the time whose explanation and decision shall be final and without appeal as well in regard to the execution of the plans the sufficiency of the work as to the true meaning of the Contract and both parties bind and oblige themselves and their foresaids to implement and perform their respective parts to each other under the penalty of £500 sterling to be paid by the party failing to the party observing or willing to observe his part thereof Alexander Low and Donaldson Rose as Cautioners bind and oblige themselves jointly and severally and their heirs executors and successors that all the conditions and covenants of this Contract incumbent upon the said John Gibb as Contractor for the said work shall be duly and faithfully implemented and performed and to the extent of £1000 sterling which sum the said Alexander Low and Donaldson Rose bind themselves jointly and severally and their foresaids to pay to the Commissioners if the said John Gibb shall fail in the execution of his part of the premises and the said John Gibb binds and obliged himself and his foresaids to free and relieve the said Alexander Low and Donaldson Rose and their foresaids from the payment and performance of the above obligations and of all damage or expense they or either of them may happen to sustain by and through the obligation of Cautionry in any manner of way and both parties consent to the registration hereof in the Books of Council and Session or other Judges Books competent that letters of horning on six days charge and all legal execution may pass upon a decree to be interposed hereto in form as effeirs and for that purpose Constitute

Their procurators and In writing whereof &c

APPENDIX XIV

(Inverness Journal Thursday 14th November, 1828)

NOTICE TO MARINERS
CAPE WRATH LIGHT-HOUSE

THE COMMISSIONERS OF THE NORTHERN LIGHT-HOUSES hereby give notice, That a LIGHT-HOUSE has been erected upon CAPE WRATH, in the County of Sutherland, the light of which will be exhibited on the night of Thursday, the 25th day of December, 1828, and every night thereafter, from the going away of the Day-light, till the return of Day-light in the morning.

The following is a Specification of the Position of the Light-house, and the appearance of the Light, by Mr. Stevenson, Engineer to the Commissioners.

CAPE WRATH forms the north-western extremity of the Mainland of Scotland in Lat. 58 degrees 36' North, and in Long. 4 degrees 56' West.

BY COMPASS , it bears from Hoyhead in Orkney West, distance of 45 miles; from the Butt of Lewis E.S.E.1/4 E., distance of 41 miles; from Rocks called Stags of the Cape, S.W. by W.1/4W., distance about one mile; from the Sunken Rock called Nun, S.S.W.3/4W.,distance of 15 miles; and from the Islands of Stack and Skerry, W.S.W., the former 28, and the latter 30 miles distant.

This Light will be known to Mariners as a REVOLVING LIGHT, exhibiting from one and the same Lantern a light of natural appearance, alternating or changing with one tinged red; which two kinds of light successively attain their most luminous effect every two minutes, and thereafter, becoming gradually less luminous, are to a distant observer totally eclipsed for a short time.

The Lantern-room is elevated 400 feet above the medium level of the sea. The light of the natural appearance will, in clear weather, be seen like a star of the first magnitude, at the distance of 8 or 9 leagues, and at lesser distances, according to the state of the atmosphere; but the red light being somewhat obscured by the coloured shades, will not be seen at so great a distance.

By order of the Commissioners of the Northern Light-houses

C.CUNINGHAM, Sec

Edinburgh, 10 Nov. 1828

N.B. The Light-houses now erecting upon Tarbetness in Cromartyshire, and Mull of Galloway in Wigtonshire, will be lighted in 1829, of which due notice will be given.

APPENDIX XV

First Statistical Account of Scotland 1791–99
Volume 3 Parish of Durness
Rev. Mr. John Thompson

Shore and Tides:

'The tides run in with great rapidity and violence upon the coast, especially on the headlands; and above all, at Cape Wrath, where their violence is increased by means of a shoal, running out north by east, from the extremity of the Cape, for 5 or 6 miles, and covered by a depth of water, measuring only from 16 to 24 fathoms. About a mile from the coast is the Staigs, a rock the top of which is always above the water, but which is, nevertheless, formidable to ships approaching the Cape by night; but a still more dangerous rock, the top of which can be seen only in neap tides, is said to lie 9 miles due north from the Cape.' (p. 578)

Birds and Quadrupeds:

'Cape Wrath has long been reckoned an excellent sheep walk; the sheep flock fed upon it was, however, much more numerous 30 years past, than at present, having been disjoined from the contiguous farm of Balnakeill.' (p. 580)

Roads:

'No roads have yet been made through this tract of country.' (p. 580)

Proposed Improvements:

'It would contribute greatly to the safe navigation of vessels upon these coasts, if a light house was erected upon Cape Wrath. The bearings of the rocks, lying off the Cape, ought also to be accurately ascertained. Some shipwrecks that have happened, within these last 10 years, upon the coast of Durness, seem to point out the necessity of these measures.' (p. 585)

APPENDIX XVI

New Statistical Account of Scotland 1834–45
Volume 15 Parish of Durness
The rev. William Findlater, Minister

'In the Parf district . . . with the exception of the light-keepers at Cape Wrath, there are only four families, shepherds, who reside in this extensive district.' (p.84)

Meteorology:
'Cape Wrath is the only place in the parish where observations have been recorded: a monthly report is transmitted to the Board of the Lighthouse Commissioners of the readings of the thermometer, barometer and rain-gauge.' (p.86)

Civil History:
'A correct survey was taken of the coast in 1827 by order of the Commissioners for the Northern Lights.' (pp.92–3)

Buildings:
'Another building of importance is the Light-house at Cape Wrath, the tower of which is fifty feet high. The building is altogether 350 feet above the level of the sea. It was built in 1827 of granite found at the Cape. Previous to its erection, seldom a winter passed without one or two wrecks; but these are now of rare occurrence.' (p.94)

Roads:
'1st-a road from the Kyle of Durness to Cape Wrath, executed by the Light-house Commissioners in 1828, 11 miles in length.' (p.110)

Harbours:
'The harbours are, Loch Eriboll, Rispond and Port Our, at the termination of the Cape Wrath road . . . A slip for boats has also been made at Clashcarnach, three miles east of the Cape, where the

light-house yacht lands the oil and necessaries for the light-house; but is seldom attempted in stormy weather with northerly winds. (pp. 101–102)

September 1834

APPENDIX XVII

Request for additional funds for special repairs to Cape Wrath Lighthouse.

Northern Lighthouse Board
84 George Street
EDINBURGH

13th August 1906
The Assistant Secretary
Harbour department
Board of Trade

LONDON

Sir,

With reference to Query No. 56 on the Accounts for the Quarter ended 31st December 1905, regarding the excess of the expenditure for certain Special Repairs at Cape Wrath Lighthouse over the sum in the Estimates – I am directed by the Commissioners of Northern Lighthouses to state, for the information of the Board of Trade that it is extremely difficult to estimate the cost of thoroughly over-hauling an old station, and in this case the excess of one hundred and thirty three pounds nine shillings and ninepence has been due:-

(1) To considerably more work having been found necessary than was anticipated, especially on certain of the roofs of certain of the buildings, which had practically to be renewed in stead of merely repaired.

(2) To the cement extension of the landing slip being washed away more than once during bad weather, and

(3) To the operations generally taking longer than was anticipated, the ultimate expense being thus increased owing to the high charges for time work.

I am therefore, as requested, to ask the covering sanction of the Board of Trade to the excess above mentioned.

I am, Sir, Your obedient Servant
C. Dick Peddie
Secretary

APPENDIX XVIII

Arrangements for Maintenance of Ferry to Cape Wrath Lighthouse and War Signal Station.

Admiralty
24 November 1919

The Secretary
H.M. Treasury
London S.W.1.

Sir,

1. I am commanded by my Lords Commissioners of the Admiralty to request that you will lay before the Lords Commissioners of His Majesty's Treasury the following proposal with regard to the maintenance of the ferry by which access is gained to the road leading to the War Signal Station at Cape Wrath.

2. The War Signal Station consists of quarters for three men, erected by Lloyd's, the Admiralty making payment in accordance with the terms of the General Agreement of the 22nd July 1903 relating to Commercial Maritime Signalling.

3. The road leading to the Station which is about ten miles long was originally constructed by the Commissioners of Northern Lights at a cost of £3520 and the County Council then took it over as a public highway. In 1912, however, the Council informed the Commissioners that as practically all the traffic was in connection with the lighthouse and the War Signal Station, a resolution would be submitted to have the road removed from the list of public highways unless the Commissioners would agree to contribute to the cost of maintaining it. The cost was estimated at £35 per annum, towards which the

Commissioners were asked to contribute £25. Of this amount Lloyd's were asked to pay £12.10s.0d and it was eventually agreed that this contribution should be shared equally by Lloyd's and the Admiralty. The Admiralty contribution of £6.5s.0d is charged to Vote 10 Part III, Subhead E and is included in the list of such cases furnished annually to their lordships of the Treasury.

4. The Commissioners of Northern Lights have now asked whether Lloyd's and the Admiralty will share with them the expense of maintenance of the ferry above referred to, which is the only means of access to the road.

5. It has hitherto been maintained by the Proprietor subject to repayment by the Commissioners of Northern Lights of half the cost of providing and maintaining the necessary boats and of maintaining the piers and the ferryman's house.

6. The property has recently been sold and the new proprietor has given notice terminating the arrangement referred to as from Whitsunday 1919 and that in future be will be at no expense with regard to the Ferry but will allow the ferryman to continue to occupy his house free of charge.

7. The County Council decline to take over the ferry and the Commissioners of Northern Lights have decided to maintain it on its present lines until a more satisfactory arrangement can be made. They state it is difficult to estimate the cost of maintenance but they think it will amount to approximately £45 per annum excluding repairs other than those of a minor character and ask that Lloyd's and the Admiralty will pay half of this sum.

8. My lords consider that as the contribution towards the cost of the repair of the roadway is shared equally between them and Lloyd's it is only reasonable that the same course should be followed with regard to the upkeep of the ferry and I am accordingly to ask that their Lordships

of the Treasury will sanction the payment out of Naval Funds of one fourth of the actual cost on condition that all Admiralty Officials and Officers and men of the Naval Service are ferried free of charge.

9. The expenditure if approved will form a charge to Vote 11, Subhead Z.

I am,
Sir,
Your obedient Servant
Alfred Anderson

APPENDIX XIX

Analysis of Claim for Grant to Repair Cape Wrath Road – Wartime Damage.

<u>Mr. Orchin</u>

<u>Cape Wrath Lighthouse Road (unclassified)</u>
<u>Sutherland County Council</u>

1. This case of a claim for reinstatement of damage caused to a public highway by Government traffic presents an unusual and difficult problem.

2. More than 100 years ago the Northern Lighthouse Board constructed a road from Keoldale Ferry to Cape Wrath Lighthouse. (See key plan in envelope at front of file). The road is 11 miles in length and was constructed to the low standard required for the transport of stores to the lighthouse.

3. In 1833 the road became a public highway, and Sutherland County Council is now the responsible highway authority. Since 1833 the Lighthouse Commissioners have contributed annually towards the cost of maintenance, originally on a 50-50 basis. In 1922 it was fixed at £50 per annum and in 1946 it was increased to £150 per annum.

4. The road is linked to the main highway system of the County by a rowing-boat ferry, which carries foot-passengers only. It is operated by the Lighthouse Commissioners. Vehicular traffic on the road is in practice restricted to one lorry, owned by the Commissioners and used for the conveyance of stores from the ferry to the lighthouse. That lorry has a specially made narrow body to allow it to pass over bridges which are only 6 feet wide between the parapets.

5. The County Council have regularly spent more on maintenance than the £50 received from the Commissioners, and during the war years spent about £100 per annum.

6. In September, 1939 the Admiralty established a signal station at the

Lighthouse and that station remained in operation until September, 1945. For transport of all stores and naval personnel the Admiralty arranged to have the use of the Lighthouse Board's lorry – clearly a sensible and economical arrangement. Thus for six years the lorry made more frequent trips, and was more heavily laden, than was the normal practice. That increased traffic caused damage to the road and on its cessation it was estimated that repairs costing £1442.10s.0d were necessary to make good the damage.

7. Since the vehicle which caused the damage is not owned by the Admiralty, I feel that no useful purpose would be served by approaching the Admiralty for an admission of liability. Nevertheless, I think that our Department should treat the case as one of damage to a public highway by extraordinary Government traffic and I recommend that an Authorisation on the Roads Vote be issued. To the estimate of £1442.10s.0d the County Council is prepared to contribute £263 in respect of the saving of maintenance, i.e. £113 in excess of their annual contribution from the Commissioners. That contribution I regard as adequate.

8. Recently the road has been rendered impassable to vehicular traffic by a washout caused by a cloudburst. The estimated cost of repair of that damage is £2000 and no contribution can be made by this Ministry since the road is unclassified. The County Council will probably look to the Lighthouse Board to find the money since the road is essential to the Lighthouse service, and the road is of little or no value to the County as a whole and the County Council have considered removing the road from the List of Highways maintainable by the Council. This question has been deferred for the moment and if the cost of repairing the road is found from other sources, the Council will continue to maintain the road as a public highway, which is clearly very desirable.

9. The expenditure of the Lighthouse Board is subject to control by the Minister under the provisions of the Merchant Shipping Act, 1894. Mr. Bailey tells me that the Lighthouse Fund is almost bankrupt.

10. If the County Council should remove the road from the List of Highways, an Authorisation from the Roads Vote for the repair works cannot, of course, be issued. The road is, however, the only approach to the Lighthouse, which cannot be supplied by sea transport, and it is essential to keep the road open. The best course is to retain it as a public highway repairable by the County Council, and I think we should take all steps to that end.

11. I recommend, therefore, that we should offer to contribute £1227 towards the repair of the road, representing the amount of damage by Government traffic during the war, (conditional upon the County Council retaining the road as a public highway) leaving the Lighthouse board to find any additional money required for immediate repairs.

12. A decision is a matter of considerable urgency, since the County Council meet on 16th December.

I shall be glad to discuss the case with you, if you desire to do so.

R.J. Samuel

Engineering (Highways) Division,
Berkeley Square House,
London W.1.

5th December, 1947

APPENDIX XX

Notice published in the Northern Times of 9 September 2005.

Highland Council

Road Traffic Regulation Act 1984

(U70 Cape Wrath Lighthouse Road)(Temporary Restriction) Order 2005.

Notice is hereby given that The Highland Council has made an Order in terms of Section 14 of the Road Traffic Regulation Act 1984 as amended entitled as above.

The effect of this Order is to :

1. Prohibit the use of the U70 Cape Wrath Lighthouse Road by vehicles with a width in excess of 7' 0' over the full length of the road.

2. Prohibit the use of the U70 Cape Wrath Lighthouse Road by vehicular traffic in excess of 7.5 tonnes MGW at Diall Bridge and Inshore Bridge No. 2 over the full extent of the said bridges.

These restrictions are imposed in order to prevent serious damage to the U70 road and bridges.

There are no alternative routes available.

This Order came into force on 1st September 2005 and shall continue in force for a period of 18 months.

The Highland Council
TEC Services   Campbell Stewart
Victoria Road
Brora kw9 6qn   Area Roads and Community
5th September 2005.   Works Manager – Sutherland

BIBLIOGRAPHY

PUBLISHED BOOK SOURCES

Allardyce, Keith, *Scotland's Edge Revisited*, HarperCollins, 1998

Bathurst, Bella, *The Lighthouse Stevensons*, HarperCollins, 1999

Clarke, Jack, *The Cape Wrath Fellowship Booklet*, Author's publication, 2001

Durness Local Studies Group, *Durness Past and Present*, Published locally, 1998

Krauskopf, Sharma, *Scottish Lighthouses*, Appletree Press, 2001

Leslie, Jean and Paxton, Roland, *Bright Lights: The Stevenson Engineers 1752–1971*, Authors' publication, 1999

Stevenson, Robert Louis, *Records of a Family of Engineers*, Chatto and Windus, London, 1912

The Bell Rock Light, Caedmon of Whitby Reprint, 2004

NEWSPAPER AND PERIODICAL SOURCES

John O'Groat Journal
Inverness Courier
Scots Magazine
Northern Times

ARCHIVE SOURCES

Northern Lighthouse Board, Edinburgh

National Archives of Scotland, Edinburgh

Manuscripts Division, National Library of Scotland, Edinburgh

Royal Commission on the Ancient and Historic Monuments of Scotland, Edinburgh Museum of Scottish Lighthouses, Fraserburgh

British National Archives, Kew
National Motor Museum, Beaulieu
Guildhall Library of the City of London (re Lloyd's of London)

First ('Old') Statistical Account of Scotland, 1791–99
Second ('New') Statistical Account of Scotland, 1834–45
Third Statistical Account of Scotland 1955–85

Report of the Island of Lewis to the Rt. Hon. Lord Seaforth by the
    Reverend Mr. Headrick, 1800

Personal Historic Notes 1871–1914, David A. Stevenson, 1927

Highland Regional Council Archives, Inverness:
Sutherland County Council minutes:
County Council in Committee
Planning Committee
Finance and General Committee
County Road Board
County Roads Committee
Education Committee
Eddrachillis and Durness School Management Committee

North Highland Archive, Wick

Highland Libraries, Am Baile